the science of
SCIENCE

the science of SCIENCE

CHANGING THE WAY WE THINK

BERNARD DIXON

CASSELL

Editor Bill MacKeith
Designers/Art Editors
Frankie Macmillan, Chris Munday,
Niki Overy
Picture Researchers Mary Fane,
Alison Renney, Rose Taylor,
Menna Williams
Design Consultant John Ridgeway
Project Director Lawrence Clarke

Contributing Editor
Dr Bernard Dixon (chapters 3-11)

Principal Contributor
Professor A. J. Meadows (chapters 1,
2)

Advisors
Eugene Garfield, founder and
president, Institute for Scientific
Information, Philadelphia
Professor John Ziman, H.O. Wills
Professor of Physics, University
of Bristol

Other Contributors
Michael Allaby, Susan Blackmore,
Paul Davies, Robin Holloway,
Anthony Martin, Zhores Medvedev,
John Newell

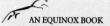

AN EQUINOX BOOK

Planned and produced by:
Equinox (Oxford) Ltd
Musterlin House,
Jordan Hill Road
Oxford OX2 8DP

First published in the UK 1989 by
Cassell, Artillery House, Artillery Row,
London, SW1P 1RT

Copyright © 1989 Equinox

Distributed in Australia by
Capricorn Link (Australia) Pty Ltd
PO Box 665, Lane Cove, NSW 2066

British Library Cataloguing in
Publication Data Dixon, Bernard The
science of science; changing the way we
think 1. Scientific knowledge, –
sociological perspectives I. Title 306'.45

ISBN 0 304 31786 1

Cover pictures

Main picture: Image Bank

Corner picture: Imagine

Printed in Spain by H. Fournier, S.A.

Contents

The Central Tradition

1

Egyptian and Babylonian science...Science in classical Greece...An Earth-centered view...How knowledge was handed on...The Copernican Sun-centered view...The Scientific Revolution...Biology and chemistry...Chinese science...Physics as the model for science...Entering the present century...PERSPECTIVE...Plato and Aristotle...The Aristotelian tradition in science...Islamic science... Studies of motion...Ideas of evolution...Chronology

What makes science different from other ways of looking at the world? Some of the answers that may come to mind do not actually distinguish science uniquely from other activities. For example, it could be said that science provides a consistent and coherent picture of the world: but so do many systems of magic. Equally, a magician might claim to predict the future just as much as a scientist. The history of how science developed is helpful here in two ways. Firstly, in showing that "the scientific method", as it is sometimes rather grandly called, is actually a set of beliefs and activities, rather than a single item. Secondly, in demonstrating that, though some progress could be made in studying the world in the prescientific era, modern science only appeared with the development of this "scientific method".

In the story of western science three components of the scientific method surface at different times, and developed in different ways. The first concerns the interlinked role of observation (or experiment) and theory. In modern science, an observation or experiment may lead to a theoretical generalization which is then tested and, perhaps, extended by further observations or experiments. Scientific progress depends on this kind of repeated interaction between practice and theory. Secondly, most modern scientists feel happier if they can express their results in quantitative – which usually means mathematical – form. Finally, quantitative theory can lead to the precise prediction of future events.

▲ *Science advances by rational argument, but intuition gives the insights that form the starting point of many scientists' work. Isaac Newton's moment of intuition was when he imagined gravity as a force acting at a distance. Thereafter science took over as Newton produced a reasoned and testable argument.*

▼ *Many systems of philosophy have used the idea of the relationship between the macrocosm (universe) and microcosm (internal or subtle world). Though often expounded in detail, as in this 17th-century illustration, this idea is not scientific – it relies on intuitive imagery, not reasoned discussion or experiment.*

Is there a real world out there?

Underlying the use of the scientific method (◗ page 54), including observation or experimentation, quantification of results, and prediction of future events, is one of the first beliefs among scientists past and present – that there is a real world out there, which looks much the same to everyone. If this sounds obvious, it must be remembered that there have been plenty of religions and philosophies which have denied it. Scientists might, if pressed, agree it is an assumption that cannot be proved, but they have seldom seen any need for a proof. Arguments against this basic scientific belief in the existence of an objective world have generally been of a fairly sophisticated kind. The opposite is true of another basic scientific belief – that the world can be investigated by the application of human reason. Most primitive magical views of the world assume that its operations are not rational, and so cannot be helpfully studied by applying human powers of reasoning. Human civilization was already well advanced before rational discussion of the universe around us began.

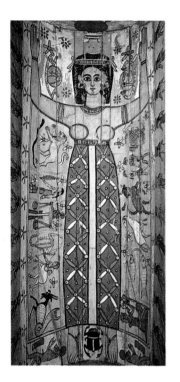

▲ *The ancient Egyptian concept of the world resulted from a belief in a large number of deities, most of whom incorporated aspects of the natural world. Interactions between these aspects were explained by stories of these deities. Here the goddess Nut is holding the Sun in the heavens. She is surrounded by astrological symbols in this 2nd-century AD depiction on a coffin base-board from Thebes.*

The ancient Egyptian picture of the world

All ancient civilizations were concerned with the study of the heavens above us. This was partly a religious concern, in the sense that the heavens had to be accounted for in any religious view of the world. Partly, the concern was practical, because the motions of the heavens provided a way of measuring time and position. The most widespread creation myth of the ancient Egyptians had the Sun god Re appearing from a watery chaos on a mound, the first solid matter, creating a pair of deities, Shu and Tefnet, by masturbation or by spitting. Shu and Tefnet (in their turn) produced Geb and Nut, the Earth and the Sky, whose children were Osiris, Isis, Seth and Nephthys. The ancient Egyptians saw the heavens and the Earth as being physical manifestations of their gods. A picture from around 1,000 BC shows the heavens as the body of the goddess Nut, leaning arched on hands and feet over the body of the Earth god Geb (Qeb), who is the Earth. In another old cosmological myth it was a great star-studded cow – Hathor – which curved above the Earth. The myths and deities enabled the ancient Egyptians to correlate human, natural, and divine life. Clearly, there is nothing scientific in such pictures, and they are not intended to be questioned rationally.

Yet, at the same time, the Egyptians had developed a surprisingly good calendar from their astronomical observations. The length of the year they determined – 365 days – is a quantitative result: should we not consider it to be "scientific"? Here we have to be careful. The Egyptian result, though quantitative, is not based on any theory of the heavens: it is a purely empirical value ("empirical" in the sense that it is what came out of the observations; from the viewpoint of the observers, there was no reason why the heavens should not appear to move at whatever rate pleased them). Hence, the best that can be said about the Egyptian astronomy is that it made some quantitative observations. Otherwise, it was entirely prescientific.

The Babylonians' view

The Egyptian picture can be compared with the roughly contemporaneous Babylonian view. Babylonians saw the heavens as an inverted bowl placed over a flattened Earth. Round the edge of the Earth's disk ran an encircling ocean, on the far side of which was a range of high mountains supporting the dome of heaven. From one viewpoint this is as unscientific a picture as the Egyptian; but, from another, it represents a major advance. The world is built up not from the unknown bodies of gods, but in terms of familiar objects. It would be possible to build a model of the Babylonian view of the world, but not of the Egyptian.

The Babylonians were correspondingly more advanced in their handling of theory and observation. They noted, for example, that the Moon's differences in appearance depended on where it was in the sky relative to the Sun. Their explanation of this suggests that they had made the theoretical deduction that the Moon shone by reflected sunlight. In terms of quantitative representation of their observations, they were also far ahead of the Egyptians. Thus they used quite sophisticated arithmetic to represent the path of the Sun against the background stars during the course of a year. Their results were sufficiently good to allow them to predict approximately where the Sun would be at some time in the future. Obviously, the Babylonians were closer to a scientific view of astronomy than the Egyptians; but, still, their interpretation of observations was entirely empirical.

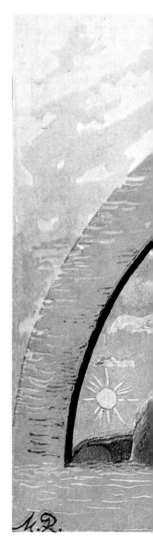

◀◀ The Egyptians had highly developed mathematical skills, which far outran their scientific reasoning. These derived initially from the need to survey the cultivable land each year after the Nile had flooded, and also from the need to organize centralized taxation in goods and labor to support the pharaohs' enormous building projects. As rule-of-thumb geometry and counting developed, examples of reckoning the area of land were recorded, as in this papyrus of 1600 BC (far left) which also shows the development of theoretical geometry.

◀ This 19th-century sketch attempts to reconstruct the world as imagined by the Babylonians, at about the same time as the Egyptians. From the top, it consists of the vault of heaven, the home of the gods, and the celestial ocean, resting on the foundations of heaven. The universe is lit by the Sun, which rises from a door in the east and sets into a hole in the west. The Earth is in the form of a round mountain, ringed by and floating upon the ocean. In the east is the bright mountain of the sunrise, in the west the dark mountain of the sunset. The isle of the blessed is in the southwest, floating on the ocean between Earth and heaven.

The Greeks were the first in Europe to examine the world about us in rational terms

The followers of Pythagoras

Initially, the ancient Greeks' picture of the world was scarcely an improvement. One of their earliest recorded thinkers, Thales (c.640-546 BC) envisaged the Earth as a disk floating on an ocean of water – an image not all that different from the Babylonians'. But a most significant development soon occurred. Pythagoras (c.570-500 BC) and his followers were led to believe from their observations that the world was governed by mathematics and, more especially, by number. The Pythagoreans were a mystical sect who favored secrecy, so it is difficult to be sure how they reached this conclusion. They seem to have started, however, from the observation that the note given out by a plucked string depends in a simple way on the length of the string. This led to an acceptance, fundamental to modern science, both that the world could best be described in mathematical terms, and that the best description would turn out to be the mathematically simplest. The most famous geometrical discovery of the Pythagoreans – the relationship between the lengths of the sides of a right-angled triangle – illustrates the same point. Geometry, as the name ("earth measurement") implies, was originally concerned with surveying and made great use of right-angled triangles. So the Pythagoreans were demonstrating how an everyday type of measurement depended at a deeper level on simple mathematical relationships.

The nature of matter

From the time of Pythagoras onward, the Greek world sparkled with new ideas about the nature of the world. The problem was that these ideas were seldom subject to experimental test: indeed, in some cases, it would have been difficult to have devised suitable tests at that time. An example is the debate over the nature of matter. Many Greeks assumed that all objects were made up of some mixture of common substances with which they were acquainted. A widely accepted list consisted of four such "elements" – earth, water, air and fire. But some Greeks held a totally different view: they supposed that all objects actually consisted of minute particles – called "atoms" – and differences between objects depended on differences between their constituent atoms. This atomic theory sounds very modern today, yet it made little headway in the ancient world. The point was that neither theory could be tested; and at least the four elements involved substances which were known to exist, whereas atoms were unobservable.

▶ *Plato established the Academy, or grove, in which philosophers could assemble to ponder and discuss philosophical topics. It used to be said that the cerebral nature of Greek science, with reason more important than observation or experiment, owed something to the nature of the Greek economy: just as slaves did all the manual work and a life of leisure was the ideal for the citizen, so theorizing was considered preferable to experimentation. However, discoveries in recent years of sophisticated machines built by the Greeks, including an astronomical clock, have qualified this view somewhat.*

◀ *This Roman-period coin from Samos shows Pythagoras pointing to a globe. Pythagoras developed a complex system of relationship and proportion based on his study of geometry and music. This took the rational principles of Greek mathematics and returned them to the realm of mystical philosophy.*

◀ *Aristotle's scientific work had great influence for almost two thousand years. In addition to his theoretical philosophy, he did important work in establishing a system of classification of birds and other animals by observing their appearance and behavior. This Arabic edition of his work dates from the 13th century AD.*

Plato and Aristotle

The two philosophers of antiquity who were to have greatest influence down the centuries were Plato and Aristotle. Plato (c.427-347 BC) followed the Pythagoreans in his emphasis on mathematics. He attached a low value to observation, but set much store by theoretical insight. His younger contemporary Aristotle (384-322 BC) had little interest in mathematics, but stressed the importance of careful observation. It was already apparent in antiquity that the two approaches produced incompatible results. When Ptolemy introduced his complex model of the Solar System (◊ page 10), he followed Plato and built up planetary orbits from combinations of circles, the most perfect form of closed path. An examination of his results makes it plain that the paths he allotted to the planets could not result from the motion of solid spheres, which Aristotle proposed

encircled an Earth that observation suggested was spherical. The idea of testing and comparing theories systematically had still to develop.

The Aristotelian inheritance

Aristotle demonstrated how observation combined with reasoning could lead to a coherent picture of the world. Although his attempts at description covered all aspects, from astronomy through physics and chemistry to biology, it was in the last area that his contribution proved most important. Biology has always been a science where classification is as important as quantitative analysis. Aristotle demonstrated how biological classification should be handled, and his work has had a lasting impact. Consequently, although his ideas on astronomy and physics were finally overthrown his influence persisted much longer in biology; some would say it can still be seen today.

Ptolemy's model of the Solar System epitomizes the virtues and defects of the ancient Greeks' way of examining nature

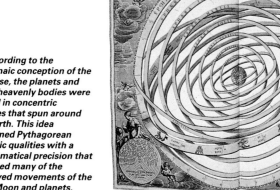

► *According to the Ptolemaic conception of the universe, the planets and other heavenly bodies were placed in concentric spheres that spun around the Earth. This idea combined Pythagorean esthetic qualities with a mathematical precision that reflected many of the observed movements of the Sun, Moon and planets.*

▲ ► *Alexandria was the intellectual center of the Hellenistic world, famed for its library (above) which housed hundreds of thousands of manuscript rolls, and for its Pharos or lighthouse. Archimedes worked here, as did Ctesibios, inventor of new forms of water-driven clock, and Heron, who designed many complex mechanical toys and demonstrated the principle of jet propulsion.*

The Ptolemaic model

The virtues and defects of the Greek examination of nature are seen best in their study of astronomy. The culmination of this work occurred in Egypt, rather than the Greek mainland or islands. Egypt formed a part of the vast empire that Alexander the Great conquered. It was thus exposed to the Greek tradition of thought, and when Alexander's empire fragmented on his death in 323 BC, this culture remained. Egypt was governed by one of Alexander's generals, Ptolemy Soter, who finished building the new seaport of Alexandria and endowed it with a museum and library. Alexandria became a center for the spread of the new Hellenistic culture which in some areas of study reached greater heights than had been attained in Greece itself. For example, part of the difficulty of testing scientific theories in Greece had been the lack of adequate instrumentation. Now quite complex devices, especially astronomical instruments for navigation and surveying, were produced. The crowning scientific achievement of the Hellenistic world was the theoretical picture of the world developed by Ptolemy of Alexandria (no relation of the kings), who flourished in the 2nd century AD.

Ptolemy's extremely complicated calculations led for the first time to a model of the Solar System which allowed the future positions of the planets to be estimated with moderate accuracy. Moreover, it was based on a detailed theory of the Solar System, not on purely empirical extrapolation. So it seems to qualify as a genuinely scientific piece of work. Yet, without detracting from its value, it clearly falls short in at least one respect – the appeal to observation. Ptolemy had begun with some basic assumptions (that the Earth was stationary, that planets moved in orbits made up of a combination of circles), and had used these in all his calculations. In modern science, he would be expected to go back at the end of his work, to see whether his results, when compared with observations, confirmed these assumptions. Ptolemy did nothing of the sort. In fact, observations which did not fit in with his theoretical model were ignored.

The transmission of knowledge

Ptolemy's work was widely recognized as one of the greatest intellectual achievements of the ancient world. This is reflected in the name we give today to the book in which Ptolemy published his results. This name – the *Almagest* – means "The Greatest", and is actually the Arabic abbreviation of the original Greek title. Its use reflects the way in which Ptolemy's ideas have been handed down to us. In the centuries after Ptolemy, western Europe declined gradually into what we now call the "Dark Ages". The disintegration of the Roman empire and the rise of Islam disrupted the growing scholarship of the Mediterranean world. The library at Alexandria was partly burnt by an invasion in AD 269, suffered worse at the hands of a Christian mob in 415, and finally expired after the Islamic takeover of Egypt in 640. For some time it seemed that Hellenistic culture had been virtually extinguished, but, by 750, once the first thrust of Moslem expansion was over, a new interest in the natural world emerged (♦ page 13). It was stimulated in part by translations from Greek to Arabic, and in part by the influx of new ideas from India and China (♦ page 18). Gradually, expertise developed until not only was Ptolemy's work translated and understood, but it was even extended. Similarly, in mathematics, Arabic scholars developed new techniques in algebra and trigonometry that proved to be of major importance for science.

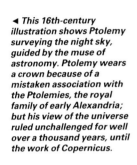

◄ *This 16th-century illustration shows Ptolemy surveying the night sky, guided by the muse of astronomy. Ptolemy wears a crown because of a mistaken association with the Ptolemies, the royal family of early Alexandria; but his view of the universe ruled unchallenged for well over a thousand years, until the work of Copernicus.*

▼ *Dioscorides, an Alexandrian army doctor of the 1st century AD, produced a pharmocopeia that included botanical descriptions of many plants and their medicinal uses, and indications on how they should be preserved. His work remained influential for many Arabic and Renaissance pharmacists and botanists.*

The Renaissance and the Copernican revolution

The influx of Greek learning from the Arabs was further disseminated through the new universities, such as Paris and Oxford. At Oxford, for example, Roger Bacon (c.1214-1292) not only revived Hellenistic knowledge, but also promoted the idea that the world should be studied via experimentation. The dangers involved in this advocacy were considerable: he spent several years in prison. For some time, the question of how, or whether, the new learning could be absorbed into Christian thinking hung in the balance. The turning point came with Thomas Aquinas (1225-1274), the youngest son of a rich Italian family. He spent many years of his life devising a synthesis of classical learning, and especially of Aristotle's ideas, with Christian theology. At first he seemed to have failed, for his work was condemned, but within 50 years of his death he was canonized for his writings. His distinction between the natural world, which classical learning could tell us about, and human salvation, which was the province of the Bible and the church, set the basic guidelines for centuries to come. There followed one of the great periods in the flowering of civilization, the Italian Renaissance of the 14th century.

The general acceptance of classical learning had two opposite effects. For many people, the new knowledge was so comprehensive that it became an essential framework into which all additional items of information had somehow to be fitted. But for some it acted as a stimulus to observe the world, both to fill gaps in classical accounts, and to explore their apparent discrepancies. Some of these latter arose from Aquinas's attempt to synthesize all older material together, in which Aristotle's ideas were the basis, but Platonic and Pythagorean ideas (◀ page 8) also infiltrated.

Nicolaus Copernicus (1473-1543), a Polish cleric well trained in mathematics, became dissatisfied with the Ptolemaic picture of the world. This was partly due to discrepancies between the observed motions of the planets and those predicted from Ptolemaic theory. Copernicus preferred a picture in which the Sun was at the center of the Solar System, rather than the Earth. Copernicus was basing himself on the kind of approach which derived from the Pythagoreans, where one sought for an underlying unity, rather than accepting the immediate appearance of things. Copernicus' theory made little impact. His bold revision of the accepted picture questioned the balance between religion and study of the natural world that Aquinas had established. Not only did the scriptures appear to assert that the Earth stood still; more importantly, current ideas concerning heaven and hell depended on an Earth-centered universe. Copernicus was well aware of this problem. The book containing his ideas – usually called *De revolutionibus*, after the initial Latin words of its title – was only published as he lay on his deathbed in 1543, and this staunch Roman Catholic's book was seen through the press by a Protestant.

Along with the Renaissance, the Reformation formed a part of the intellectual background to modern science. In principle, the reformers were no more sympathetic to science than the Vatican, if science appeared to question religious beliefs. However, the divisions between the reformed churches made them generally less effective in controlling the flow of discussion and publications. On the positive side, some aspects of reformed religion proved advantageous to the development of science. It was helped by the consignment of miracles to biblical times and by the emphasis on utilitarian studies. This more favorable climate became apparent in the 17th century.

▲ *St Thomas Aquinas presented the most fully worked out scholastic philosophical system in the 13th century, developing the ideas of Aristotle within the Christian context. He clearly distinguished between the roles of reason and faith in acquiring complementary but different kinds of knowledge of the world.*

▲ ▲ *Islamic science was crucial in the survival of ancient knowledge into the Renaissance era; and it added many contributions of its own. These included work in life sciences such as botany (above, a detail from a 1218 Arab manuscript on the theriac, an antidote to poison). Several encyclopedic surveys of plants have survived.*

▲ *The astrolabe was developed by Arabic astronomers in order to measure the height of the Sun, Moon, stars and planets. This allowed the user to estimate the time, and calculate latitude and longitude. The device was suspended by its ring, and sightings were taken by aligning a pointer on the pivoted section.*

How Aristotle reached the "West"

The Greek scientific tradition had been adopted by the Arabs. Ancient Greek texts were translated into Arabic and studied. The Arabs were mainly concerned with the medical, astronomical and mathematical heritage of ancient Greece. Averroës (Ibn Rushd, 1125-1198), who lived in both Spain and Morocco, taught that Aristotle "comprehended the whole truth – by which I mean that quantity which human nature, in so far as it is human, is capable of grasping". In Iran, Avicenna (Ibn Sina, 980-1037) brought Aristotle up to date, lecturing on all branches of Aristotle's learning. The Greek scientific tradition came to western Europe through contacts between Muslims and Christians in Arab Spain and Sicily. In the 12th and 13th centuries many works of Greek science were translated from Arabic into Latin, but the most important translations were made direct from the Greek.

◄▼ *Nicolaus Copernicus developed his revolutionary theory of the Sun-centered universe in order to offer more accurate predictions of planetary positions and to simplify the immensely complex calculations needed to maintain the Ptolemaic system. He also may have considered the heliocentric idea to be more esthetically satisfactory. His ideas were not well known until promoted by Galileo.*

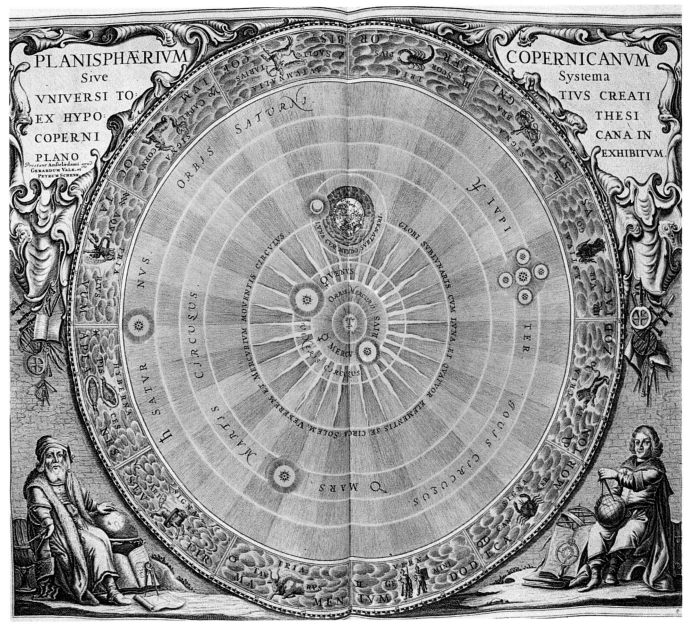

Isaac Newton proved clearly for the first time that modern science was superior to the learning of the ancients

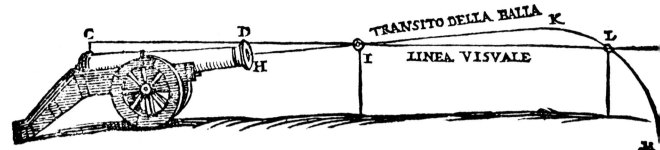

▲ The inventions of gunpowder and the cannon stimulated the study of ballistics. Galileo challenged the Aristotelian idea of how objects moved. Aristotle argued that an object was naturally in a state of rest, and moved because it was pushed or pulled. Galileo on the other hand claimed that motion is the more natural state, and that it was necessary to explain not so much why things move as why they stop. This line of reasoning allowed Galileo to develop his important and mathematically sound explanation of forces and motion.

The way things move

Aristotle's description of motion was queried quite early on during the Renaissance. His claim that objects only move when they are pushed or pulled did not seem to match everyday experience. When a stone is thrown in the air, what pushes it, or pulls it, after it has left the thrower's hand? Furthermore, the nature of motion was simple enough to be explored experimentally with crude apparatus and described theoretically with relatively simple mathematics, and it was involved in many of the burning scientific questions of the day.

In Italy Galileo carried out experiments on how bodies fell, while Johannes Kepler in Prague was establishing a set of empirical laws for the motions of the planets. The first important step in relating terrestrial experiments to astronomical observations was taken by the French philosopher, René Descartes, who showed that any object put into motion would tend to continue moving in a straight line. If planets move round the Sun, it must be due to some deflecting force, which came to be called "gravitation", centered on the Sun. The Dutch scientist Christiaan Huygens showed how the size of this force could be estimated for motion

in a circle, and his contemporaries in England – Edmond Halley (1656-1742), Robert Hooke (1635-1703) and Christopher Wren (1632-1723) – applied this result to deduce what kind of force might be coming from the Sun. The problem in all this was that the planets do not move in circular orbits. It was Isaac Newton who showed that this attraction can produce either elliptical or circular orbits.

Newton's achievement had an immense impact; it was the first time that modern learning had clearly been proved superior to the ancients. Newton's contemporaries were particularly impressed by his ability to make unexpected predictions which were subsequently shown to be correct, for example, that the Earth was not perfectly spherical, but slightly flattened, by an amount he calculated. Yet Newton also left questions for his successors to investigate. For example, his results, strictly speaking, applied only to a Solar System consisting of the Sun plus one planet. Subsequent generations of scientists had to determine what difference additional planets made. This systematic testing and extending of scientific knowledge from one generation to the next is a characteristic of modern science.

► Galileo presents his telescope to the doge of Venice. Among his many claims to fame, Galileo took up the earlier Dutch invention of the skyglass, and produced the first usable telescope. Observations of the Moon made by Galileo with his telescope reinforced his belief in the heliocentric view, clearly showing that the Moon has mountains and craters which reflect the light of the Sun. Equally telling was his discovery that there are many more stars than are visible to the naked eye, and the fact that Jupiter, too, has moons. He showed that the universe as described in Ptolemy's calculations was not complete, but his opponents in the Vatican refused to accept that the telescope could offer acceptable evidence with which to challenge views held for more than a thousand years.

The Scientific Revolution

Although Copernicus inspired a few followers, his ideas only began to make headway when new observations indicated that all was not well with the accepted picture of the world. Toward the end of the 16th century, the Danish observer, Tycho Brahe (1546-1601), established that comets could move freely through regions that Aristotle had claimed were filled with a transparent solid. The same point followed even more forcibly from observations made by the Italian scientist, Galileo Galilei (1564-1642). His invention of the astronomical telescope in 1609 led Galileo to note discrepancies between what he saw through it, and what Aristotle had supposed. Though neither Tycho's, nor Galileo's observations directly confirmed the Copernican picture, their undermining of established doctrine helped clear a path for it. But when Galileo began to support Copernicus in his writings, he soon came into conflict with the Roman Catholic hierarchy. In the 17th century, the growth of science inevitably took place further north, on the Atlantic seaboard of Europe.

Galileo's innovations were not restricted to astronomy. Whereas Aristotle had supposed that motions in the heavens and on Earth had to be explained in quite different ways, Galileo realized that they could actually be similar. Moreover, he began to show via experimentation how motion could be described mathematically. In doing this, he was tackling one of the key scientific questions of the 17th century – could all types of motion be described in the same way mathematically and, if so, what should the description look like? Most of the great names of 17th-century science contributed to this discussion – Johannes Kepler (1571-1630), René Descartes (1596-1650), Christiaan Huygens (1629-1695) and many others. But the final step, which synthesized all this previous work, was not taken until towards the end of the century by Isaac Newton (1642-1726). His *Principia*, published in 1687, provided a unified description of motion. (The full title, translated from Newton's original Latin, is *The Mathematical Principles of Natural Philosophy*.) The title tells us something of the impulse that led to modern science: for, once the *Principia* appeared, modern science was irrevocably launched on its course. "Natural philosophy" meant in the 17th century the study of nature via observation, experiment and theory. "Mathematical principles" tells us that such a study must be quantitative, and that mathematics is the language which best describes the universe. So the two strands that had been handed down from antiquity – the power of systematic observation and the importance of mathematics (◀ page 8) – were finally united.

Newton's achievement in providing a new unified picture of the world had two major consequences. In the first place, he established a model, a powerful source of inspiration for succeeding generations of scientists. Secondly, Newton's work had an enormous impact on nonscientists. His astonishing ability to make accurate predictions led to a general acceptance not only that science was a new way of looking at the world, but that its claims must be taken seriously.

Newton and, independently, Gottfried Leibniz (1646-1716) in Germany devised a new type of mathematics, now called the "calculus" (◆ page 78), which could be readily applied to the quantitative discussion of how bodies move. During the 18th century, this new mathematics was extensively explored, leading to ever-deeper insights into the nature of motion. Newton's initiative indicated the need for mathematics to keep pace with scientific research. Ever since, mathematical techniques have been always pursued hand in hand with science.

▼ René Descartes produced an explanation of the physical world that owed more to his philosophy of knowledge than to experimental observation. He relied on deductive reasoning, building up a series of logical consequences from apparently incontrovertible fundamental tenets. In this way, he argued that the universe must be infinite, and that there could be no such thing as a vacuum. He also argued for the conservation of matter and of momentum. Although he began with the idea of a good God creating the Universe, he derived all further developments in the physical universe from reason, allowing no room for divine intervention in nature.

▲ Isaac Newton was generally considered to provide the culmination to the Scientific Revolution. He took the insights of Galileo and summarized them in his three laws of motion. From these, he propounded the theory of gravitation, conceiving of the force of gravity, and showing its fundamental role in explaining the motions of the universe. His work on light and optics laid the foundations for the modern study of that subject too. Newton was perhaps the first to achieve a distinguished social and political position on account of his scientific achievement. He became a member of parliament and master of the mint.

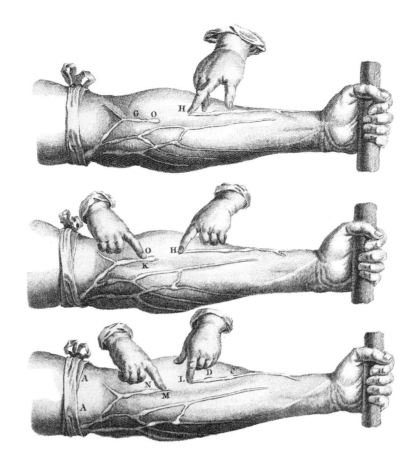

► *The Flemish anatomist Andreas Vesalius conducted the first highly detailed anatomical studies of the human body, presenting his discoveries in brilliantly finished engravings (1543).*

◄ *In the 17th century the study of the human body was brought out of the realms of secrecy and sorcery to which it had been condemned since Roman times. The most important challenge to the authority of the Roman physician Galen came from the English physician William Harvey who showed that the blood circulates around the body, rather than ebbing and flowing from heart to limbs, as Galen had taught. He demonstrated this by showing that a vein, once blocked, must refill with blood on the far side of the blockage. He calculated the flow of blood through the heart, and argued that a closed loop of blood vessels must exist. His theory predated the discovery of capillary blood vessels, by which the blood passes from arteries to veins.*

▼ *Carolus Linnaeus (Carl von Linné) introduced the modern system of binomial classification for plants and animals. According to this system, each species is located within a genus, and the name is the genus name followed by the species. The system allowed him to investigate the similarities and the differences between species.*

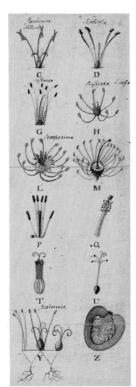

The birth of modern science: biology and chemistry

Areas of science beyond Newton's main concerns were influenced by his example but also by other traditions. For example, the Renaissance had stimulated a new interest in the study of plants, animals and, especially, Man. The origins of modern medicine actually date to the same time as the origins of modern astronomy. A new approach to human anatomy – *De humani corporis fabrica (On the Structure of the Human Body)* by Andreas Vesalius (1514-1564) – was published in 1543, the same year as that in which Copernicus' book appeared (◄ page 12). This medical concern with structure also figures in contemporary studies of plants and animals. In these, it was combined with attempts to list the creatures and plants then known, and to put them into some kind of order. Systematic study was becoming essential as a result of the increasingly common long-distance voyages which brought back descriptions, and sometimes specimens, of strange forms of life. Other developments, such as the invention of the microscope showing hitherto invisible forms of life, also increased the pressure for systematic listing. This aspect of the biological sciences reached a recognizably modern state toward the end of the 18th century, when the Swedish naturalist, Carolus Linnaeus (1707-1778), introduced the system of classification which is still essentially in use today. Classification is in some ways a prescientific activity; but Linnaeus' approach both tried to apply objective criteria and have some theoretical basis.

About the same time, geology began to develop into a proper science, and here, too, an important element was classification. But geologists not only classified rocks: they also began to theorize about how rocks formed. Some of these theories were backed by chemical experiments. This was not surprising, for of all the branches of science, it was chemistry that most clearly emerged in a modern guise by the end of the 18th century.

ANDREÆ VESALII ANATOMIA

VENETIIS APVD   IOAN: ANTON: ET IACOBVM   DE FRANCISCIS

Organisms as machines

The Renaissance fascination with new forms of technology extended to an interest in the analogies between the human body and a machine. Leonardo da Vinci (1452-1519), for example, not only made detailed drawings of muscles and bones, he also constructed models to help him see how they worked. This impulse to see parallels between the human body and machinery formed the basis for one of the fundamental advances in 17th-century biology – the discovery of the circulation of the blood by the English physician, William Harvey (1578-1657). The analogy here was between the human heart and a water pump. Harvey's work is often cited as the origin of the science of physiology.

Descartes took the idea of the human body machine much further. He believed that mind should be regarded as something distinct from body, the latter being purely a mechanical device. Since he also believed that only Man had a mind, this led him to see all other creatures as automata. (Descartes and his followers therefore regarded any form of vivisection as permissible, since machines cannot feel pain.)

Although Descartes' view was extreme, modern science, as it developed, clearly tended increasingly to identify living processes with nonliving models. Toward the end of the 18th century, the Italian, Luigi Galvani (1737-1798), found during his study of animal muscles that their contraction involved electrical effects, which he attributed to the production of a special kind of electricity by animals. However, his fellow-countryman, Alessandro Volta (1745-1827) subsequently demonstrated that animal electricity was identical with ordinary electricity generated by machine.

This lent further color to the belief that animals work on the same basic physical principles as the inanimate world.

In the 19th century, a similar conclusion began to be drawn about the chemistry of animals. It was sparked off by the German chemist, Friedrich Wöhler (1800-1882), who showed that a simple inorganic compound, ammonium cyanate, could easily be transformed into the organic substance, urea. As its name implies, organic chemistry had been thought to be uniquely related to living processes. Although it took much of the 19th century to establish the point, no one finally doubted that the chemical compounds found in the human body were essentially the same as those which could be created in the laboratory.

Chemistry comes of age

Alchemy flourished from classical times onward. Though it represented a kind of practical chemistry, its theoretical notions set it far apart from modern chemistry. One of the main aims of alchemists was to learn how to transmute common metals into gold, something that had to be rejected as impossible before chemistry could advance. A reappraisal of aims began at much the same time that Copernicus was rethinking astronomy.

The Swiss Paracelsus (1493-1541), a character as flamboyant as his name, helped deflect alchemy from its original emphasis on transmutation to a new concern with the preparation of medicines. This path proved fruitful in terms of practical results, but chemistry still lacked theoretical foundations. A first attempt at laying these was made in the decades before and after 1700. The German physician, Georg Stahl (1660-1734), defined chemistry as the search for chemical compounds, their resolution into constituent elements and their recombination into new compounds. The unifying principle which was involved in these chemical changes he called "phlogiston". It was a kind of insubstantial essence which was given up (or taken in), typically in the form of heat, when chemical changes occurred.

Experimental chemistry developed rapidly in the 18th century. The particular focus of interest was gases. The Scot Joseph Black (1728-1799) showed that Aristotle's element of air actually consisted of more than one chemical component. His work was followed up by Joseph Priestley (1733-1804) in England and Carl Scheele (1742-1786) in Sweden, who extended it to show that several different gases could be isolated or prepared experimentally. Priestley described his attempts to explain his results in terms of phlogiston to a French scientist, Antoine Laurent Lavoisier (1743-1794), during a visit to Paris. Lavoisier then carried out his own investigations, and they led him to a theory of chemical combination which did away with phlogiston. In cooperation with colleagues, he then not only defined elements in the modern way, but revised the chemical naming system so that the names of compounds reflect the elements they contain. In consequence, by the time Lavoisier died on the guillotine during the French Revolution, he had provided the basic scientific requirements for the development of modern chemistry.

▲ There was a less clear break between the prescientific study of alchemy and the scientific discipline of chemistry than in some other fields of science. However, Antoine Lavoisier, by showing that combustion depends on a measurable substance, such as oxygen, rather than an insubstantial "principle" (phlogiston) contained in matter, launched chemistry on firmly materialistic lines.

Regarding the universe itself as an organism, the Chinese tended to describe it in qualitative rather than quantitative terms

▲ *An ancient Chinese geomancer's compass, used for astrological purposes. The Chinese regularly used compasses for navigation by the 10th century AD, but long before that they were used to determine the subtle energy flows of the Earth to find the most propitious location for temples and other buildings.*

Science in China: a different tradition

Why did modern science begin in western Europe in the 16th and 17th centuries and not elsewhere? An obvious alternative tradition to examine is the Chinese, for Chinese culture was not only highly advanced at an early date, it also possessed greater continuity than other cultures. In addition, developments in China were partly shielded from west European influence by geographical factors – mountains and deserts on the landward side and long stretches of ocean. The organization of the Chinese state had reached by about 200 BC a form which lasted for centuries. The bureaucracy was recruited via competitive examinations which were based on the writings of Confucius (551-479 BC). These were essentially humanistic in approach and content – the Chinese never came to believe in the concept of a supreme god who ruled heaven and Earth. The mandarins produced by this system formed a hierarchy which governed China under the overall rule of the emperor. Their administrative role was supposed to consist in the application of Confucian principles to problems as they arose: they had no codified legal system by which to work.

▲ *Chinese science has always been strongly practical and the prediction and detection of earthquakes has been a major problem for the huge, but highly centralized country. By the 2nd century AD a seismograph had been built which enabled government officials to detect the direction and strength of earthquakes instantly. These modern posters exemplify another side of Chinese science, urging the populace to be on the lookout for natural indications that an earthquake may occur, by observing unusual behavior in their animals. This subtle observation of nature was a tradition that derived from the Daoist philosophy.*

Chinese theoretical views of the universe were not more advanced than those of the European classical world, but their observations were much more systematic. (Indeed, they still have some use today.) This reflects not only the stable bureaucratic regime in China, but also the official concern with changes in the heavens. This was partly related to the measurement of time throughout the country, but even more with the supposed implications of celestial events. To the Chinese, the heavens were organized in the same way as their own country. The emperor was identified with the Pole Star and the rest of the hierarchy with the stars moving round the pole. At the back of this picture was a belief that the universe was a living organism, in contrast with the Greek view which saw it as a mechanism. The Chinese also differed in their study of mathematics. Whereas Greek mathematics tended to see the world in geometrical terms, the Chinese preferred to develop arithmetic.

Confucius lived at much the same period as Pythagoras (c.572-c.497 BC) and for many centuries the levels of Chinese and Hellenistic culture were generally similar. But when Europe descended into the Dark Ages, a sophisticated culture, including study of the natural world, continued to flourish in China. It was during this period that the inventions of printing, gunpowder and the magnet were diffused into Europe from China, where they had first appeared while European learning was still at a low level. Nor were these all: in most matters relating to practical activities the Chinese were ahead of the Europeans. Indeed, they remained so in some areas even after the 17th century. In some instances – for example, the study of earthquakes, more common in China – the reasons are obvious. But, for example, the Chinese also quite early on took some of the important steps in botanical classification that were not finally taken in Europe until the time of Linnaeus (◀ page 16).

Had visitors from outer space arrived on Earth at any time prior to the 16th century, they would have pointed to China as the most scientifically advanced country. Why therefore did modern science not appear first in China? First, the idea of a universe governed by laws was not fundamental in China, as it came to be in Europe; the Chinese legal system was not based on a codified set of laws. Similarly, the lack of belief in a supreme deity meant that the concept of universal law was generally absent. Even in mathematics, something like the logical structure of Greek geometry was never established in China. Another factor may have been the Chinese image of the universe as an organism. This led to statements about the world being couched in qualitative, rather than quantitative terms. Perhaps, too, the humanistic training of all the country's leaders may have told against a high value ever being assigned to scientific thought. Even the stability of Chinese society may have precluded the development of modern science there. China never experienced anything like the influx of new knowledge that triggered off the Renaissance in Europe. The English scholar, Joseph Needham, quotes from a letter by Albert Einstein:

"The development of western Science has been based on two great achievements, the invention of the formal logical system (in Euclidean geometry) by the Greek philosophers, and the discovery of the possibility of finding out causal relationship by systematic experiment (at the Renaissance). In my opinion one has not to be astonished that the Chinese sages have not made these steps. The astonishing thing is that these discoveries were made at all."

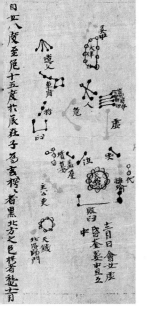

▲ Chinese astronomers, like their early counterparts in the West, incorporated astrology in their systems, and the identification of constellations was therefore important. Chinese astronomers developed the technique for mapping the heavens in two dimensions which has since been universally adopted. The star map of AD 940 shown here uses a map projection resembling the Mercator projection (named for the Flemish geographer who used it in 1568).

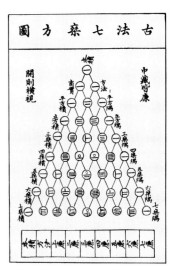

▲ Mathematics in China was highly advanced, although the theory of algebra was never developed. This table of about AD 1100 shows what is now known as Pascal's triangle. Starting with 1 at the top, each number is the sum of those to the left and right in the row above. The sequence is valuable in the study of probability.

Physics came to be seen as the model of how science should be done, until, with the Darwinian revolution, the biologists came back

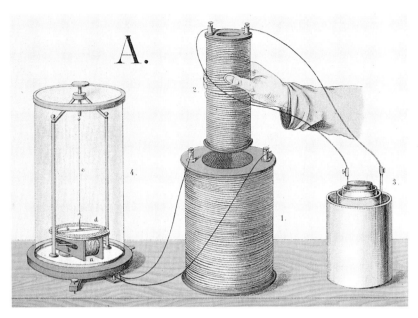

▶ ▼ *The British scientist Michael Faraday was one of the last men to be able to make a major contribution to the studies of both physics and chemistry. Perhaps his most important work, however, concerned the connections between magnetism and electricity. In one of his experiments (right) he passed a current through a cylindrical coil. When he moved another coil through the field of the first, a current was set up (induced) in the second coil. Faraday's work in this area led to the development of the electric motor and generator. In addition, Faraday set up the principles and practice of electrolysis, which proved an important contribution to the understanding of chemical compounds.*

Post-Newtonian developments

Although physics and chemistry proceeded on rather separate paths during the 19th century, it was already clear that they overlapped in their treatment of matter as formed from atoms. This overlap was brought to the fore in the early years of the century with the discovery of electrolysis. When an electrical current (associated with physics) was passed through a solution, it produced elements (associated with chemistry) at its points of entry and exit. It was also electricity that provided the most significant new development beyond Newtonian physics. Experiments, especially by Michael Faraday (1791-1867), showed not only that electricity and magnetism were interrelated, but that the way they interacted was quite different from the Newtonian model of gravitation.

In practical terms, Faraday's invention of the electric motor, transformer and dynamo provided the basis for the modern electrical industry (♦ page 29). Studies of electricity and magnetism provided the stepping stone for many 19th-century advances in physics. Thus it was subsequently shown that both light and radiant heat were electromagnetic in nature. Nineteenth-century physicists came to feel that they had isolated all the important forces in the world, and so were well on the way to providing the finishing touches to a world view based on an understanding that had begun with Newton. By the end of Faraday's life, his belief in the unity of all sorts of physical and chemical activity had been largely vindicated.

As a result of this achievement, physics was seen as the model for how science should be done. Sciences which did not follow this model – many branches of biology, for example – were regarded as backward and worthy of less esteem. But, in the mid-19th century, the biologists struck back. Darwin's theory of evolution by natural selection provided a basis for interpreting all the work that had hitherto been done on classification. Moreover, it suggested new types of observation that could be made. Indeed, a measure of the importance of the concept of evolution is that it proved fruitful over a whole range of sciences – astronomy and geology, as well as biology, although evolutionary theory was clearly different from a theory in physics.

▲ ▶ *Long before Darwin proposed his theory of evolution, sportsmen had developed a practical knowledge of the effects of breeding thoroughbreds and mixed strains of livestock, horses and some birds. Darwin drew on this reservoir of knowledge in his "Origin of Species" to describe the variations possible within a single species. A pigeon-fancier himself, he devoted several pages of his book to pigeons. The cartoon of 1874 (right), some 15 years after the debate in Oxford between the Darwinians and the creationists, caricatured Darwin's belief that the ape is a close relative of the human.*

Ideas of evolution: Lamarck and Darwin

In classification schemes, such as that proposed by Linnaeus, each species was expected to remain the same throughout time. This belief came to be questioned in the 18th century for various reasons, such as the increased interest in breeding plants and animals, and the discovery of fossil species which no longer existed on Earth. A number of people, including Erasmus Darwin, the grandfather of Charles Darwin, began to speculate that a particular species of living things might gradually acquire a different set of characteristics, so evolving into a different species.

The first person to put forward a coherent theory of evolution was the Frenchman, Jean-Baptiste Lamarck (1744-1829). Lamarck recognized that, if such changes occurred, they must be caused by environmental pressures. He supposed that such pressures produced systematic changes in individuals during their lifetimes, and these changes could then be inherited by their offspring. Lamarck's views never became popular, though attempts to revive them have been made at intervals since.

The breakthrough came with Charles Darwin (1809-1882) and his book "Origin of Species", published in 1859. Darwin not only accumulated far more evidence in favor of evolution than Lamarck had available, he also put forward a mechanism which could allow it to work. This mechanism – called "natural selection" – also depended on environmental pressure, but in a totally different way from Lamarck's proposals. Darwin supposed that some genetic differences always existed between the individual members of a species. If the environment changes, certain of the characteristics produced by these differences might prove helpful to survival in the new circumstances. Individuals with these characteristics would then be better placed to have offspring, and so the whole species would gradually change over generations until they all bore these characteristics.

Genetics and Darwinian evolution

The idea of natural selection was clearly in the air – Alfred Wallace (1823-1913) thought of it at the same time as Darwin. The question of how genetic characteristics of parents were distributed between their children was essentially solved by one of Darwin's contemporaries, Gregor Mendel (1822-1884), a monk in what is now Czechoslovakia. However, his work went unnoticed at the time, so that the answer did not become known until some years after Darwin's death. Then, in the early part of the 20th century, Thomas Morgan (1866-1945) extended it to include consideration of the other question Darwin's theory raised – how changes in the genetic material (now called "mutations") occurred and were disseminated. Darwinian evolution is therefore an interesting example of a theory which was put forward successfully long before it could be properly developed.

Into the 20th century

Developments during the 20th century have gone a considerable way toward making the theory of evolution more quantitative. The initial step was the growth of a new science of genetics. Continuing study of genetic material led after World War II to the identification of the way genetic information passed from parents to offspring at the chemical level. This, in turn, has led to the growth of biotechnology, which allows the characteristics of offspring to be manipulated systematically. Such manipulation is a form of experimental evolution, and brings some of the basic elements of Darwinian evolution into the laboratory for investigation. A quite different strand which has come to the front in recent years is the study of how plant and animal populations can change with time. The growth of this branch of ecology has led to quantitative studies of how natural selection operates on particular populations over many generations.

While in the 20th century biology has become more similar to 19th-century physics, physics itself has thrown up a number of problems. The discovery of subatomic particles led in the 1920s to a new description of motion, which diverged from the Newtonian description for very small objects. This new "quantum mechanics" seemed to reveal a much less well-defined world than Newton's. For example, it appeared that, when the position of a subatomic particle was fully determined, nothing could be said about the way it moved. Correspondingly, when the motion of such a particle was fixed, its position became indeterminate. In consequence, the predictability of Newton's world was seen to be the result of averaging over the activities of many somewhat indeterminate particles. So physical laws were not definitive statements; rather, they were statements about statistical probability.

Einstein could never accept this as the final conclusion: he

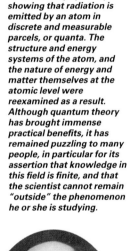

▼ The German physicist Max Planck (1858-1947) together with Einstein laid the foundations for a revolution in physics by showing that radiation is emitted by an atom in discrete and measurable parcels, or quanta. The structure and energy systems of the atom, and the nature of energy and matter themselves at the atomic level were reexamined as a result. Although quantum theory has brought immense practical benefits, it has remained puzzling to many people, in particular for its assertion that knowledge in this field is finite, and that the scientist cannot remain "outside" the phenomenon he or she is studying.

▼ Albert Einstein (1879-1955) made contributions to quantum theory, but is best known for his two theories of relativity. In the special theory (1905) he argued that the speed of light is the only constant in the universe, and that time, mass and energy must vary to preserve this constant. These shifts cause a body to appear to shrink, to become heavier and cause time to slow at high speed. They have been demonstrated experimentally (♦ page 52) but remain contrary to common sense. In his general theory (1915) he added gravitation to the argument, showing that space too is not constant but is curved by the gravitational fields within it.

Le Petit Parisien

SUPPLÉMENT LITTÉRAIRE ILLUSTRÉ

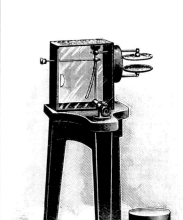

◄ ▲ *French physicists Pierre (1859-1906) and Marie (1867-1934) Curie pioneered the study of the world inside the atom. They explored radioactive decay, whereby an atom of one element gives off radiation in the form of neutrons and protons (alpha decay), electrons (beta decay) or high energy radiation (gamma decay) from its nucleus, and transmutes into an atom of another element. They used the electroscope (above) to discover the radioactive element radium in 1898. Again, the practical contributions of their work are matched by the revelation of the puzzling world of the nucleus – a world which, though well below the limits of the most powerful microscope, can yet be studied by use of high-energy devices such as synchrotrons.*

commented, "God does not play dice". Yet his own work on relativity also led to new problems of understanding. For example, the "twin paradox" was a matter for dispute until quite recently. (This asserted that, if one twin remains on Earth and the other goes off on a space voyage, then when they meet again they will have aged differently.)

Looking back from the vantage point of present-day science, it seems clear that the various requirements for science to flourish came together after many ups and downs in western Europe during the 17th century. But this does not mean that scientific method then reached a final state which has remained constant since. New advances in science have repeatedly raised questions about the nature of science, and no doubt they will continue to do so in the future.

24

Precursors of modern science

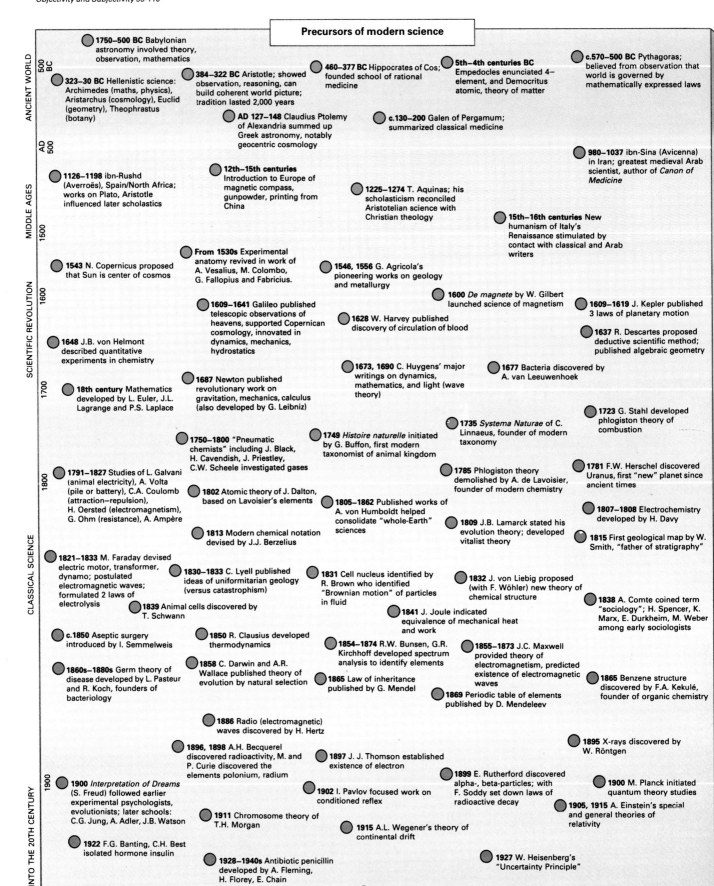

ANCIENT WORLD

500 BC

1750–500 BC Babylonian astronomy involved theory, observation, mathematics

323–30 BC Hellenistic science: Archimedes (maths, physics), Aristarchus (cosmology), Euclid (geometry), Theophrastus (botany)

384–322 BC Aristotle; showed observation, reasoning, can build coherent world picture; tradition lasted 2,000 years

460–377 BC Hippocrates of Cos; founded school of rational medicine

5th–4th centuries BC Empedocles enunciated 4–element, and Democritus atomic, theory of matter

c.570–500 BC Pythagoras; believed from observation that world is governed by mathematically expressed laws

AD 500

AD 127–148 Claudius Ptolemy of Alexandria summed up Greek astronomy, notably geocentric cosmology

c.130–200 Galen of Pergamum; summarized classical medicine

MIDDLE AGES

980–1037 ibn-Sina (Avicenna) in Iran; greatest medieval Arab scientist, author of *Canon of Medicine*

1126–1198 ibn-Rushd (Averroës), Spain/North Africa; works on Plato, Aristotle influenced later scholastics

12th–15th centuries Introduction to Europe of magnetic compass, gunpowder, printing from China

1225–1274 T. Aquinas; his scholasticism reconciled Aristotelian science with Christian theology

1500

15th–16th centuries New humanism of Italy's Renaissance stimulated by contact with classical and Arab writers

SCIENTIFIC REVOLUTION

1600

1543 N. Copernicus proposed that Sun is center of cosmos

From 1530s Experimental anatomy revived in work of A. Vesalius, M. Colombo, G. Fallopius and Fabricius.

1546, 1556 G. Agricola's pioneering works on geology and metallurgy

1600 *De magnete* by W. Gilbert launched science of magnetism

1609–1619 J. Kepler published 3 laws of planetary motion

1609–1641 Galileo published telescopic observations of heavens, supported Copernican cosmology, innovated in dynamics, mechanics, hydrostatics

1628 W. Harvey published discovery of circulation of blood

1637 R. Descartes proposed deductive scientific method; published algebraic geometry

1648 J.B. von Helmont described quantitative experiments in chemistry

1673, 1690 C. Huygens' major writings on dynamics, mathematics, and light (wave theory)

1677 Bacteria discovered by A. van Leeuwenhoek

1700

1687 Newton published revolutionary work on gravitation, mechanics, calculus (also developed by G. Leibniz)

18th century Mathematics developed by L. Euler, J.L. Lagrange and P.S. Laplace

1723 G. Stahl developed phlogiston theory of combustion

1735 *Systema Naturae* of C. Linnaeus, founder of modern taxonomy

1749 *Histoire naturelle* initiated by G. Buffon, first modern taxonomist of animal kingdom

1750–1800 "Pneumatic chemists" including J. Black, H. Cavendish, J. Priestley, C.W. Scheele investigated gases

1781 F.W. Herschel discovered Uranus, first "new" planet since ancient times

1800

1791–1827 Studies of L. Galvani (animal electricity), A. Volta (pile or battery), C.A. Coulomb (attraction–repulsion), H. Oersted (electromagnetism), G. Ohm (resistance), A. Ampère

1785 Phlogiston theory demolished by A. de Lavoisier, founder of modern chemistry

1802 Atomic theory of J. Dalton, based on Lavoisier's elements

1807–1808 Electrochemistry developed by H. Davy

1805–1862 Published works of A. von Humboldt helped consolidate "whole-Earth" sciences

1809 J.B. Lamarck stated his evolution theory; developed vitalist theory

1813 Modern chemical notation devised by J.J. Berzelius

1815 First geological map by W. Smith, "father of stratigraphy"

CLASSICAL SCIENCE

1821–1833 M. Faraday devised electric motor, transformer, dynamo; postulated electromagnetic waves; formulated 2 laws of electrolysis

1830–1833 C. Lyell published ideas of uniformitarian geology (versus catastrophism)

1831 Cell nucleus identified by R. Brown who identified "Brownian motion" of particles in fluid

1832 J. von Liebig proposed (with F. Wöhler) new theory of chemical structure

1838 A. Comte coined term "sociology"; H. Spencer, K. Marx, E. Durkheim, M. Weber among early sociologists

1839 Animal cells discovered by T. Schwann

1841 J. Joule indicated equivalence of mechanical heat and work

c.1850 Aseptic surgery introduced by I. Semmelweis

1850 R. Clausius developed thermodynamics

1854–1874 R.W. Bunsen, G.R. Kirchhoff developed spectrum analysis to identify elements

1855–1873 J.C. Maxwell provided theory of electromagnetism, predicted existence of electromagnetic waves

1865 Benzene structure discovered by F.A. Kekulé, founder of organic chemistry

1860s–1880s Germ theory of disease developed by L. Pasteur and R. Koch, founders of bacteriology

1858 C. Darwin and A.R. Wallace published theory of evolution by natural selection

1865 Law of inheritance published by G. Mendel

1869 Periodic table of elements published by D. Mendeleev

1886 Radio (electromagnetic) waves discovered by H. Hertz

1895 X-rays discovered by W. Röntgen

INTO THE 20TH CENTURY

1900

1896, 1898 A.H. Becquerel discovered radioactivity, M. and P. Curie discovered the elements polonium, radium

1897 J. J. Thomson established existence of electron

1899 E. Rutherford discovered alpha-, beta-particles; with F. Soddy set down laws of radioactive decay

1900 M. Planck initiated quantum theory studies

1900 *Interpretation of Dreams* (S. Freud) followed earlier experimental psychologists, evolutionists; later schools: C.G. Jung, A. Adler, J.B. Watson

1902 I. Pavlov focused work on conditioned reflex

1905, 1915 A. Einstein's special and general theories of relativity

1911 Chromosome theory of T.H. Morgan

1915 A.L. Wegener's theory of continental drift

1922 F.G. Banting, C.H. Best isolated hormone insulin

1928–1940s Antibiotic penicillin developed by A. Fleming, H. Florey, E. Chain

1927 W. Heisenberg's "Uncertainty Principle"

1953 F. Crick, J. Watson proposed DNA double helix

Empiricism and Practicality

2

Technology before science...Scientific knowledge and technological advance...Close interactions between science and industry...PERSPECTIVE...Early practical theoreticians...Development of the steam engine... Chemical and electricity generating industries take off...From telegraph to radio...The military stimulus

Sophisticated technology appeared long before there was significant scientific insight into the world about us. The Great Pyramid of Giza was built in Egypt some 50 centuries ago. Though it demanded a considerable range of skills, including the ability to design something shaped like a pyramid, no science was involved. On a smaller scale, quite complex skills were already then developing in such areas as pottery, or the extraction and working of metals. The potter's wheel had been invented by about 3000 BC, and potters early developed procedures for making and firing their wares. Similarly, the recognition of minerals and the consequent smelting of ores were skills that grew steadily from very early days. Copper, for example, was already being cast in molds by 3500 BC. All these developments were empirical – that is, based on trial-and-error methods – rather than based on any scientific theory.

However, in the world of Greek culture, a few technical innovations do seem to have resulted from theoretical insight. The work of Archimedes (c.287-212 BC) is an obvious example. Archimedes was especially interested in the way liquids and solid objects move. One of the inventions attributed to him – the Archimedean screw – is still in use for irrigation of crops in arid countries. This screw, which when turned lifts water from one level to another, was a result of Archimedes' interest in fluid motion. Equally, his introduction of a system of pulleys to raise heavy weights derived from his interest in the motion of solid objects.

Practical science in the Renaissance

Technological innovation, like scientific discussion, decreased drastically in Europe during the Dark Ages, but it recovered much more rapidly. From AD 800 onward, European craftsmen were experimenting with new methods and machines. For example, long before the Renaissance of European culture, windmills had been invented and, along with waterwheels, were being used to provide power for a variety of activities.

Methods of transmitting this power were also introduced: the most important for the future was the crank, which could transform rotary motion into forward-and-backward motion, or vice versa. But the most significant developments during the Middle Ages related to metallurgy. These ranged from the discovery of new ores, through new methods of obtaining metals from them (including, eventually, the blast furnace) to a variety of new applications, such as the manufacture of cannon. The center for much of this activity was south Germany and north Italy, which also become the center of Renaissance culture in the 15th and 16th centuries. It is characteristic of the leading figures of the Renaissance that they were as concerned with practical matters as with theoretical ideas. The notebooks of Leonardo da Vinci (1452-1519) illustrate this innovative mixture well, though some of his contemporaries made more immediately practical contributions. But it was not in the central areas of their concern, such as architecture, that science first made an impact on practice. This came rather in instrument-making, where an interaction between scientists and craftsmen began in the 17th century and has continued ever since. An obvious example is the invention of the telescope by Galileo Galilei (1564-1642).

◄ Early civilizations in many parts of the world have been characterized by large-scale building projects which involved moving large quantities of earth and stone. This painting of the construction of the pyramid of Cheops in Egypt shows the large-scale organization required; on the other hand, little true scientific knowledge was needed.

▼ The Greek scientist Archimedes designed a screw that would lift water to a higher level, with immense practical benefits for irrigation. This device owed much to Archimedes' interest in fluid motion.

The wedding of science and technology

The telescope was an innovation based on an existing technology – the manufacture of lenses for spectacles – but its invention led to a new growth in the manufacture of optical instruments. Another example, which affected many more people, was timekeeping. Clocks had been mounted on public buildings in western Europe from the end of the 13th century onward. By the 17th century, scaled-down versions were available for use domestically. But none was particularly accurate; for there was no good way of controlling the rate at which they went. Galileo was the first to realize that a pendulum swinging backward and forward kept equal time on each swing, and so could be used to control the going rate of clocks. Later in the 17th century, the Dutch scientist, Christiaan Huygens (1629-1695), applied the discovery to the invention of the pendulum clock.

The impact of new scientific knowledge was here direct, but science also had an indirect effect on important developments in the 18th century. The interesting example is the steam engine. It was first realized in the 17th century that the atmosphere exerts a high pressure at the Earth's surface. We do not usually notice it, because the pressure acts equally on all sides. But a body with a vacuum on one side and the atmosphere on the other will experience a strong pressure. This was strikingly demonstrated by Otto von Guericke (1602-1686) in Germany in the middle of the 17th century. He made two metal hemispheres, put them together to form a close-fitting sphere, and then pumped out the air from between them. The resultant atmospheric pressure on the hemispheres was such that two teams, each containing eight horses, could not pull them apart.

Experiments like these soon raised the question whether atmospheric pressure could be made to do useful work. It was Huygens' assistant Denis Papin (1647-1712) who first suggested how this might be done by using steam. When water was heated in a vertical tube, fitted with a piston, the steam formed pushed the piston upward. If the tube was then cooled, the steam condensed into water again, and the outside atmospheric pressure forced the piston down into the resultant partial vacuum. By alternate heating and cooling, continuous up-and-down motion could be produced.

▼ *The Industrial Revolution depended crucially on improvements in the art of iron-founding and steel-making. These developments were characterized by the bridge at Ironbridge, England – the world's first iron bridge of its size – near to one of the earliest industrial centers at Coalbrookdale. With the new techniques of working metal it became possible to design more and more sophisticated machinery, including boilers capable of withstanding high pressures.*

▲ *The English engineer Thomas Newcomen devised one of the first practical steam engines to pump water out of mines. The piston was connected by a heavy beam to a pump shaft in the mine, and balanced so that the piston naturally tended to revert to the raised position. After steam from the boiler was passed into the cylinder, cold water was sprinkled on the outside of the cylinder to cause the steam to condense, drawing the piston down, and pumping water from the mine. The earliest such engines required the stream of cold water to be turned on and off by hand, but Newcomen added an automatic tap. The relatively simple ironwork involved in this engine meant that only low steam pressure could be achieved.*

The steam engine

Papin's atmospheric engine became known in England, where he worked for some years, and the first fairly practical source of steam power was built there. Thomas Savery (c.1650-1715) was mainly concerned with the need to remove water from mines. This had always been a problem for miners, but it increased in importance as mines grew in number and size, and proved a major stimulus to the development of the steam engine. Savery's device relied on steam and atmospheric pressure like Papin's, but is really better described as a steam pump than a steam engine. It failed in its main objective of draining mines, but could be used for lifting water over smaller heights. A significant descendant of Papin's engine appeared a little later, in 1712, and was designed by Thomas Newcomen (1663-1729), an English metalworker.

One way in which scientific method aided new technology was in emphasizing the importance of experiments and quantitative measurements. John Smeaton (1724-1792) realized that improvement of steam engines depended, in part, on the ability to compare the performances of different engines. His measurements of the efficiency of contemporary engines allowed him to make appreciable improvements in their consumption of fuel for a given amount of work. But steam engines remained grossly inefficient until the latter part of the 18th century, when the Scotsman, James Watt (1736-1819), introduced fundamental new ideas into their design.

Watt was trained as an instrument-maker and worked for the University of Glasgow, so he was acquainted with the scientific advances of his day. He started to think about steam engines when he was given a model of a Newcomen engine to repair. His study led him to realize that the great drawback of these engines was their rapid changes in temperature, as first hot steam was introduced to the cylinder, then cold water to condense the steam. This alternate heating and cooling used a lot of fuel inefficiently. Watt therefore devised a new type of engine in which the steam was condensed in a separate container attached to the main cylinder. Equally importantly, he began to move away from a reliance on atmospheric pressure to do the work. Instead, he experimented with introducing the steam alternately on either side of the piston, so pushing it backward and forward.

These improvements were helped and, in part, made possible by increasingly accurate ways of machining metals at the end of the 18th century. The English engineer, Richard Trevithick (1771-1833), was introduced at an early age to the Newcomen engines used in the mines of southwest England, where he was born. He soon saw the value of smaller, high-pressure engines, and, by 1801, had built a steam carriage that could carry passengers along a road. This was not the first such experiment – pride of place goes to the Frenchman, Nicholas-Joseph Cugnot (1728-1804), who built one in 1769 – but Trevithick's work pointed the way forward to 19th-century railway engines.

▼ *The steam engine meant that power could be made available wherever it was required, whether within a factory, for the engine of a locomotive, or as a mobile power source such as the traction engine. For the most part the backward-and-forward motion of the piston was translated into the circular motion of the flywheel for ease of use. The traction engine had great repercussions in changing the amount of manual labor required for agriculture, as can be seen in this steam plowing operation of about 1860.*

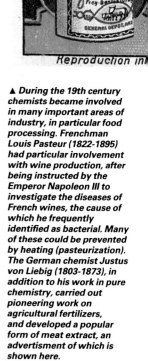

Reproduction in

Science and industry

During the first half of the 19th century, most benefits in terms of stimulating new ideas continued to flow from technology to science. Thus, one of the significant new areas of 19th-century science was thermodynamics (the study of heat flow and the work heat can do). The Frenchman, Sadi Carnot (1796-1832), who introduced the basic ideas of thermodynamics, was particularly impressed by the pervasive importance of steam power. But, despite the value of his theoretical work, it was not until many decades later that the design of steam engines benefited from it in any significant way.

Science was certainly involved in the development of 18th-century technology, but it was science that was already well established: there was usually little feedback to further developments in science. For example, John Smeaton (1724-1792) in England and his contemporaries in France carried out a number of important experiments on the efficiency of waterwheels, which led to considerable improvements. Their investigations were based on the mechanics of Newton, Huygens and Leibniz, but did not in turn feed back to produce new scientific developments. Much the same can be said of other areas, such as agriculture. Here, the stimulus of new studies of plants and animals helped in establishing the use of phosphate fertilizers and in the development of the sugarbeet industry; but connections between the basic science and the agricultural improvements were typically indirect, and feedback was limited. It was only in the latter part of the 19th century that science and technology began to interact closely, so that it became necessary for industrial firms to employ scientists.

▲ *The French physicist Sadi Carnot was the theoretician who studied the principle of the operation of the steam engine in terms of thermodynamics. His analysis made it possible to compare the performance of an actual steam engine with the theoretical optimum. In practice, this was of little use, and most steam engine design was carried out in a pragmatic, rather than theoretical, fashion. The heat engines that most nearly approached Carnot's ideal were the so-called Stirling engines, developed in the 1820s; but practical difficulties in putting these machines to useful work meant that they played only a minor role until modern times.*

▲ *During the 19th century chemists became involved in many important areas of industry, in particular food processing. Frenchman Louis Pasteur (1822-1895) had particular involvement with wine production, after being instructed by the Emperor Napoleon III to investigate the diseases of French wines, the cause of which he frequently identified as bacterial. Many of these could be prevented by heating (pasteurization). The German chemist Justus von Liebig (1803-1873), in addition to his work in pure chemistry, carried out pioneering work on agricultural fertilizers, and developed a popular form of meat extract, an advertisement of which is shown here.*

◄ *Among the scientific developments which most impinged on the general public and helped to create a large-scale chemical industry was the discovery in 1856 of the first artificial dye, aniline purple, or mauveine. The new color soon became fashionable, and remained so until the 1870s, as seen in this painting of 1872. Soon many other artificial dyes expanded the palette of the textile designers.*

AMPAGNE.

able Extrait de Viande Liebig.   Pressurage des raisins.

Voir l'explication au verso.

The chemical industry

Several industries which expanded at the end of the 18th century – such as soap manufacture, glassmaking and, expecially, textiles – required chemicals to carry out their work. Natural resources were not always adequate to meet the new demands, and it became necessary to search for methods of synthesizing chemicals. This was especially true in France, where a long series of wars hampered imports. So it was a Frenchman, Nicolas Leblanc (1742-1806), physician to the Duke of Orleans, who invented a way of converting readily-available salt into the soda that was urgently required by industry.

In the Leblanc process, scientific knowledge was invoked to replace a naturally-available product by the same chemical manufactured industrially. But 19th-century chemists began to discover new chemicals with properties that differed from those of naturally-occurring products. The dye industry provides a good example. The textile industry used vast quantities of dyes, but the problem with many natural dyes was that the colors they produced were neither very bright, nor very fast. At the end of the 1850s, William Perkin (1838-1907) in England accidentally stumbled on a new dye, mauve or "aniline purple", whilst carrying out some chemical experiments. This proved so much more satisfactory than the natural dyes then available that chemists all over Europe began to look for new dyes. By the end of the 19th century, the manufacture of dyes had become a major science-based industry, especially in Germany, where its development was encouraged by Perkin's teacher, A.W. Hofmann (1818-1892).

The electricity generating industry

After Michael Faraday's series of experiments showing that electricity and motion could be transformed one into the other, it took some decades before practical generators were developed. The people responsible for such advances often combined scientific and technical backgrounds. The German Werner von Siemens (1816-1892) – who introduced the name "dynamo" – was one of a family of four brothers with scientific and engineering skills. More unusually, the great American inventor Thomas Edison received no formal scientific education.

Scientific advances led to a revolution in communications in the late 19th century

Electricity in communication

A system of mechanically-operated semaphore stations was introduced in France during the Revolutionary Wars of 1792-1802. Use of the semaphore system spread abroad, especially to Britain and the United States, but scientific progess soon rendered it obsolete, and the semaphore telegraph was displaced by the electric telegraph. For the last 100 years, electricity has provided the basis for almost all forms of rapid long-distance communication.

Attempts had been made in the 18th century to transmit signals using static electricity, but viable systems only became possible when the electric battery appeared. Alessandro Volta (1745-1827), an Italian professor of physics, built the first battery at the end of the 18th century as part of his researches into electricity, and it rapidly became the standard source of electrical current.

In 1820, the Danish physicist, Hans Christian Oersted (1777-1851) discovered that the passage of such a current through a wire could deflect the needle of a nearby magnet. His identification of a connection between electricity and magnetism established a major new area of research in physics – electromagnetism. Equally, it suggested a new method of communication over long distances; for it meant that a pulse of electricity sent down a wire could momentarily deflect a magnetic needle at the other end. By creating successive deflections of the needle, it would be possible to send a message.

The electric telegraph

The idea of an electric telegraph was developed in Germany, especially by Baron Schilling (1786-1837), one of whose instruments was seen by an Englishman, William Cooke (1806-1879), a student at Heidelberg in the 1830s. Cooke returned to England with the intention of developing this type of communication system, particularly for the expanding railway network. However, he ran into problems and turned to Charles Wheatstone (1802-1875), a professor of physics in London, for advice.

The two entered into partnership to develop the electric telegraph commercially. By the mid-century, they had installed several thousand miles of telegraph line in Britain.

The electric telegraph spread even more rapidly in the United States, and the message code devised there by Samuel Morse (1791-1872) came into universal usage. The proliferating networks in different countries were soon being interconnected. This was easy enough across land frontiers, but water created a greater barrier. As soon as an appropriate insulating material (gutta percha) had been found, cables clad with this material could be laid along the sea floor. This worked well over shorter distances, such as England to France, but the link between Britain and North America proved much more difficult to establish. It took until 1866 before a transatlantic telegraph was operating satisfactorily. Again, a physicist was involved in the success – in this case, William Thomson (1824-1907), who, under his later title of Lord Kelvin, is remembered as one of the greatest scientists of the 19th century.

The telephone

The development of the telephone also involved science, but of a different kind. During the 19th century, there was considerable interest in the properties of sound. One of the pioneers in such studies was the German, Hermann von Helmholtz (1821-1894), who combined his interests in physics and physiology to provide new information on the nature of hearing. His work attracted the attention of the Scottish-American inventor Alexander Graham Bell (1847-1922), who was concerned with teaching the deaf. Bell was led to experiment with the mechanical reproduction of human speech and its transformation into electrical variations that could be transmitted along a wire. The results formed the basis for the modern telephone.

▼ **Messages could be sent by the electric telegraph across distances limited only by their physical connections by wire, and at a rate limited by the ability of operators to encode and transmit their messages. Charles Wheatstone first developed a two-needle telegraph, in which the current in the wire deflected the needles on a screen. For speedier or unattended transmission, in 1858 he devised the tape machine (below): the operator encoded the message onto tape in advance, and the receiving device recorded the message onto paper.**

New advances in physics aid communication

By the end of the 19th century, new advances in physics rapidly affected methods of communication. Thus, the concept of radio waves was put forward by James Clerk Maxwell (1831-1879) as part of his theoretical investigation of electromagnetism in the 1860s and 1870s. In 1885, such waves were detected experimentally by the German physicist, Heinrich Hertz (1857-1894). His ability to transmit radio waves over short distances suggested that they might be used for purposes of communication over much longer distances. Within 20 years of their first detection, Guglielmo Marconi (1874-1937) had transmitted radio signals across the Atlantic.

It is true that inventors with little knowledge of theory enjoyed some success in advancing electrical communications. An obvious example is the American, Thomas Edison (♦ page 29). Yet the hand-in-hand growth of science and electrical communication in the 19th century contrasts clearly with the general rule-of-thumb development of steam engines. Even Edison's ideas were influenced, in part, by reading the collected works of that great scientific experimenter, Michael Faraday (♦ page 20).

▲ *The telephone, in which sounds are themselves directly transduced into electrical impulses, transmitted along the wire, and reconstituted into sound at the receiving end, was invented by Alexander Graham Bell in 1876. When linked to the automatic exchange, invented in 1889 by Almon B. Strowger, it became possible to speak to distant people from the comfort of the living room or office. This cartoon of 1887 predicted that, 75 years thence, people would be likely to conduct their love affairs by phone.*

◄ ▲ *Guglielmo Marconi sent wireless messages a few kilometers in 1896, and across the Atlantic in 1901. A wireless telegraphy link was set up between Paris and Casablanca in 1907 (left) – invention of the coherer by Édouard Branly (1844-1940) had made wireless telegraphy possible. Voices, rather than Morse code, could be broadcast after the invention of the triode vacuum valve in 1907, and general broadcasting began in the 1920s. The soprano Nellie Melba (above) broadcast singing into an early microphone in 1920.*

On s'abonne sans trais dans tous les bureaux de poste

Dix-huitième Année   DIMANCHE 24 NOVEMBRE 1907   Numéro 888

DR BRANLY

CASABLANCA

MARCONI

LES PRODIGES DE LA TÉLÉGRAPHIE SANS FIL.
On communique entre Paris et Casablanca

See also
Styles of Science 33-46

The military stimulus to invention

Military needs have always been a stimulus to technological innovation. Here, too, science provided only a little input until the 19th century. Thus, Galileo tried to study the way in which shot was propelled from guns (◀ page 14). Although his ideas were basically correct, the complicated effect of the atmosphere on bodies passing through it meant that his results were not applicable to military requirements. However, both the chemical industry and the electrical industry of the 19th century provided important new items to the military. The former developed more powerful and stable explosives, whilst the latter led to various forms of communication. Both played a major role in World War I, the "chemists' war". But it was World War II, the "physicists' war", that underlined the now inseparable link between science and technology. A list of important technological advances in that war includes such familiar items of our present life as atomic bombs, computers, rockets, radar and jet engines. All of these involved scientific, as well as technical advances. The obvious example is the atomic bomb. The totally unexpected discovery by physicists just before World War II that uranium atoms broke down in an unexpected way (labeled "fission") was only fully understood by a handful of academic scientists. Yet, in less than a decade, the discovery led to the production of a usable weapon. Radar is an equally good example of the interaction between science and the military, for it, in turn, led after the war to the appearance of a new branch of science — radio astronomy. The story of the development of television in Britain also illustrates the impact of military requirements on technical advance. Computer development during the war concentrated on the analysis of enemy messages and, to some extent, the control of heavy guns. These two areas of analysis and control have remained central to much computing since. Similarly, the military uses of rockets at the end of the war have led directly to the "Star Wars" debate of today. But they have also led to the achievements of space research which have totally altered understanding of a whole range of sciences in the last quarter of a century. These developments in space have only been possible because industrial firms have moved to levels of engineering precision never before envisaged. The exploration of space is an excellent example of present-day trends — the practice of engineering is now based far more on scientific knowledge than on empirical "know-how".

▼ **The hydrogen bomb, first exploded by the United States in the Pacific in 1952, represented the recreation by scientists of the reactions that fuel the Sun itself. During World War II, many scientists in all the combatant nations had been involved in war work, including, crucially, the development of radar in Britain (inset), and of the atomic bomb in the United States. Many involved in the latter argued that the bomb should never be used.**

Mission-oriented and curiosity-oriented science...
Chance has a role in scientific discovery...International
cooperation...PERSPECTIVE...What kind of people
become scientists?...Six ways of doing science...
"Planned" science...A laboratory-continent...The role
of the individual scientist...Scientific disciplines...
J.B.S. Haldane

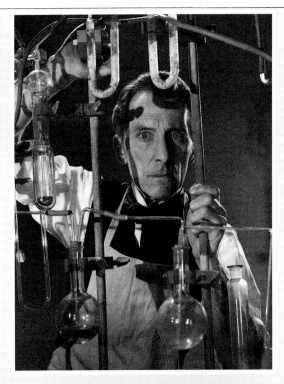

▲ *Peter Cushing in*
"Frankenstein Must be
Destroyed" (1960). The
subject of Mary Shelley's
novel, Frankenstein created
a creature like a man and
has come to symbolize the
mad scientist.

Unlike "accountant", "butcher", "pianist" or "clerk", the term "scientist" embraces a wide variety of occupations. One scientist can be found doing experiments at a laboratory bench in Cambridge, Massachusetts, recording in a notebook figures obtained by comparing the tensile strengths of a novel range of alloys. Another spends week after week living with and observing the behavior of mountain gorillas in central Africa. Another passes much of his or her time in committee rooms, managing huge research projects. Some scientists are theoreticians. With a penchant for calculation and contemplation, they never go near a laboratory. Others work like Sherlock Holmes or Hercule Poirot, piecing together disparate clues in pursuit of their prey – the microbe responsible for a newly-recognized infection like Legionnaires' disease, for example. Despite the caricature of the mildly eccentric, white-coated boffin, which is commonplace in novels and comic strips, scientists are an extremely variegated group – more so than most other professions.

The motives for doing science vary too. The spectrum ranges from the disinterested quest for new information, without any tangible goal in view, to the solution of immediate problems in agriculture, transportation and other practical fields. The former (pure, basic or fundamental science) is concerned solely to compile increasingly accurate pictures of the physical and biological world. Sometimes termed "curiosity-oriented" science, its only justifications are intellectual and cultural. The lack of immediate practical applications has made this kind of science vulnerable to economies in times of economic stringency. Over the long term, pure science does, of course, generate data and insights which are later turned to practical benefit. But that is not its *raison d'être*.

Projects in applied science, on the other hand, are initiated because those providing the finance want clearly identified returns such as an improved antirheumatic drug, electric light bulb or helicopter stabilizing device. This is often called "mission-oriented" research. Much of it, in specialities such as mechanical, civil, electrical and electronic engineering, is synonymous with technology. Today, one of the fastest growing disciplines is biotechnology – the manipulation of animal, plant and microbial life to yield useful products and processes.

In areas such as medical research, the distinction between pure and applied science becomes blurred. Some of the investigations carried out in medical research institutes are concerned with the basic chemistry and genetics of living cells. They hardly differ from similar studies conducted inside laboratories devoted to pure science. The term "strategic research" is increasingly used to describe fundamental work whose results may be required to solve foreseeable practical problems in future.

Imagination and creativity

Psychologists and psychiatrists are fond of debating whether scientists are born or made. Lawrence Kubie, for example, argues that the motive for entering science is often a need to gratify unconscious neurotic desires. In extreme cases, he insists, this can lead to cheating (♦ *page 82). He describes one neurotic scientist "who had proved his case, but was so driven by his anxieties that he had to bolster an already proven theorem by falsifying some statistical data." British psychologist Liam Hudson (b.1933) believes that the type of person who tends to become a scientist is one who likes to tackle questions where clear answers are likely to be found – in contrast to the arts-oriented individual who prefers more open-ended questions. He extends this contrast between "convergers" and "divergers" to differentiate activities within science. Many rank-and-file researchers appear to match Hudson's stereotypes. Yet many of the greatest scientists have a streak of creativity that seems closer to that of the artist. Given the heterogeneity of the scientific community, it is unlikely that even a narrow majority of its members match any one psychological analysis. It does appear that the emphasis placed on rationality in science teaching, and in the presentation of research findings in the scientific literature (*♦ *page 78), may discourage people from entering a field they believe to require mental approaches quite different from their own.*

Six Scientists

Dr A   Research director trained in biochemistry

Employment
Head of a 40-strong research team, multinational pharmaceutical company in Basel, Switzerland

Objective
To develop drugs which combat viral diseases, comparable with the antibiotics which attack bacteria

Principal working tools
Well-equipped laboratory to synthesize and purify novel chemicals, and computers to assess their likely activity. Animal house

Style of work
1. Decides which chemicals are promising antiviral agents
2. Assesses budgets for projects and agrees them with the research director and company board
3. Directs synthesis and testing
4. Processes results for significance by statistical analysis

Profile
Dr A's team contains two types of scientist (each supported by technicians). His chemists work on synthesizing molecules with slightly different structures, in the hope that one will show antiviral activity, thereby indicating further structural changes that may achieve greater potency. His microbiologists screen the chemists' products for antiviral activity. This is done by adding measured quantities to specific viruses multiplying in cells growing in glass vessels and measuring the diminution of virus growth, if any. The reliability and standardization of these tests is crucially important.

Dr B   Theoretical physicist

Employment
Team leader, Fermi National Accelerator Laboratory, near Chicago, Illinois

Objective
To evolve mathematical models, which explain the internal structure of the atomic nucleus

Principal working tools
Library, computer, databases

Style of work
1. Studies data generated by particle accelerators
2. Researches and studies contemporary theories in subatomic physics

Profile
At one time believed to be a fundamental unit of matter, the nucleus of the atom is known to have a complex structure of its own. Dr B is trying to work out how certain forces inside the nucleus account for its physical behavior although she does not herself carry out any experiments. She relies instead on data derived from the more practical world of high energy physics, and ideas thrown up by other theoreticians. Dr B is also concerned about the complexity of contemporary theories of the subatomic world. Because nature is usually elegantly simple, these ideas are probably erroneous. So, just as Albert Einstein created new theoretical models to supplant the Newtonian picture of the universe, Dr B is one of the theoreticians whose task today is to formulate a more satisfying portrait of nature.

Dr C   Animal behaviorist

Employment
Research Fellow, University of Geneva

Objective
To assess the intelligence and social behavior of mountain gorillas

Principal working tools
Field research, Virunga volcanoes, Rwanda, Africa

Style of work
Monitors family group recording their movements by long-term observation in the wild

Profile
Dr C is curious to know whether the remarkable intelligence shown by gorillas in captivity is also apparent in the wild. Do the animals need to use their brainpower to solve physical tasks day by day? Do they behave intelligently in dealing with each other? Dr C's method of answering her questions about intelligent behavior in gorillas – indeed, the *only* way of answering them – is by close, unremitting watchfulness. This is science in the tradition of natural history, as practiced by Gilbert White who, in the late 18th Century, wrote his *Natural History and Antiquities of Selbourne*, to record the changing English countryside through the seasons. It is also the method of the younger Charles Darwin – though as the years passed he began to relate his observations more consciously to an emerging theory as to how the panoply of life on Earth had risen and changed.

Dr D   Consultant scientist

Employment
Partner in Scientific Consultancy,
Cambridge Science Park, UK

Objective
To solve practical problems brought
to the company by small
manufacturing companies

Principal working tools
Well equipped all-purpose
laboratory plus access to more
specialized equipment as required

Style of work
Invents and improves gadgets

Profile
Much closer to the media caricature
of the white-coated boffin is Dr D.
Unlike Drs A, B and C, he has moved
away from the subject in which he
took his first degree (chemistry) and
is now a polymath whose work
covers electronics, microbiology,
and several other disciplines too.
Virtually all of the problems brought
to him are thoroughly practical –
how to prevent mildew growing on
a new type of plasterboard, for
example, or how to detect errors in
the operation of a semi-automatic
production line making mechanical
toys. On a typical day, he is to be
found fiddling with a light-sensitive
photoelectric cell, which he is
mounting inside a novel design of
heat-resistant shield for operation
inside a furnace used at a nearby
factory. It is part of a new system of
temperature monitoring, and is the
fourth adaptation of a design
evolved by Dr D many months ago.
The gadget has been patented, and
will be marketed commercially.

Dr E   Geneticist

Employment
Professor, University of Adelaide

Objective
To establish a theoretical model to
explain the way in which living cells
regulate their internal chemistry

Principal working tools
Laboratory with analytical
and cell culture equipment

Style of work
Pieces together evidence from
several different lines of enquiry
(for example, the decoding of
genetic messages or how bacteria
resist destruction by antibiotics)
and gathers data from research
journals and own experimentation

Profile
Interest in Dr E's work has, in recent
years, focused on the question of
how the chemical machinery by
which cells release energy from
foodstuffs and build up structural
materials is regulated. Why, at any
one time, do not all of those
chemical reactions proceed at full
pace? What switches them on and
off? How do the various parts of
metabolism work so harmoniously –
a harmony drastically destroyed in
cancer? Dr E has constructed a
model of cell regulation that fits the
facts. It has even spawned
predictions confirmed by further
experiments. Part theoretician, part
experimentalist, he has applied
logic, systematic work and
imaginative speculation to a
problem whose solution has
required insights from several,
traditionally separate disciplines.

Dr F   Physiologist

Employment
University of Loamshire

Objective
To publish lots of papers as quickly
as possible and without much
original thought

Principal working tools
Laboratory with analytical and other
equipment. Animal house

Style of work
1. Monitors latest publications in
his field and selects lines of
investigations to replicate
2. Performs test – copying
experimental method already
established – and writes up results

Profile
Dr F is virtually impotent as an
innovator, devoid of imaginative
creativity, and bereft of practical
skills. He simply copies what other
investigators do. His findings are of
interest simply because they have
never been reported before. Some
day, another researcher may well
peruse the data and use the figures
to draw new conclusions. It is
possible, for example, that the two
sets of measurements, compared
and contrasted, will yield new
insights into the relationship
between differences in kidney
function and the evolutionary links
between hamsters and rabbits. But
Dr F fails to make that intellectual
leap and very soon has to move on
to a new project because he does
not know what to do next with this
one. Replication of research findings
is necessary in science, but Dr F is
conspicuous in doing nothing else.

Mistakes in science are no disgrace; what matters is to learn from what has happened

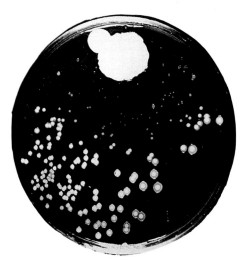

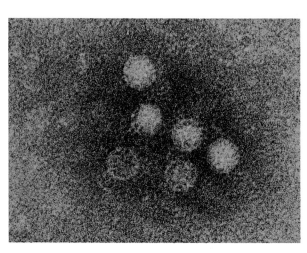

▲ *One summer day in 1928, a spore of the mold Penicillium fell on nutrient medium in a glass dish which British bacteriologist Alexander Fleming (1881-1955) was inoculating with staphylococci. Rather than being incubated as usual, the plate seems to have been left on the bench, allowing penicillin produced by the mold to come into contact with the growing bacteria. As shown on the original plate the then-unknown antibiotic curbed the growth of the staphylococci – an action which later proved of enormous practical significance. But Fleming's chance observation, which he misinterpreted, was not developed for another decade, when it was taken up by Howard Florey (1898-1968) and Ernst Chain (1906-1979), who isolated and purified penicillin – the first wonder drug.*

◄ *Rhinoviruses, a major cause of the common cold, were another discovery owing much to chance. In the early 1960s David Tyrrell and colleagues at the Common Cold Research Unit, Salisbury, England, were trying to isolate disease-causing viruses by inoculating nasal secretions into cells growing in a solution of salts. When something went wrong with the solution, Tyrrell borrowed a batch from another laboratory. Very soon he found what he was looking for – because the solution was more acidic than expected.*

▼ *Computer graphics illustrate the molecular configurations of histamine, study of which led to the development of firstly antihistamines to treat hay fever, and later a powerful series of drugs to combat peptic ulcers. Both have been triumphs for scientific drug design – in this case the production of substances capable of blocking "receptors" on cells normally sensitive to something harmful.*

A discovery by accident

Because science is unique as a human activity in continually breaking new ground, because outstanding science is truly revolutionary, and because scientists are concerned with the unknown, it is also a field in which error is permissible. Mistakes are no disgrace; what matters is whether those making them learn from what has happened. One occasion when a researcher capitalized on a capricious accident occurred in 1940, when the Russian hormone expert Andrew Nalbandov, working in the United States, was trying to discover ways of helping patients whose pituitary gland had been destroyed by disease or injury. He was using chickens and removing the gland by the operation known as hypophysectomy. Despite attempts at replacement therapy – providing the hormones the birds no longer received from the pituitary – they always died. Then, quite suddenly, most of one group of chickens survived for many weeks and even months. As nothing else had changed, Nalbandov presumed that his surgical technique had improved. But then the next group of birds again died after the operation. Some months later, there was a second period when they all survived. Examining his laboratory records, Nalbandov found no factors that could have made any possible difference. There was no evidence that an infection was to blame. Nalbandov was baffled.

The actual explanation began to emerge at two o'clock one morning when Nalbandov was driving home from a party and noticed lights still burning in the animal rooms. "I thought that a careless student had left them on, so I stopped to turn them off," he recalls. "A few nights later I noted again that the lights had been left on all night. Upon enquiry it turned out that a substitute janitor, whose job it was to make sure at midnight that all the windows were closed and doors locked, preferred to leave the light on in the animal house in order to be able to find the exit door. Further checking showed that the two survival periods coincided with the time when the substitute janitor was on the job. Controlled experiments soon showed that the hypophysectomized chickens kept in darkness all died, while chickens lighted for two periods nightly lived indefinitely."

Further tests revealed that the explanation was simplicity itself. Chickens spending the night in the dark do not eat. When combined with the removal of their pituitary gland, this produces a severe degree of hypoglycemia (low blood sugar) from which they cannot recover. But even brief periods of illumination are sufficient to encourage birds to eat, thereby taking in sufficient sugar to prevent the fatal hypoglycemia.

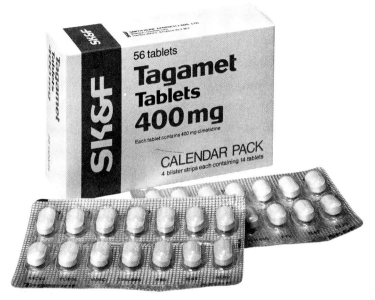

A discovery by design – cimetidine

*In contrast, the development of cimetidine followed
a totally rational course. The story began with some
"pure science" at the Wellcome Research
Laboratories in Britain in 1910, when researchers
found that histamine made smooth muscle
contract and lowered blood pressure. The similarity
between its effects and the symptoms which
appeared during inflammation and following shock
produced by injury and allergy led to the realization
that histamine released at these times was the
immediate cause of the symptoms. In turn, that
triggered off a search for drugs to prevent the ill
effects. Such substances were found and are now
widely used as antihistamines to treat hay fever
and related conditions. They work as inhibitors,
blocking off "receptors" – specific patches on
sensitive tissues which respond to histamine.*

*Meanwhile, other scientists realized that
histamine also stimulated the secretion of
hydrochloric acid by the stomach wall. As excess
acid production is the root cause of peptic
ulceration, researchers tried giving antihistamines
to animals and human ulcer victims. But it did not
work. Although the drugs blocked off histamine
receptors in muscle, they had no effect on acid
secretion. The receptors in the stomach must be
different. Reasoning along these lines led Dr (now
Sir) James Black and his colleagues at Smith Kline
and French Research Ltd to begin in 1964 a
program of work designed to locate chemicals
capable of blocking those specific receptors.
Assuming that any blocking agent would have a
very similar structure to histamine, they decided to
synthesize a large number of related histamine
analogs. Four years later, after screening 200 of
them, they detected the first, weak but significant,
activity. Altering that molecule further, by
lengthening its side chain and making further
modifications, they eventually produced
cimetidine. Now known as a H2-receptor
antagonist, it was first marketed in 1977 and is
widely used to treat peptic ulcers and the
hyperacidity which often precedes ulceration.*

▲ **Tagamet (cimetidine),
developed by James Black
and colleagues at the UK
laboratories of Philadelphia-
based Smith Kline & French
Laboratories, is a product of
rational drug design which
has brought relief to
thousands of peptic ulcer
sufferers. The first billion-
dollar drug in history,
Tagamet is unlikely to have
emerged had Black not
been given a rare degree of
freedom to develop his
ideas.**

Cooperation in science

Since World War II, there has been a spectacular growth in research involving huge teams drawn from several different institutions, usually in fields where costs have rocketed and made cooperation essential. The outstanding example is subatomic physics – now called high energy physics. A typical paper in this field published around 1950 and titled "Angular distribution of neutrons from targets bombarded by 190 MeV deuterons" was written by three authors whose detection equipment was a simple Geiger counter. Over 30 years later, a comparable paper headed "Inclusive hadron scattering from 50 to 175 GeV V/c" was composed by no fewer than 36 researchers, working in 11 different institutions. The energy applied by their equipment had increased 1,000 times, and the scientists (supported by large engineering facilities) had replaced the elementary Geiger counter by an elaborate facility costing millions of pounds. That equipment would be used for experiments other than the one reported in the paper, each being planned and conducted by a "collaboration" between a large number of teams and individuals.

Gone are the days when an atomic physicist could perform important experiments more or less alone on the laboratory bench, using equipment purchased through a modest budget from the university physics department. The reality facing a new recruit has been described by Dr Chris Damerell, from the Rutherford Laboratory in Britain, as follows: "He finds himself joining an international team of scientists whose success depends on their ability to push proposals through various national and international committees, to manage massive budgets, to negotiate tight contracts with engineering firms, and to organize the analysis of hundreds of magnetic tapes of data on several large computers in different countries. Worst of all, he finds himself working in an environment which superficially has more the atmosphere of a giant steelworks than that of the quiet contemplative physics department where he has been trained so far." Damerell further compares the structure of the high energy physics community, consisting of compact groups from which ever-expanding collaborations are formed, with that of families within a large city.

Although it is still conceivable to imagine a lone physicist performing a solitary experiment with a Geiger counter, the results are unlikely to be of any significance. By replacing this simple detector with a more sophisticated version, however, and by boosting the power of particles employed as projectiles in subatomic collisions, incomparably more information may be gleaned from each experiment. One reason is that certain questions can be answered only by detecting and identifying most or all of the products of such a collision, and measuring their momentum so as to reconstruct possible parent particles from which the observed ones have decayed. Moreover, some of the most interesting experiments entail collisions between high energy neutrinos, which interact so rarely that massive detectors weighing hundreds of tons are required to monitor them. The growth of collaborations has stemmed, therefore, from two factors. First the need for higher powers meant that university machines were gradually closed down and replaced by "national" machines. As costs escalated further, this led in Europe to the establishment of CERN (Conseil Européen pour la Recherche Nucléaire) in Geneva, where even more powerful accelerators are shared by several nations. Second, as experiments became more complex to plan, execute and analyze, teamwork – in the form of "collaborations" – became increasingly necessary.

▲ *The Big European Bubble Chamber (BEBC) was one of CERN's earlier pieces of equipment jointly funded by the organization's member countries. It consists of a 3.7 meter-diameter cylinder containing liquid hydrogen. Between 1973 and 1984 it was used to take some 6.3 million photographs of interactions between subatomic particles in high-energy accelerators.*

► *Installation of a 65-tonne superconducting coil, part of the equipment needed for electron–positron collision experiments due to commence at CERN, Geneva, in 1989, marks one stage toward some of the largest scientific "collaborations" ever seen. A typical CERN collaboration involves scientists from, say, Amsterdam, Cracow, Munich, Oxford and CERN itself. Rather like a cabal of criminals planning a sophisticated robbery, which may require a locksmith, two drivers, a forger and a fence, a collaboration arises through informal verbal contact between members. They begin to discuss which groups will provide equipment, how to organize the experiment and make best use of their limited, costly time on the machine, and how and where to analyze the resulting data. Sometimes the existence of multiple sources of finance leads to politicking and bartering. One country, for example, may be under government pressure to purchase a home-made computer. If the collaboration as a whole feels that one from elsewhere is more suitable, that country may agree to substitute a less sensitive item of equipment.*

A Laboratory Continent

The continent of Antarctica holds many attractions for scientific research. Almost totally covered by permanent ice to an average depth of more than two kilometers, and experiencing extremes of cold and dryness, it serves as a vast natural laboratory for work in numerous fields of science, including glaciology, meteorology, auroral physics and various earth sciences. Antarctica is also an impressive showpiece of international scientific collaboration, where teams from different nations work together on projects, share research facilities and technology and pool their observations and experimental results.

Recognition of the continent's value to the worldwide scientific community came with two important events in the late 1950s. International Geophysical Year (IGY) 1957-1958 marked a culmination of the postwar trend away from journeys of exploration and short-term, privately-organized expeditions. In that year, 44 research stations manned by some 800 scientific and logistic personnel from 12 nations were established. Their findings and observations yielded much new information about the nature of the continent's ice sheet and geology – as well as supplying important new clues relating to the Earth's geological history, its magnetic field and the atmosphere.

A further stimulus to scientific research was provided by the Antarctic Treaty of 1959. Along with its political clauses freezing territorial claims and guaranteeing nonmilitarization, it encouraged cooperation and ensured freedom of scientific investigation in any part of the continent.

▶ **Negotiating a crevasse 40m deep in the Nye Glacier, Antarctic Peninsula. Scientists collecting specimens in such sites take great care to avoid contaminating their material. In addition to holding appropriate qualifications in, for example, marine biology, research workers in Antarctica have a greater need of physical fitness than their counterparts in temperate climes.**

▼ **The unique conditions of Antarctica have attracted scientists from every other part of the world, and led to the establishment of an increasing number of research stations. The work carried out there ranges from studies on the growth of sea birds to the analysis of the ice sheet as a detailed chronological record of global pollution.**

▶ **A glaciologist collects samples inland from the Halley Station on the Brunt Ice Shelf. The Antarctic Ice Sheet, which contains 90 percent of the world's total fresh water, provides an invaluable record of industrial activities such as radioactive and gaseous discharges, natural events such as volcanic activity, and climatic changes over thousands of years.**

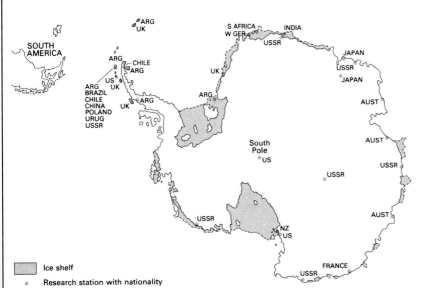

Ice shelf

• Research station with nationality

International Antarctic Glaciological Project

One project founded in the spirit of the 1959 treaty was the International Antarctic Glaciological Project (IAGP), begun in 1969. It unites expeditions from Australia, France, Japan, Britain, the United States and the Soviet Union, and is run by a coordinating council of representatives from the participant teams which meets yearly to compare results and plan future operations.

IAGP exists to carry out a concerted investigation of the East Antarctic ice sheet, drawing from technological advances such as satellite observation, remote sensing and computer simulation. Using the technique of radar altimetry, for example, by which radar signals emitted from an overflying airplane penetrate the ice and reflect upward from its base, detailed maps of both ice elevation and the underlying topography can be built up. Sophisticated radar systems can even discern internal layers within the ice. IAGP workers measure the flow of ice with the help of a satellite which helps to fix the location of a point and record any displacement on subsequent measurement.

In a research project undertaken by a joint Russian–French IAGP team, samples of ice taken from deep boreholes are studied and analyzed for information on the ice's structural properties and trace elements within it – giving evidence of temperature changes, and atmospheric accumulation of carbon dioxide and radiation. The borehole at the Russian Vostok station is 2,000m deep and will give information on climatic history and global pollution going back 160,000 years.

▲ *A field party traveling by Skidoo in the Antarctic Peninsula. During the 1986-1987 austral summer, the United States alone sponsored 255 researchers and 74 experiments in the great white continent. There were 57 stations operating, manned by scientists from 18 nations.*

▼ *A crabeater seal joins a scientist to negotiate the icy waters of Antarctica. Centered on the ecology of krill – a potential source of protein – there is increasing interest in the interrelations between the continent's animals and plants.*

Science is not so organized as to exclude the independent scientist

▶ Although he has done
contract work for NASA in
the United States and much
smaller organizations
elsewhere, independent
scientist James Lovelock
has for many years enjoyed
the freedom to pursue
many diverse interests. One
product of Lovelock's
rumination is the "Gaia
hypothesis", which
portrays the whole of life on
Earth as a single, self-
correcting system.

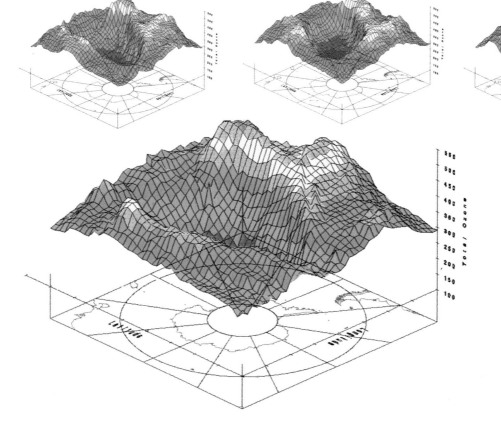

◀ ▲ It was James Lovelock
who first suggested that
the fluorocarbons which are
used as propellants in hair
sprays and other aerosols
might be destroying the
protective layer of ozone in
the Earth's upper
atmosphere. Evidence that
he was right in his
speculation comes from
these daily plots of the
ozone hole at the South
Pole, located in 1986 by the
NASA Climate Data System
(team leader Donald F.
Heath) and the National
Space Science Data Center
through the World Data
Center-A for Rockets and
Satellites.

An independent scientist

It is often argued that operating independently as a scientist is hardly possible now that science is a highly organized profession. One person who disproves that view is James Lovelock, who works from his home in the English countryside. He is famed for his invention of the electron capture detector, which has revolutionized environmental analysis, and as the author of the "Gaia hypothesis" according to which the entire biosphere of the Earth comprises a self-regulating organism. Lovelock has received the accolade of being elected a Fellow of the Royal Society (♦ page 88) and his research has attracted the interest of many different organizations, including NASA, who have approached him about serving as a consultant. But his motives for pursuing particular topics have seldom if ever been immediate financial reward: "I wanted to be able to do scientific creative work without any constraints from employers or customers who, even with the best will in the world, tend to interfere. Gradually, I found that the answer lay in doing only those things which were truly interesting or which curiosity inspired. Strangely, the work done to answer such questions as 'I wonder if' almost always led to bread and butter in two or three years' time."

Detection of chlorofluorocarbons

During a summer visit to his holiday cottage in western Ireland, Lovelock noticed that the air was sparklingly clear when the wind blew from the Atlantic, but hazy when the wind came from continental Europe. Could this be smog, carried from industrial cities in Europe? Meteorological colleagues assured Lovelock that air pollution would not travel that far, and suggested instead that the haze might originate with strange exhalations in the Irish bogs.

Next year, Lovelock took his electron capture detector on holiday with him, intent on analyzing the air on a hazy day to see whether it contained any solely manmade substance(s). Common pollutants such as sulfur dioxide would not count, because they originate in nature too. But when Lovelock detected chlorofluorocarbons – the gases used to propel aerosol sprays – he felt convinced that human pollution was to blame.

Lovelock discovered that chlorofluorocarbons also occurred, in lower concentrations, in air sweeping in from the Atlantic. Were they really traveling all the way from America? Or were chlorofluorocarbons building up in the world's atmosphere generally, because they were highly stable and not broken down in the environment?

Lovelock made several unsuccessful efforts to secure funding for a global sampling operation – one of his grant applications was rejected on the grounds that it was frivolous. Eventually he was able to confirm that the gases were indeed accumulating worldwide. This was the discovery which led to fears that aerosol propellants could be destroying the ozone layer. The phenomenon would never have come to light without the enquiring mind and obstinacy of a solitary scientist.

Self-employed scientists

Self-employed scientists now comprise a growing fraternity in the United States and other countries too. Although some disciplines such as particle physics are ruled out on grounds of expense and a lack of paying customers, many brands of science are appropriately carried out in this way. Microbiologists, for example, can sell their services to food and other companies, tracing contamination, identifying microbes responsible for spoilage, and advising on hygiene and sterility procedures. Some consulting scientists set up laboratories specializing in analytical and investigative techniques. For others, the working tools are computerized databases and modern techniques of data and information processing. In fields such as pharmaceuticals, consultants often combine their scientific skills with expertise in market research. Paralleling changes in other areas – the "cottage industry" style of publishing, for example – the trend toward freelance science brings many benefits to employers, who are freed from the overheads involved in having permanent staff. At the same time, successful consulting scientists combine high earning power with freedom from the bureaucracy and daily routine that often accompany work in a large institution.

▼ Dian Fossey observing silverback mountain gorillas in Rwanda typifies the scientist as a natural historian. By meticulous observation, and by living very close to her subjects, such a researcher is able to discern patterns of behavior and social interactions that could never be understood through laboratory work or by theoretical speculation. Even the "harder" sciences have benefited by this sort of investigation, as when Tufts University, Boston, researchers monitored the spread of intestinal bacteria among primates in the wild in Africa.

Maps of Science

▶ *The relationships between different sectors of science can be shown as a map, using the technique of "multi-dimensional scaling", developed by the Philadelphia-based Institute for Scientific Information. Firstly, heavily-cited papers in a particular field are presented as a cluster in such a way that the closeness between papers reflects the degree to which they have been cited together by other authors. These clusters are then clustered successively to produce a mega-cluster or global map of science.*

▼ *Based on the principle of "co-citation strength", but drawn to a finer scale, this map shows relationships within the biomedical and physical sciences. As in the global map, the distances from one circular cluster to another reflect the strength of the intellectual links between those domains. The sizes of the individual circles correspond to the numbers of heavily-cited key papers in the clusters.*

Global map of science

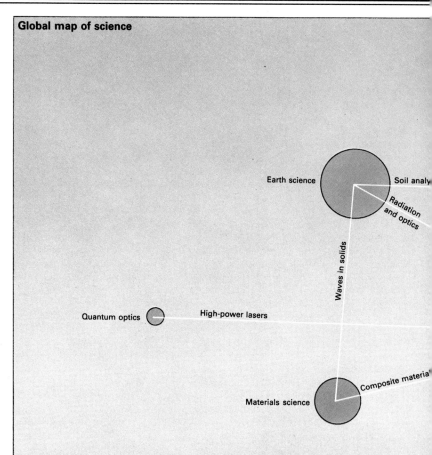

Biomedical and physical science

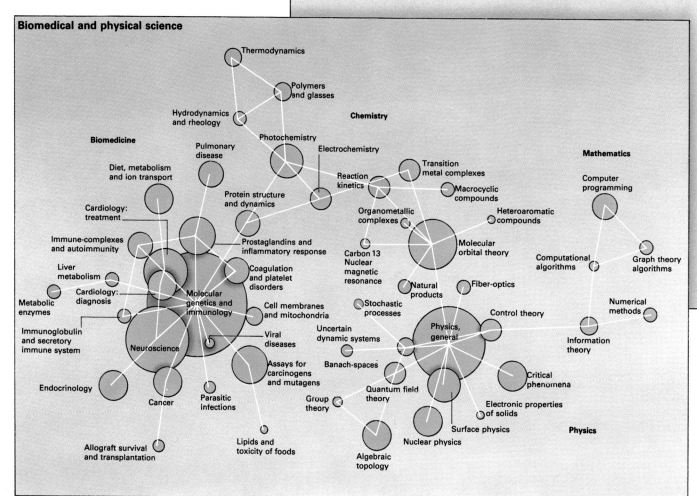

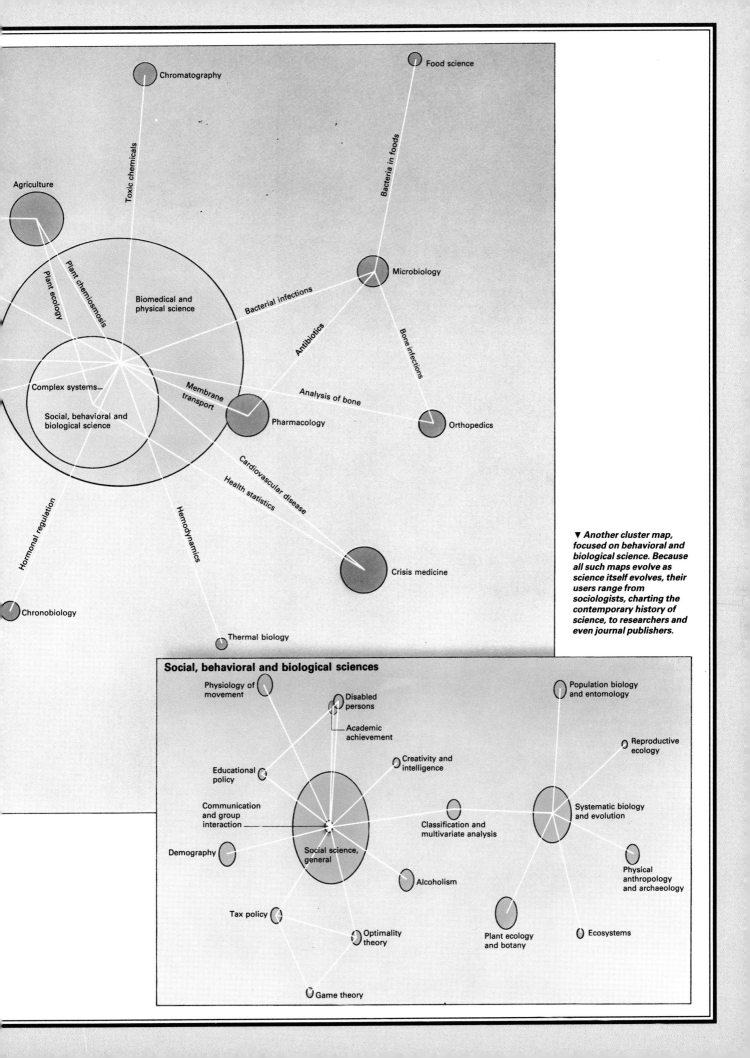

Chromatography

Food science

Toxic chemicals

Bacteria in foods

Agriculture

Plant chemiosmosis

Plant ecology

Biomedical and
physical science

Bacterial infections

Microbiology

Antibiotics

Bone infections

Complex systems

Membrane
transport

Analysis of bone

Social, behavioral and
biological science

Pharmacology

Orthopedics

Cardiovascular disease

Hormonal regulation

Health statistics

Hemodynamics

Crisis medicine

Chronobiology

Thermal biology

▼ Another cluster map,
focused on behavioral and
biological science. Because
all such maps evolve as
science itself evolves, their
users range from
sociologists, charting the
contemporary history of
science, to researchers and
even journal publishers.

Social, behavioral and biological sciences

Physiology of
movement

Disabled
persons

Population biology
and entomology

Academic
achievement

Reproductive
ecology

Creativity and
intelligence

Educational
policy

Communication
and group
interaction

Classification and
multivariate analysis

Systematic biology
and evolution

Demography

Social science,
general

Physical
anthropology
and archaeology

Alcoholism

Tax policy

Optimality
theory

Plant ecology
and botany

Ecosystems

Game theory

J.B.S. Haldane

J.B.S. Haldane (1892-1964) was polymathic in his interests and achievements to a degree that is now virtually unknown. He was the son of the British physiologist J.S. Haldane, who cheerfully sent him underwater in an oversized diving suit at the age of 13 to assist his studies on decompression sickness. "Jack" Haldane began work with the vitamins pioneer F.G. Hopkins (♦ page 56) in Cambridge, but soon became interested in enzymes. Unlike other biologists of his time, Haldane was not content to know that enzymes were catalysts which promoted particular chemical transformations in living cells. Having read mathematics (as well as classics and philosophy) at Oxford, he set out to devise equations expressing their rates of reaction – resulting in an analysis which he expounded in the now-classic book "Enzymes" (1930).

Realizing that enzyme activity must be controlled by genes, which somehow switch them on and off, Haldane turned next to the science of genetics. Working with the Briton R.A. Fisher (1890-1962) and the American Sewall Wright (b.1889), he laid the foundations of the mathematical study of population genetics, showing how genes and mutations spread during the process of evolution. Meeting Lionel Penrose (1898-1972) precipitated a further extension of this line of enquiry, which led him, virtually single-handedly, to turn the formerly descriptive science of human genetics into a rigorous quantitative subject.

Alongside these and other pioneering efforts in plant and animal breeding and other disciplines, Haldane never lost his interest in physiology. He continued to work on respiration and other bodily processes, often using himself as an heroic experimental subject.

Haldane was also a highly skilled popularizer of science, writing brilliantly clear articles on scientific phenomena and ideas for the communist "Daily Worker" and books such as "Daedalus, or Science and the Future" (1924) and "Everything has a History" (1951). An avowed Marxist, Haldane finally broke with the Communist Party after the Lysenko affair and in 1957 emigrated to India, later becoming a citizen of that country. Among his unique epitaphs are an obituary he wrote for himself, and the poem "Cancer's a Funny Thing", which begins with the words: "I wish I had the voice of Homer, To sing of rectal carcinoma..."

► *"A with-knobs-on variant of us all" (to quote his friend Sir Peter Medawar), J.B.S. Haldane could have made a successful career as a mathematician, classical scholar, philosopher, scientist, journalist, or imaginative writer, and to some extent he was all six. Haldane made pioneering contributions in physiology, biochemistry and genetics – notably the mathematical theory of natural selection. He was a supremely effective popularizer of science, and took an active part in political life. Here, a few months before the outbreak of World War II, he publicizes the inadequacy of government policy by eel-fishing in an uncompleted "Anderson" air-raid protection trench, alongside members of the Unemployed Workers Movement. (Haldane's 1938 book "ARP" on air-raid protection was one of the earliest attempts to apply mathematics to strategy.)*

▲ *In 1957 Haldane and his second wife Helen Spurway took up posts at the Indian Statistical Institute in Calcutta. He adopted Indian citizenship and (above) dress. Later he set up the Genetics and Biometry Laboratory at Bhubaneswar in Orissa with the backing of the chief minister, and founder of the Kalinga Prize, Biju Patnaik.*

Ideas of Science

4

*The hypothetico-deductive method...Causality...
Control and reproducibility in experimental science...
Inductive thinking...PERSPECTIVE...Ideals in science...
Mapping the cause of cancer...An abuse of statistics...
The Scientific Method*

As we have seen, science is a heterogeneous profession. Its members embrace both intuition and objectivity. It is also deeply affected by social, political and economic pressures. Furthermore, science as experienced from the inside by its own practitioners does not always accord with science as portrayed from the outside by philosophers and sociologists (♦ page 63). Nevertheless, there are certain attitudes which, while not unique to the profession, are held with peculiar tenacity by all physicists, chemists, biologists and other specialists who call themselves scientists.

Preeminently, scientists are committed to the search for, and belief in, *rational* answers to questions about the nature of life and the physical universe. And in pursuing those answers, they try to adhere to particular habits of thought that have proved reliable in the past in the painstaking process of building up increasingly dependable pictures of the world.

Scientists are human, like everyone else, rather than desiccated calculating machines. They make mistakes and have flashes of inspiration. So it is not difficult to find examples to contradict the image of scientists as single-mindedly objective in their outlook. At the same time, there *is* a cast of mind that binds all scientists together – an acute regard for intellectual rigor, a critical stance toward evidence, and an insistence on due caution when conclusions are drawn.

Central to scientific investigation is the formulation of hypotheses, the validity of which can be explored by collecting evidence (through experiments or observation) and by deductive reasoning (♦ page 54). There is no place in science for metaphysics or even for intellectual reflection that is totally divorced from evidence and observations concerning the real world.

While the wholesale collection of data through induction is an inelegant and usually costly approach to science (♦ page 56), it does have the virtue of being founded on concrete observations and phenomena. The stepwise process of reasoning known as deduction, on the other hand, is foreign to science if it takes place in a vacuum, isolated from the material world. Some scientists would cite the Aristotelian tradition of scholastic theology – illustrated by St Thomas Aquinas's proofs of the existence of God – as an example. But deduction allied to hypothesizing and practical investigation is an essential tool of science. Sometimes an hypothesis is expressed as a model – a conceptual construct (for example, a depression on a weather map) which indicates relationships as they are thought to obtain in the real world. Research scientists disagree over whether, in testing their hypotheses, they are guided more by the tactic of verification or that of falsification (♦ page 64). Certainly, an hypothesis that cannot be subjected to any such test is unlikely to be of significant value in advancing science.

Ideals in science

The ideas of science discussed in these pages are to some degree ideals too, in the sense that some advances occur in a far less tidy and intellectual fashion. Even without cheating (♦ page 82), researchers may decide to place on one side data that do not conform to a cherished hypothesis. Luck and accidents (♦ page 36) play their part. Historically, too, some of the greatest breakthroughs have stemmed from neither observation nor experiment but from wishful thinking and blatantly unscientific ideas as was the case with Johannes Kepler's laws of planetary motion.

Similarly, Copernicus' later decision to place the Sun rather than the Earth at the center of the universe was not a simple, elegant outcome of new astronomical observations. Its origin was the semireligious notion, traceable to Plato, that the Sun ought to be at the center because it represented the greatest worth of all things in nature. Even today, scientists have occasional flirtations with irrationality – as shown by physicists who have been seduced by claims of paranormal metal-bending and then had to retract their views in the light of further experience (♦ page 120). Nevertheless, scientists recognize that their success in their craft is likely to depend on the degree to which they adhere to the "hypothetico-deductive" approach and its associated ideas, such as controlled experiments.

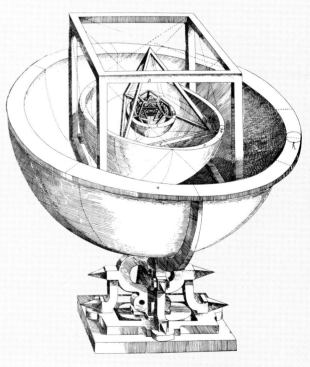

▲ Although Johannes Kepler was a brilliant mathematician, his representation of the Solar System was also founded upon the "harmony of the spheres" and his mystical belief in a power from the Sun which steered the planets in their courses.

Ideas of cause and effect have undergone modification in the light of modern physics

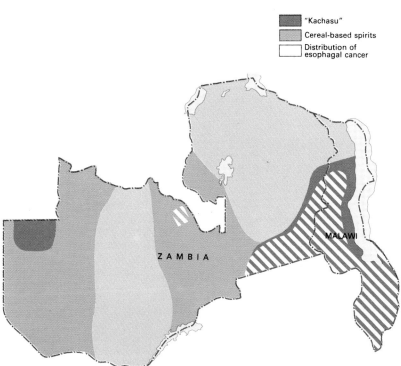

"Kachasu"
Cereal-based spirits
Distribution of esophagal cancer

ZAMBIA

MALAWI

▲ **Journeying through central Africa in the mid-1960s, Neil McGlashan solved the problem of why clusters of esophageal cancer correlated with areas in which people drank illicitly distilled spirits. He pinpointed Kachasu as the drink which caused the cancer. At first he suspected copper and zinc in the drink, which had originated from the tubing and crude stills used to distill Kachasu from a corn and sugar beverage. But that idea was trounced by the discovery of high amounts of these metals in liquor consumed in areas with low cancer rates. The real culprit proved to be dimethyl-N-nitrosamine, produced by "wild" yeasts which had contaminated the fermentation.**

The pattern of esophageal cancer

For many years, medical scientists were perplexed by the extremely patchy distribution of esophageal cancer in central Africa. Claims regarding the cause of this tumor centered upon everything from smoking and diet to particular elements in the soil. But none of these alleged links stood up to critical examination. The real breakthrough in fathoming the problem came in the early 1960s when Dr R.J.W. Burrell painstakingly plotted the homes of esophageal cancer victims on maps of regions where the disease was especially common. After trying to correlate the cancer incidence with several likely environmental, social and geographical factors, he spotted a marked clustering of patients' homes around shebeens – stores of illicitly distilled spirits. Moreover, the distribution of cases altered from time to time, and Burrell noticed that this happened whenever the police located and then closed particular shebeens.

Although extremely clear in retrospect, the relationship between spirit drinking and tumor formation was not at all easy to discern at the time, for two reasons. First, there was a latent period between ingestion of the alcohol and the appearance of cancer. Second, many victims – especially the Bantu – did not come to immediate medical attention but preferred instead to hide away in stoic fatalism. Within a few years, Burrell's research had set another investigator, Neil McGlashan, on the track of the real culprit, which proved to be dimethyl-N-nitrosamine. Produced by "wild" yeasts which had contaminated the fermentation, this was later also found in pickles eaten in a devout Muslim area of northern Iran where esophageal cancer rates were high but alcohol consumption was virtually unknown.

Cause and effect

One of the most elementary (yet easily forgotten) ideas that guides scientific investigation is the relationship between cause and effect. A Martian arrives on Earth and, after six months of diligent observation, concludes that because policemen are invariably seen around the scenes of criminal acts, they are responsible for them. A farmer notices that sheep which devour a specific type of vegetation also develop unusually tough wool, and he draws the obvious conclusion that a particular plant has caused the fleece to change. Both are wrong. Unfamiliar with Earthlings and their ways, the Martian has been misled by the clustering together of (a) crimes and (b) police officers. The farmer has been impressed by a similar proximity of two phenomena and applied common sense to work out what is happening. In fact, his flock contains some sheep of a new breed which he bought as lambs at auction last year and which (a) relish the taste of a particular plant found in his fields and (b) tend to develop slightly wiry wool. These two phenomena are quite separate. There is no causal relationship between them.

The basic fallacy behind the cases of the Martian and the farmer is the same. When we observe a close – perhaps invariable – relationship between A and B, commonsense may compel us to believe that A causes B. What we ought to do is to consider two rival explanations. B may cause A. Or both A and B may result from C – a third factor, perhaps as yet unidentified.

Disputations about the link between tobacco and lung cancer devolve on these arguments. Decades ago, physicians began to realize that the disease was commoner among smokers, its prevalence reflecting the number of cigarettes smoked each day. Although the obvious conclusion seemed appropriate, it may have been wrong. Perhaps certain individuals had a genetic tendency both to smoke and to develop lung cancer? If so, antitobacco propaganda could have had no effect in curbing the disease.

Only during the 1950s did a meticulous scrutiny of smoking patterns by Richard Doll and Austin Bradford Hill make the commonsense verdict irresistible. One type of evidence that could not be squared with alternative interpretations was the reduced risk of contracting cancer among individuals who gave up the habit. Another was historic parallels between increased smoking and increased lung cancer – particularly among women, who began later than men in most countries.

An important caveat is necessary regarding causality. Until this century, scientists believed that *all* things and phenomena would prove to be explicable on this basis. Like a gigantic machine, the universe was thought to consist of endless sequences of causes and effects – the actions and reactions of forces as described by Isaac Newton, for example. But the dawn of modern physics led to a realization that in the subatomic world, matter and energy behaved in a more bizarre fashion, which could not be described so simply. It also focussed attention on the way in which orderly behavior sometimes emerges from disorderly behavior at a lower level. For example, a quantity of dye, placed at one end of a bathful of water, will spread throughout the water at a rate which can be calculated and predicted – but the movement of individual molecules of dye through the water is random. Likewise, many of the physical laws which govern the universe reflect the net result, the pattern, that emerges from a background of disorder.

◄ As demonstrated in this 19th-century poster, many proprietary medicines had spurious reputations as remedies. Their success reflected the fact that most illnesses cure themselves.

▼ A false-color scanning electron micrograph taken inside the human windpipe shows (top right quarter) the growth of malignant cells. Although the linking of smoking and lung cancer suggests the obvious conclusion, its appearance in nonsmokers and its absence in many heavy smokers indicate that the relationship is not a simple one. However, the much greater prevalence among smokers, and their better chances if they abstain, confirm that tobacco smoke does cause lung cancer.

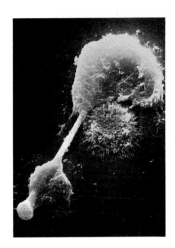

▲ A macrophage, which normally destroys foreign material in the lung, is itself impaled on an asbestos needle in this false-color scanning electron micrograph. The specimen comes from a person suffering from asbestosis. This condition is caused by exposure to asbestos – though it can take years before the effect is seen.

Probability and statistics

Probability is another key principle of scientific investigation and explanation. In one sense, the health effects of smoking can be quantified exactly. Smokers run about double the risk of contracting coronary heart disease as compared with nonsmokers. They are several times as likely to develop chronic bronchitis. And their chances of contracting lung cancer are some 25 times higher. But these dangers must be expressed as probabilities. Given two groups of people, differing only in that one consists of smokers, we can confidently predict that about 25 times more individuals in that group will succumb to lung cancer. What we cannot be certain about are two things. First, the figure may not be exactly 25; it might be 24, 26, or possibly even higher or lower, but will average out at 25 the larger the size of the group. Second, it is impossible to make a firm forecast about any single individual in either population. Some nonsmokers develop lung cancer, just as some very heavy smokers avoid the disease.

This is why scientists have to amass vast quantities of data, even when studying apparently straightforward problems. If, for example, investigators wish to compare atmospheric pollution in two different cities, they cannot simply measure sulfur dioxide and other pollutants in one sample of air from each location on a single occasion. They will need to set up several sampling points in the two cities, and make hundreds of different measurements on separate days, at different times of day, and under varying weather conditions. By averaging out these figures, they can then draw a meaningful comparison between air pollution in the two places. Scientists as disparate as meteorologists and epidemiologists use such methods.

An ornithologist, for example, wanting to study alterations in plumage of wild ducks of a particular species at one nesting site over several years, could waste enormous amounts of time counting and recording every single bird. It is far more convenient, and cheaper, to concentrate on a sample. The whole exercise is designed (a) to make manageable a complex, numerically large area of study, and (b) to generate reliable information from the whole by examining only a part. Statistical techniques will indicate the characteristics and size of sample, and the measurements and observations, required to produce meaningful results.

But statistics, while they cannot "prove anything", can certainly be misleading. Some years ago the distinguished British physician Sir Douglas Black drew attention to the claim by a critic of the pharmaceutical industry that "despite the discovery of insulin, as many people die of diabetes as before". In one sense, this statement is literally true. Diabetes is a contributory cause of death among almost as many people suffering from the disease as it was before Frederick Banting (1891-1941) and Charles Best (1899-1978) isolated the sugar-regulating hormone during the 1920s. But the bald statistic requires further interpretation. First, the world's population has doubled over the past half-century, from 2,000 million to 4,000 million. Second, many diabetics now die beyond the age of 70, whereas before 1920 they would not have survived their youth.

The way in which statistics are brandished in advertising campaigns nowadays illustrates an important divergence between the methods of the scientist and of the lobbyist. When writing a paper, a scientist certainly indulges in advocacy (♦ page 78), but he or she ought to take the widest possible view of a particular problem. The lobbyist selects data to support a predetermined case.

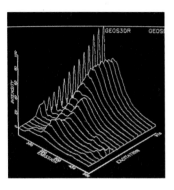

▲ *The gathering of data is fundamental to most observational and experimental science. Telling presentation of results can help analysis and promote better communication of findings. Computer graphics, for this reason, are widely used in science. This image, for example, is a three-dimensional display of variations in the amount and intensity of emission from a chemical compound excited by ultraviolet light. The graphic was produced from data collected by a fluorometer linked to a personal computer.*

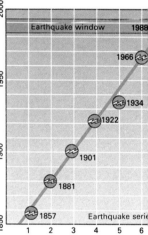

▲ *Since 1857, the Parkfield section of the San Andreas fault in California has experienced five earthquakes which have displayed remarkably similar features. These include the location of the epicenter, the magnitude, and the incidence of pre-shocks. The pattern of recurrence is, moreover, so regular, that scientists monitoring seismic activity there are able to offer a prediction that the next major quake will occur before 1993.*

◄ Seismologists rely on a range of instruments to amass the data they need. Laser distance-ranging devices are positioned in a triangular network across the earthquake zone, at 5-30 km distance one from the other. The technology is sensitive to minute changes in lengths, from which crustal strength can be computed. Using two-color laser systems, like this one, scientists can allow for atmospheric interference.

Predicting earthquakes in California

The study of earthquakes depends on statistics and probabilities. Data on Earth movements must of necessity be sampled, and lack of knowledge about how quakes are triggered means they can be predicted only in terms of likelihood.

Earthquakes are believed to result from sudden slippage between blocks in the upper crust. The great fault lines that mark the boundaries of the Earth's crustal plates are the lines of weakness where such slippage characteristically occurs. "Swarms" of minor quakes, which indicate accumulating strain in a high-friction segment of these faults, are likely precursors of a major earthquake. Measurement of strain, particularly of accelerations in accumulation rates, may thus provide data from which predictions can be made.

The San Andreas fault in southern California is one of several plate boundary sections around the world reckoned to be a candidate for a great earthquake in coming decades. Detailed surveys of landforms and sediments lying across the fault zones point to an average recurrence interval of 140-150 years – the last great quake on the Mojave segment was in 1857.

Instruments are now in place to gather statistics relating to the rate of shear stress accumulation in the crust along key stretches. They include laser distance-ranging devices which monitor minute changes of distance between points either side of the fault. Analysis of the data – which show a steady increase in strain accumulation – allows the long-term probability of earthquake occurrence to be calculated. Taken together with observations of strain release – in the form of modest quakes recorded at points along the fault – different segments of the fault zone can be allocated a different probability measure, the chance of an earthquake of a given magnitude occurring within each segment being expressed as a percentage likelihood.

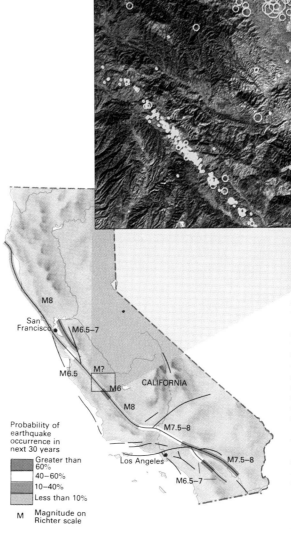

Probability of earthquake occurrence in next 30 years

Greater than 60%
40–60%
10–40%
Less than 10%

M   Magnitude on Richter scale

◄▲ Probability of earthquake occurrence in California has been estimated by geologist Allan Lindh of the US Geological Survey. Zones where crustal strain has been accumulating are thought to be where the danger of release in a massive earthquake is at its greatest. The Parkfield area, magnified in the satellite photograph above, is just such a zone. Small earthquakes (occurrences between 1975 and 1984 are located in the yellow rings) are likely to signal the approach of failure stress in the crust. Shocks from the earthquake at Coalinga in 1983 (top right) may affect the timing of the next Parkfield quake.

The control in experiments

A key idea in research is the "control". When designing an experiment, a scientist often needs to incorporate several such controls so that the results point unambiguously to the correct conclusion. In determining whether a new soap powder is better than its forerunner, for example, a consumer group should not be content with just a single wash. If a batch of garments were to emerge unusually white on that day, this *might* be correctly attributed to the formulation of the product. Alternatively, the improvement might be due to another factor such as the slightly higher temperature of the machine or its greater efficiency on that occasion. Before being certain, the investigator should carry out a controlled experiment with matched pairs of tests, using old and new powders in identical machines in which temperature, time and all other factors are standardized.

Some years ago a newspaper decided to investigate the value of starch blockers – slimming aids that allegedly interfere with the digestion of starch and thus impair the body's uptake of calories. Six volunteers were chosen, weighed and put on the pills. Two dropped out of the trial, but a month later the other four were weighed again. One, having lost very little weight, adjudged the treatment a failure. Another had shed 3.6kg and believed it had been successful. The third was disappointed not to have shed weight, while the fourth had lost 2.3kg but felt sure that the pills were not responsible. The newspaper concentrated on the "successes" and was delighted that the experiment had clarified a previously contentious issue. In fact, no conclusions whatever could be drawn from the trial, because it was not based on controlled tests. Not only was there no group, matched for build, diet and other factors but *not* put onto the starch blockers. In addition, the organizers did not check to ensure that their guinea pigs' weights were stable and neither rising nor falling at the outset.

The technique which should have been applied is that of the "double-blind" trial used to evaluate new pharmaceuticals. Patients are divided randomly to give two groups, matched for age, sex and other relevant attributes. Individuals in the first group receive the drug and those in the second an inactive "placebo" with the same appearance. Neither the patients nor doctors giving the treatment know who is receiving what, nor do the doctors who assess the patients' condition. These precautions ensure that all possible bias is ruled out.

▼ *A variation on the idea of the "control" used to verify results is seen in an experiment conducted by Professor Carroll O. Alley of the University of Maryland in 1975-1976, designed to demonstrate Albert Einstein's 1908 prediction that gravity affects clocks. An array of atomic clocks was flown aboard a US Navy aircraft (below right) on a 32km loop at an average 9,100m above the Chesapeake Bay. In a series of five 15-hour flights, these clocks gained an average of 3-billionths of a second per hour compared with "control" clocks housed in a trailer on the ground (below left). Einstein's calculations predicting that clocks run slower at ground level than in an aircraft flying in weaker gravity at high altitude were confirmed to within one percent.*

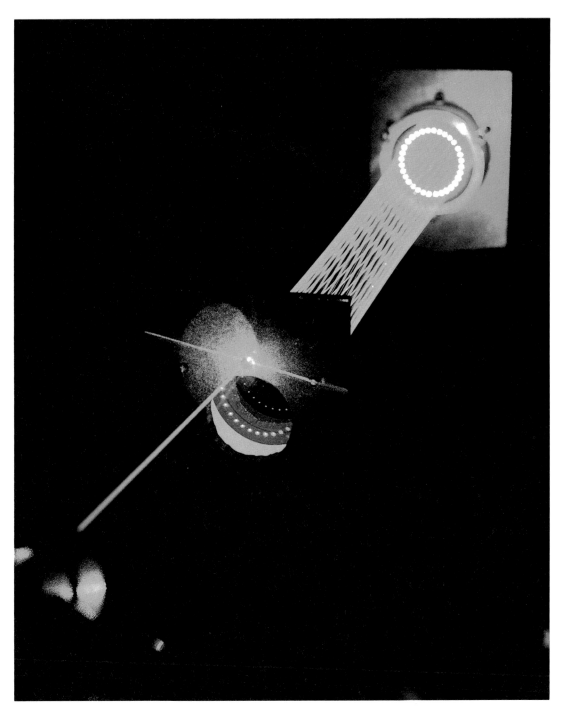

◄ Laser beams criss-cross in an interferometer at Massachusetts Institute of Technology designed to detect gravitational waves. Such waves were predicted by Einstein's general theory of relativity but have yet to be accepted. According to Einstein a gravity wave, passing through space, should generate a transient curvature, within which it should be detectable by its effect on the motion of mechanical systems. But only one person – Professor Joseph Weber working at the University of Maryland – has reported success in constructing apparatus capable of responding to gravity waves. Although there is no suggestion that Weber has reported bogus findings, scientists will not agree on the existence of gravitational waves until they have been independently confirmed.

Reproducibility

Scientists' claims command assent only after they have been accepted by the scientific community (◆ page 71). Thus another vital principle of research is reproducibility. Experimental observations must be recorded under specified conditions, which are described in detail in a research paper so that other investigators can confirm what has been reported. There are two principal reasons for this safeguard. First, scientists make errors such as misreading their equipment (◆ page 121) – which may on occasions be malfunctioning – or overlook the need for particular controls. Sometimes, only when findings are cross-checked in separate laboratories do such mistakes and mis-interpretations come to to light. Second, there are scientists who cheat (◆ page 82), and their fraudulence may be exposed only when other scientists consistently fail to reproduce their work. Current work at the California and Massachusetts Institutes of Technology aimed at detecting gravity waves, for example, if successful will include the vital element of replication of results.

Scientific Method – The Discovery of DNA

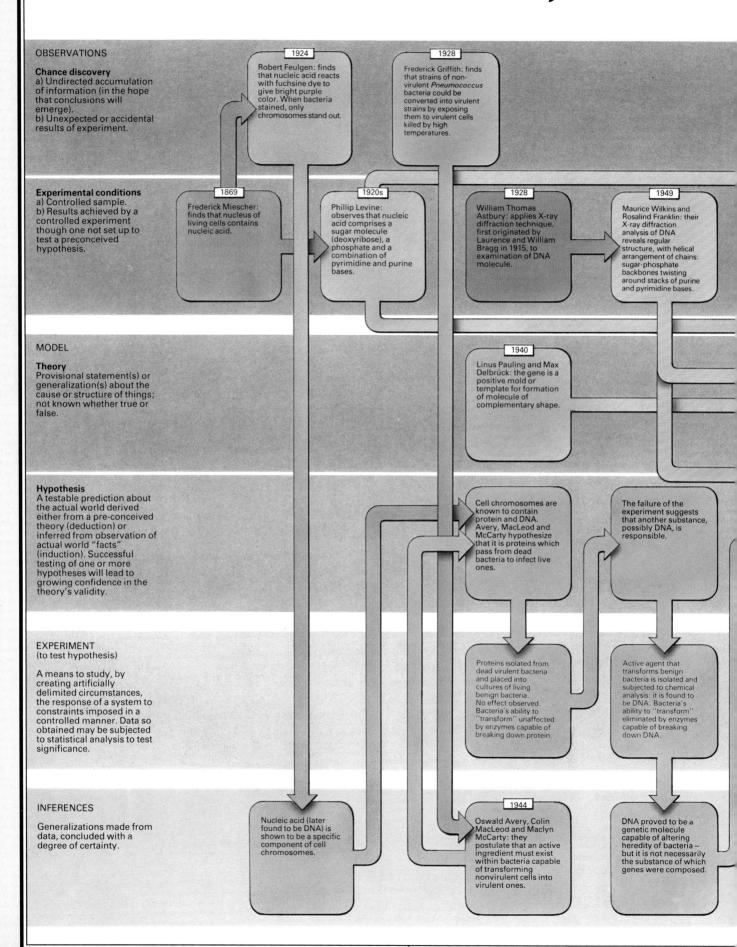

OBSERVATIONS

Chance discovery
a) Undirected accumulation of information (in the hope that conclusions will emerge).
b) Unexpected or accidental results of experiment.

Experimental conditions
a) Controlled sample.
b) Results achieved by a controlled experiment though one not set up to test a preconceived hypothesis.

MODEL

Theory
Provisional statement(s) or generalization(s) about the cause or structure of things; not known whether true or false.

Hypothesis
A testable prediction about the actual world derived either from a pre-conceived theory (deduction) or inferred from observation of actual world "facts" (induction). Successful testing of one or more hypotheses will lead to growing confidence in the theory's validity.

EXPERIMENT
(to test hypothesis)

A means to study, by creating artificially delimited circumstances, the response of a system to constraints imposed in a controlled manner. Data so obtained may be subjected to statistical analysis to test significance.

INFERENCES

Generalizations made from data, concluded with a degree of certainty.

1924 — Robert Feulgen: finds that nucleic acid reacts with fuchsine dye to give bright purple color. When bacteria stained, only chromosomes stand out.

1928 — Frederick Griffith: finds that strains of non-virulent *Pneumococcus* bacteria could be converted into virulent strains by exposing them to virulent cells killed by high temperatures.

1869 — Frederick Miescher: finds that nucleus of living cells contains nucleic acid.

1920s — Phillip Levine: observes that nucleic acid comprises a sugar molecule (deoxyribose), a phosphate and a combination of pyrimidine and purine bases.

1928 — William Thomas Astbury: applies X-ray diffraction technique, first originated by Laurence and William Bragg in 1915, to examination of DNA molecule.

1949 — Maurice Wilkins and Rosalind Franklin: their X-ray diffraction analysis of DNA reveals regular structure, with helical arrangement of chains: sugar-phosphate backbones twisting around stacks of purine and pyrimidine bases.

1940 — Linus Pauling and Max Delbrück: the gene is a positive mold or template for formation of molecule of complementary shape.

Cell chromosomes are known to contain protein and DNA. Avery, MacLeod and McCarty hypothesize that it is proteins which pass from dead bacteria to infect live ones.

The failure of the experiment suggests that another substance, possibly DNA, is responsible.

Proteins isolated from dead virulent bacteria and placed into cultures of living benign bacteria. No effect observed. Bacteria's ability to "transform" unaffected by enzymes capable of breaking down protein.

Active agent that transforms benign bacteria is isolated and subjected to chemical analysis: it is found to be DNA. Bacteria's ability to "transform" eliminated by enzymes capable of breaking down DNA.

Nucleic acid (later found to be DNA) is shown to be a specific component of cell chromosomes.

1944 — Oswald Avery, Colin MacLeod and Maclyn McCarty: they postulate that an active ingredient must exist within bacteria capable of transforming nonvirulent cells into virulent ones.

DNA proved to be a genetic molecule capable of altering heredity of bacteria – but it is not necessarily the substance of which genes were composed.

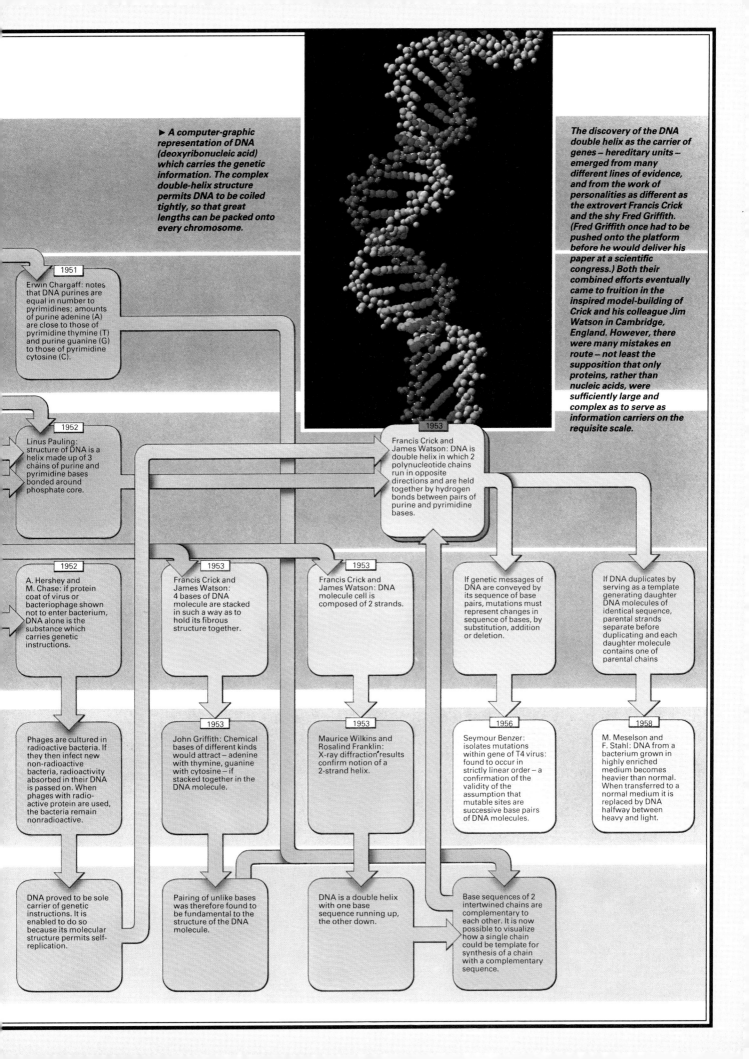

▶ A computer-graphic
representation of DNA
(deoxyribonucleic acid)
which carries the genetic
information. The complex
double-helix structure
permits DNA to be coiled
tightly, so that great
lengths can be packed onto
every chromosome.

*The discovery of the DNA
double helix as the carrier of
genes – hereditary units –
emerged from many
different lines of evidence,
and from the work of
personalities as different as
the extrovert Francis Crick
and the shy Fred Griffith.
(Fred Griffith once had to be
pushed onto the platform
before he would deliver his
paper at a scientific
congress.) Both their
combined efforts eventually
came to fruition in the
inspired model-building of
Crick and his colleague Jim
Watson in Cambridge,
England. However, there
were many mistakes en
route – not least the
supposition that only
proteins, rather than
nucleic acids, were
sufficiently large and
complex as to serve as
information carriers on the
requisite scale.*

1951
Erwin Chargaff: notes
that DNA purines are
equal in number to
pyrimidines; amounts
of purine adenine (A)
are close to those of
pyrimidine thymine (T)
and purine guanine (G)
to those of pyrimidine
cytosine (C).

1952
Linus Pauling:
structure of DNA is a
helix made up of 3
chains of purine and
pyrimidine bases
bonded around
phosphate core.

1953
Francis Crick and
James Watson: DNA is
double helix in which 2
polynucleotide chains
run in opposite
directions and are held
together by hydrogen
bonds between pairs of
purine and pyrimidine
bases.

1952
A. Hershey and
M. Chase: if protein
coat of virus or
bacteriophage shown
not to enter bacterium,
DNA alone is the
substance which
carries genetic
instructions.

1953
Francis Crick and
James Watson:
4 bases of DNA
molecule are stacked
in such a way as to
hold its fibrous
structure together.

1953
Francis Crick and
James Watson: DNA
molecule cell is
composed of 2 strands.

If genetic messages of
DNA are conveyed by
its sequence of base
pairs, mutations must
represent changes in
sequence of bases, by
substitution, addition
or deletion.

If DNA duplicates by
serving as a template
generating daughter
DNA molecules of
identical sequence,
parental strands
separate before
duplicating and each
daughter molecule
contains one of
parental chains

Phages are cultured in
radioactive bacteria. If
they then infect new
non-radioactive
bacteria, radioactivity
absorbed in their DNA
is passed on. When
phages with radio-
active protein are used,
the bacteria remain
nonradioactive.

1953
John Griffith: Chemical
bases of different kinds
would attract – adenine
with thymine, guanine
with cytosine – if
stacked together in the
DNA molecule.

1953
Maurice Wilkins and
Rosalind Franklin:
X-ray diffraction results
confirm notion of a
2-strand helix.

1956
Seymour Benzer:
isolates mutations
within gene of T4 virus:
found to occur in
strictly linear order – a
confirmation of the
validity of the
assumption that
mutable sites are
successive base pairs
of DNA molecules.

1958
M. Meselson and
F. Stahl: DNA from a
bacterium grown in
highly enriched
medium becomes
heavier than normal.
When transferred to a
normal medium it is
replaced by DNA
halfway between
heavy and light.

DNA proved to be sole
carrier of genetic
instructions. It is
enabled to do so
because its molecular
structure permits self-
replication.

Pairing of unlike bases
was therefore found to
be fundamental to the
structure of the DNA
molecule.

DNA is a double helix
with one base
sequence running up,
the other down.

Base sequences of 2
intertwined chains are
complementary to
each other. It is now
possible to visualize
how a single chain
could be template for
synthesis of a chain
with a complementary
sequence.

See also
The Central Tradition 5-24
Styles of Science 33-46
The Philosophy of Science 63-70
Objectivity and Subjectivity 99-110

56

► **The English statesman Francis Bacon (1561-1626), who was Lord High Chancellor under James I of England, believed he was born to serve not only his country but humanity as a whole through his search for goodness and truth. He saw as the central axis of science the recognition of patterns among exhaustive collections of facts. Bacon's method of induction was extended by John Stuart Mill (1806-1873) and more recently by the mathematician Karl Pearson (1857-1936) (far right), who wrote: "The classification of facts and the formulation of absolute judgements upon the basis of this classification...is peculiarly the scope and method of modern science." Few scientists now see induction as more than a very minor part of scientific method.**

Induction

The process of reasoning from particular instances to make general propositions is known as induction. It is the opposite of deduction (◊ pages 9, 15), reasoning from the general to the particular. It was the Englishman Francis Bacon (1561-1626) who, in "Novum Organum" (1620), first presented inductive logic as the logic of scientific discovery as opposed to the logic of argument, deductive logic.

As a scientific method, induction requires the accumulation of large quantities of information in the hope that conclusions will somehow emerge. Sometimes, this does indeed happen. Early studies in meteorology, for example, depended on the widespread gathering of data concerning atmospheric pressure, temperature and other variables. But even here, the indiscriminate collection of figures was soon superseded by the formulation of hypotheses which could be tested and which in turn yielded heuristic models. These expressed both the predictions on which weather forecasting is based and indicated precisely what intensity of information was required to generate dependable routine forecasts. By itself, induction is a mindless and expensive way of garnering results which, with greater forethought, could be collected more quickly to yield more immediate and precise conclusions. A scientist skilled at "thought experiments" is less dependent on practical experiments at the laboratory bench.

By itself, induction is an inefficient method of obtaining results. A strongly contrasting talent – the ability to conduct "thought experiments" – was possessed in abundance by the French bacteriologist Charles Nicolle (1866-1936) and

Louis Pasteur (1822-1895). "Nicolle did relatively few and simple experiments," wrote the American microbiologist, Hans Zinsser (1878-1940). "But every time he did one, it was the result of long hours of intellectual incubation, during which all possible variants had been considered and were allowed for in the final tests. Then he went straight to the point, without wasted motion. That was the method of Pasteur, as it has been of all the really great men of our calling, whose simple, conclusive experiments are a joy to those able to appreciate them." In contrast, the uninspired, mindless collection of data as practiced by Dr F (◊ page 35) is science of the most humdrum kind.

The British mathematician Karl Pearson (1857-1936) was one of the greatest exponents of Baconian induction – the notion that science advances by the wholesale collection of facts, from which conclusions somehow emerge. He was probably one of the last scientists to believe in induction as a universal basis for doing scientific research. "The classification of facts, and the formulation of absolute judgements upon the basis of this classification – judgements independent of the idiosyncracies of the modern mind – is peculiarly the scope and method of modern science," he wrote in "The Grammar of Science" (1892). Pearson was one of the founders of modern statistics (◊ page 50), and evolved the chi-squared test used to determine whether a difference between two sets of statistics is meaningful or insignificant. His development of this and other techniques stemmed from his work in applying statistics to biological problems of heredity and evolution, as well as to issues in the social sciences.

5

Seminal Techniques

*New investigative methods herald scientific advance...
Development of the electron microscope...The impact
of cell fusion techniques...PERSPECTIVE...How new
techniques are disseminated...Interaction of science
and technology: the computer*

In addition to feats of intellect, hard work, and flashes of inspiration, one potent factor behind the advance of science is the advent of new methods of investigation. The light microscope, introduced in its simplest form during the 17th century but brought to perfection in the 19th, revealed previously hidden dimensions of the natural world. Microbes – by definition, organisms seen only under the microscope – were unknown before it was invented. The telescope, in its various incarnations, had also revealed new worlds in and beyond our galaxy. The carbon-dating of archeological specimens, increasingly sensitive techniques of chemical analysis such as chromatography, novel ways of monitoring the movement of wild animals by attaching radio transmitters to them, and modern "noninvasive" techniques of scanning the human body, are just a few of many developments that have spawned enormous amounts of knowledge by placing powerful new tools into scientists' hands.

King of the citations

One indication of the value of a paper after it has appeared in a scientific journal is the number of times it is cited by other scientists when they write up their work for publication (♦ page 76). The fact that they cite the earlier paper means that they have found something useful in it.

Top of the all-time league table is the 1951 report by American Dr O.H. Lowry (b.1910) and his colleagues of a novel method of finding out how much protein a solution contains. Based on a color change which can be measured in a spectrophotometer, this was immediately welcomed as a simple, quick and inexpensive improvement on previous assays. Because protein concentrations need to be determined for many different purposes (from routine urine tests in hospital laboratories to research into industrial microorganisms) Lowry's technique was soon being used all over the world. Other scientists cited his paper 50,000 times between 1961 and 1975 – five times more than the second most highly cited paper at that time. It has now been cited more than any other publication in the history of science.

The enduring impact of a useful technique is illustrated by the ever increasing citations – over 1,700 by end-1987 – of the 1963 paper in which the American R. Bruce Merrifield announced his solid-phase peptide synthesis technique. For this work of greatly speeding up peptide synthesis, Merrifield received the 1984 Nobel Prize for Chemistry.

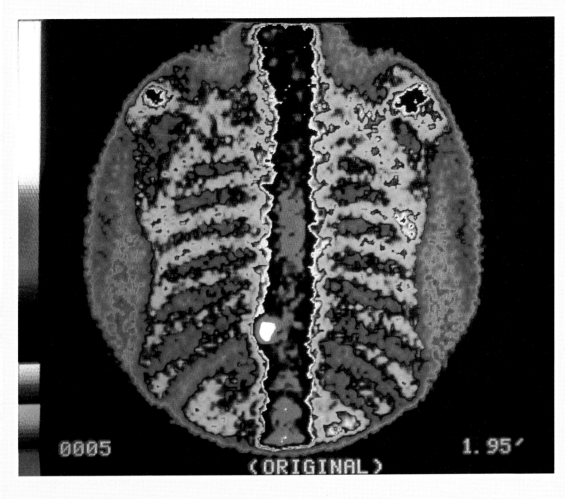

◄ *Novel methods of looking inside the body are giving medical scientists more and better information than was possible when X-rays were used just to spot broken bones. Here a white area indicates a bone tumor in a "scintigram" of the spine and ribs. The photograph was taken with a camera that detects gamma radiation from a substance, injected into the patient beforehand, that has concentrated in the cancer. Other brain and whole body scanning techniques permit scientists not only to detect structural changes in the deep tissues of the body but also to "see" metabolic processes as they happen.*

0005   1.95'
⟨ORIGINAL⟩

With powers a hundred times greater than light microscopes, the electron microscope greatly advanced both physical and biological sciences

► *Ernst Ruska (b.1906) had to wait 53 years, until 1986, to receive a Nobel prize for designing the first electron microscope. Ruska showed that Ernst Abbe (1840-1905), another distinguished German pioneer of optical instruments, was mistaken in arguing (in 1878) that further improvements in microscopy were ruled out by the laws of diffraction. Ruska also confounded critics who believed that exposure to a beam of electrons would burn his specimens to a cinder.*

The electron microscope

Particularly potent because it has found innumerable applications in both physical and biological sciences has been the electron microscope. Based on the notion of replacing light with electrons, focused by magnetic fields rather than glass lenses, the first such machine was devised by the German physicist Ernst Ruska (b.1906) around 1930. Then a doctoral student at the Technical University of Berlin, Ruska described his work in a thesis which is probably the most productive PhD dissertation ever written.

At first, the electron microscope was used only to study metals, and was soon providing new information about their fine structure. Once the original idea that the electron beam would destroy biological specimens was shown to be untrue, however, other investigators began to harness the powerful new machine to study fruit flies, bacteria, and eventually the entire range of microorganisms and plant and animal tissue. As ever in science, there was some opposition to this innovation. "Let's not have an electron microscope," said the eminent Belgian bacteriologist Jules Bordet (1870-1961). "It is troublesome enough to interpret the images we get from light microscopes." Nevertheless, the capacity of the new instrument to resolve far smaller objects (magnifying up to 200,000 times) found it increasingly in demand by microbiologists.

Ernst Ruska joined his brother Helmut to persuade Siemens to manufacture the instrument commercially, the first one being ready in 1938. By the end of World War II, most of the 50 instruments produced were being used in biology laboratories and hospitals. Meanwhile, the Russian-born American Vladimir Zworykin (1889-1982), working for RCA, had made further improvements, and the

◄▼ *Unlike the transmission electron microscope, in which electrons pass through a thin specimen and focus on a screen, the electron beam in a scanning electron microscope scans a specimen's surface, which emits secondary electrons that are focused as an image. A three-dimensional (but less magnified) image is formed, as in the images of etched aluminum (Cambridge University, 1952), and (below) of a ferromagnetic layer (using a Siemens instrument, 1959).*

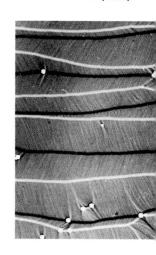

electron microscope found an even wider range of applications, particularly in studying the fine structure of muscle.

At first, electron microscopy was limited to specimens that were sufficiently small not to block the flow of elecrons completely. Viruses, for example, although already known to exist from experiments on their infectivity, were revealed for the first time. They and other microbes such as bacteria are visualized by treating them with electron-opaque substances. These either contrast them with their background or "shadow" them – throwing the organisms into relief to produce pictures rather like aerial photographs of cars caught in drifting snow. The major difficulty with early electron microscopy was that even the thinnest sections of plant and animal tissues, cut using a microtome for examination under the light microscope, were still too thick to allow the beam of electrons to pass through.

Only during the 1940s did microscopists devise ways of cutting much thinner slices. Because of their delicacy, these needed to be embedded in a hard plastic such as methyl methacrylate for mounting on the copper grids which replaced the glass slides used in the light microscope. A later tactic was to raise the voltage of the electron beam (rather like increasing the illumination). This provided even finer detail with some specimens, although there was disappointment that the visualization of living bacteria by this means added very little to scientists' knowledge of their structure. One of the latest innovations is the scanning electron microscope, which provides three-dimensional images of thick specimens by scanning their surface with an electron beam focused to a point while a synchronized television screen displays the transmitted or scattered electron activity.

▼ *With artificial color added to the black-and-white original, this scanning electron micrograph shows a human nerve growing across the surface of a silicon chip. As used in this hybrid example (taken as part of a research effort to marry biological and solid-state electrical circuits) the SEM is a uniquely powerful instrument for highlighting the topography of surfaces – whether of microbes, integrated circuits, or malignant cells in living tissue.*

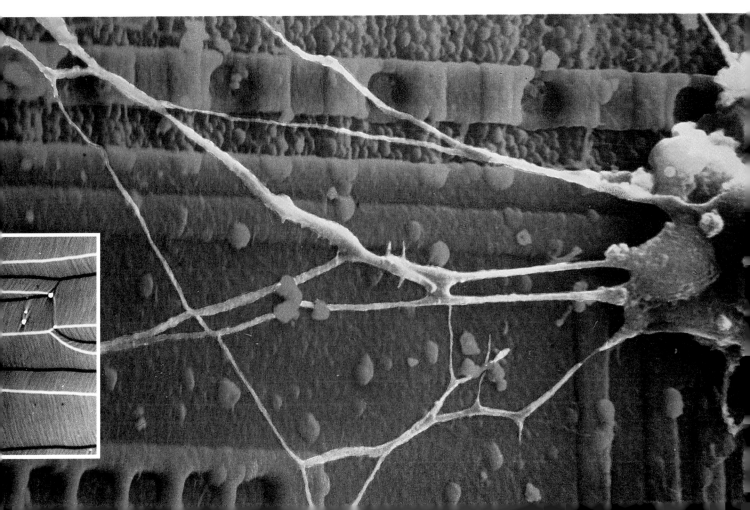

A technique based on manipulation of living tissues rather than on hardware, cell fusion has opened another "Pandora's box" for cell biologists and other scientists

Cell fusion

A technique based not on a single piece of equipment but on the ingenious manipulation of living tissues is cell fusion. Although a discovery of the 1960s, it has already had a considerable impact on many facets of scientific research. It has also facilitated the manufacture of "monoclonal antibodies" by one type of hybrid cell, and their vigorous exploitation by biotechnology companies throughout the world. The development of cell fusion owes much to the British biologist Henry Harris (b.1925), who in 1960 joined the staff of the John Innes Institute, then in Hertfordshire. There he worked alongside a researcher who was studying bread mold and other fungi. Their thread-like hyphae often fuse together as part of their normal process of reproduction. Although working on something else at the time, Harris began to wonder whether he could induce this phenomenon – in which quite different nuclei come together to share the same cytoplasm – in animal cells. If so, it might prove of great value in studying their genetics. In 1962, Harris read a paper published in *Experimental Cell Research* in which a Japanese researcher, O. Okada, reported that certain cancerous cells sometimes fused together under the influence of a particular virus. Moreover, small doses of ultraviolet light destroyed the infectivity of the virus, without affecting its ability to cause cell fusion.

The turning point came the following year when Henry Harris was appointed to a chair at the University of Oxford, and was soon collaborating with the virologist John Watkins. Approaching the National Institute for Medical Research in London for a supply of the virus used by Dr Okada, they were told that they could have something called Sendai virus thought to be the same thing. Harris decided to try to cross the species barrier by fusing two sorts of cells, one derived from human cancer tissue, the other from a mouse malignancy. One day in October 1964, he and Watkins carried out the critical experiment, which was immediately successful. Not only by examining the cells under the microscope before and afterward, but also by monitoring radioactive labels placed in their nuclei, they proved that they had indeed fused together the cells of man and mouse.

▲ *During the 1960s, the physiologist Henry Harris pioneered one of the seminal techniques of modern biological science – the fusing of different types of cell to combine their genetic material. Harris is now Regius Professor of Medicine at the University of Oxford, and his technique has found many different applications.*

▶ *One practical use of cell fusion is in engineering novel varieties of plants carrying combinations of characteristics whose genes would never come together through natural breeding. Because plant cells (unlike those of animals) are surrounded by a thick wall, the material forming a barrier has to be stripped away chemically, leaving naked protoplasts that will fuse together as easily as the animal cells originally studied by Henry Harris. This scanning electron micrograph shows the fusing of protoplasts from tobacco cells.*

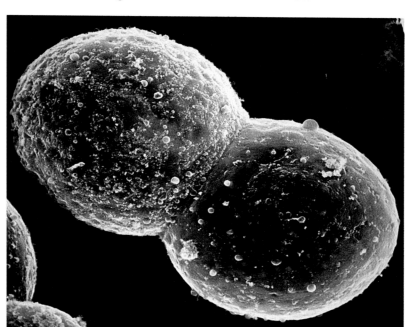

Unlike Dr Okada, who had been interested solely in the process of fusion, Harris went on to show that his cells were viable and that their genes were operational. Soon, he recalls, "it was clear that it was possible to fuse essentially any animal cell with any other and that, for cell biologists, Pandora's box was open." Developed and extended by several other research groups, Dr Harris's work has had innumerable practical repercussions. It has thrown new light on the mechanisms that regulate the expression of genes, and those that determine malignancy. It has also facilitated precise methods of mapping the genes, and thus locating the sources of hereditary characteristics, on mammalian chromosomes. This had made possible the charting of a detailed map of the human gene complex, which will almost certainly lead in future to methods of treating inherited diseases by gene therapy.

The most tangible outcome, however, was to make possible the achievement of the Argentinian César Milstein (b.1927) and the German Georges Köhler (b.1946) in the mid-1970s, when they fused malignant and antibody-generating cells to create "hybridomas". These produce monoclonal antibodies – extremely pure versions of those which the body assembles in response to infection. Their applications range from diagnosis and the purification of pharmaceuticals to research (such as the tracing of particular types of tissue) and the prospect of cancer therapy via "magic bullets" (monoclonals coupled with cell poisons and targeted on malignant tissues).

◄ *César Milstein, an Argentinian scientist working with his German colleague Georges Köhler in Cambridge, England, developed one of the most novel and important uses of cell fusion – the formation of hybridomas. Made by fusing malignant and antibody-generating cells, these are capable of producing extremely pure "monoclonal antibodies", whose uses range from diagnosis to purification of drugs. Milstein and Köhler shared the Nobel Prize for Physiology in 1984.*

◄ *Hybridoma cells, seen here in a scanning electron micrograph, have two key attributes of their parent cell types – the potential immortality of cancer cells, and the capacity of immunologically competent cells to manufacture antibodies that specifically match particular proteins or other antigens. Unlike the mixed antibodies that are normally produced by white blood cells during the immune response, the clones of cells generate pure antibodies.*

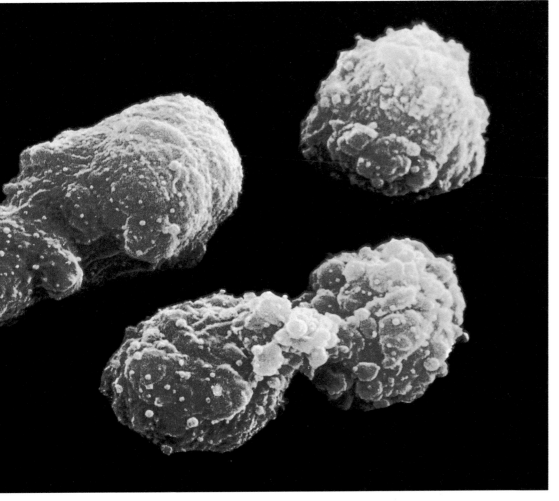

See also
Empiricism and Practicality 25-32

▲ The miniaturization of electronics over the past four decades has been staggering. The scanning electron micrograph shows a tiger beetle holding a VLSI (very large-scale integrated circuit) capable of handling over 16 kilobytes of information. Using such devices, the power of Manchester University's Mark 1 computer (1949) can be packed into a tiny fraction of the space that it occupied.

The introduction of computers

Observing how science and technology interact is rather like watching a tennis match. Just as the ball goes backward and forward from one end to the other, so progress in technology leads on to progress in science, which in turn leads to an advance in technology and so on. The development of the electronic computer is a good example of this process in operation.

The first practical computers were mechanical; they relied on a whole series of intermeshing gear wheels. The older generation of scientists and engineers still remember the mechanical desk calculators they used less than 30 years ago. World War II created great pressure for new means of rapid computation – for purposes ranging from weapon control to decoding enemy messages – and this, combined with theoretical advances by such people as John von Neumann (1903-1957) in the United States and Alan Turing (1912-1954) in Britain led to the first electronic computer.

Early versions of electronic computers were very clumsy, for they relied on a great number of valves – enclosed glass tubes with most of the air removed which could be used to regulate the flow of electricity. Such valves had short lifetimes, and it rapidly became clear that a more reliable electronic switching device was essential. Research into the properties of semiconducting solids led at the end of the 1940s to the appearance of the transistor. This device, for which the inventors received a Nobel prize, not only had a much longer lifespan, it also occupied much less space than the old-fashioned valve.

Within a decade, a new generation of computers appeared which were based on the technology of transistors.

After the transistor

Transistorized computers were immediately seized on by scientists for use on problems involving large-scale computation. One such topic was meteorology. The mathematical equations governing the motions of the Earth's atmosphere are well established, but their use as a basis for weather forecasting requires vast numbers of calculations. Weather forecasts have improved as computers have become more powerful.

During the 1960s pressures continued, especially from the United States' space program, to produce still smaller and more reliable computers. This led to the development of integrated circuits, which contain an entire electrical circuit on a single silicon chip. Integrated circuits were also used to construct a new generation of smaller computers – the minicomputers. These were sufficiently cheap and flexible to be linked directly to experimental apparatus, so allowing analysis of data at the same time that it was produced.

The next step came with the development of very large-scale integration (VLSI). Instead of putting a few circuits on a chip, this technique can put a whole computer on it. One result has been the microcomputer – almost every scientist nowadays expects to have access to these. At the other end of the scale, it has led to computers that can be used for major studies of artificial intelligence: you have to be a very good chess player now to beat a computer. We have reached the stage where use of a powerful computer is an essential part of designing and manufacturing new computers. Computers are effectively feeding on themselves. The next generation of computers should be able to go a stage further and take decisions in areas previously reserved for human intelligence.

Philosophers of science...The falsification principle of Karl Popper...Critics of Popper...Scientific revolutions... From heretics to scientists of renown...PERSPECTIVE... The transience of scientific theory... Science – a social activity...Birth of a modern theory of vitamins... Science a series of "research programs"...Computer-testing a theory

Although scientists follow certain proven principles in making observations and conducting experiments (◀ page 54), they tend not to analyze their work in philosophical terms. "Ask a scientist what he conceives the scientific method to be, and he will adopt an expression that is at once solemn and shifty-eyed," wrote the British Nobel laureate Sir Peter Medawar (1915-1987) – "solemn because he feels he ought to declare an opinion, shifty-eyed because he is wondering how to conceal the fact that he has no opinion to declare." When invited to contemplate such matters, Medawar argues, even the greatest researchers sometimes misinterpret their own approach. When Charles Darwin, for example, claimed in his autobiography: "I worked on true Baconian principles, and without any theory collected facts on a wholesale scale", he acknowledged the indiscriminate fact collecting known as Baconian induction (◀ page 56) simply because that was the fashionable view about how scientists were *supposed* to work.

The people who write most of the books about scientific method are the philosophers of science, while most studies of how science evolves come from sociologists and historians. As recorded in monographs, specialized journals and conferences, their work is largely separate from the day-to-day world of research. The majority of physicists, chemists and biologists pay little attention to the fine disputations that preoccupy these external observers. Nevertheless, their work is valid and important in revealing dimensions of science that are unnoticed by, or of no interest to, its active practitioners.

A challenge to the objectivity of science

When peering down a microscope, planning an experiment, or writing up their results, virtually all scientists adopt the attitude which philosophers call "naive realism". They believe in the existence of an external world of atoms and molecules, mountains and rivers, plants and animals. And they see their craft as that of describing and explaining reality ever more correctly. Science, in short, is objective in its approach, in contrast to the subjectivity of personal experience (◀ page 99).

Recent years have seen the emergence of philosophers and historians of science who come very close to denying this interpretation of what scientists are doing. They do not simply highlight the role of factors such as religion in shaping particular scientific beliefs, but see the whole of scientific theory as reflecting social influences, ideological resonances, and the power wielded by institutions and individuals, and dismiss as naive the idea that it reflects an independent natural world. Although neither Popper (◀ page 64) nor Kuhn (◀ page 66) portray science solely in these terms, the new wave does have its roots in their interpretations. Popper argues that scientific ideas are the free creations of inventive minds, formulated to be falsified. They are not imposed by external reality. Kuhn's picture of revolutions also emphasizes the transience of scientific theories by focussing on wholesale conceptual reorganizations in which all previous ideas go into the melting pot and are seen in a new light afterward.

But the new wave of philosophers and historians of science goes much further. They focus their attention solely on the social, political, historical, commercial and other influences on science, and give scant attention to the "philosophy of science" as it has been studied by earlier philosophers. Their opponents, while agreeing that science is a highly social profession (◀ page 85), interacting continuously with society in its wider sense, continue to believe that the earlier approach is a legitimate and meaningful activity.

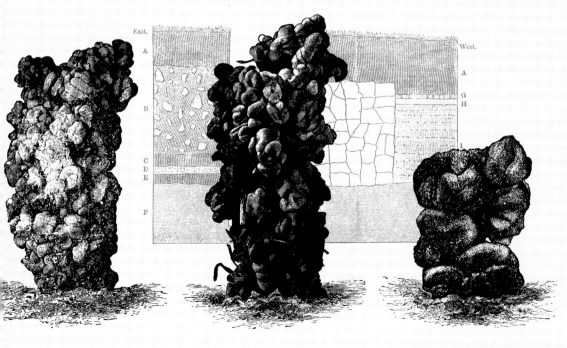

◀ *"I wrote on true Baconian principles, and without any theory collected facts on a wholesale scale, by printed enquiries, by conversations with skillful breeders and gardeners, and by extensive reading," wrote Charles Darwin about his theory of evolution. Darwin's interest in collecting is illustrated by his worldwide survey of worm casts, like these from India and France, from his book "The Formation of Vegetable Mould through the Action of Worms". But in this study and his work on evolution, Darwin's mind was by no means free of ideas, which his observations would either support or repudiate. It was just that Baconian induction was the fashionable view about how scientists were supposed to work.*

Karl Popper's is the most influential analysis in recent decades of the principles that guide science

Popper's falsification criterion

The most influential analysis of science's guiding principles has in recent decades been the "hypothetico-deductive" system described by the Austrian-born British philosopher Sir Karl Popper (b.1902) in *Logik der Forschung* (The Logic of Scientific Discovery, 1934). This had its origins in the Vienna circle of logical positivism, a ruthlessly concrete school of philosophy according to which no statement about the world could be meaningful unless it was, at least in principle, empirically verifiable. In other words, a claim that 565656 is the telephone number of London's National Gallery is meaningful because it can be checked. But a statement that poetry is orange cannot be confirmed, and therefore has no meaning.

Popper argued that this verification criterion went much further than condemning nonsense and metaphysics. It also ruled out much if not the whole of natural science, because scientific laws, being general in character, could not be proved by any number of finite observations. Using verification as the touchstone, one could not, for example, be entirely certain of the truth of a statement such as "Green plants harness the Sun's rays by means of chlorophyll" because no one had been able to check that this applied to every green plant in existence.

▼ *In his "The Logic of Scientific Discovery", published in 1934, Austrian-born Sir Karl Popper (b.1902) put forward his "hypothetico-deductive" scheme – the most influential recent analysis of the guiding principles of science. It emphasizes the importance not of verifying new ideas but of trying to falsify them empirically.*

The alternative suggested by Popper was the falsification principle: even a single unambiguous piece of evidence against a general statement is sufficient to destroy its credibility. Although the claim "All swans are white" is quite impracticable to verify, it is disproved by just one observation of a black swan. Scientific laws cannot be proved, but they can be tested. According to Popper, much of science is devoted to systematic attempts to refute these laws and hypotheses.

Popper's analysis also reconciles two interpretations which run through much of the discussion of how science works – the romantic or poetical view founded upon intuitive insight, and the rational or analytical view based upon logic and the evidence of the senses. According to the first of these views, wrote Sir Peter Medawar, "truth takes shape in the mind of the observer: it is his imaginative grasp of *what might be true* that provides the incentive for finding out, as far as he can, what *is* true. Every advance in science is therefore the outcome of a speculative adventure, an excursion into the unknown." According to the alternative, rational interpretation, "truth resides in nature and is to be got at only through the evidence of the senses: apprehension leads by a direct pathway to comprehension, and the scientist's task is essentially one of *discernment*."

What usually occurs, said Popper, is that a scientist alternates between intuitive and critical modes of thought – sometimes very quickly indeed. The imaginative phase is necessary for the individual to make a guess about some aspect of nature, and formulate a hypothesis to explain it. During the rational phase which follows, that body of ideas is subjected to rigorous criticism. By experiment, observation and induction, the scientist tries to falsify an hypothesis, which cannot be accepted (and even then only temporarily) until it has survived severe scrutiny. As with a composer writing a symphony, imagination and intellect must be harnessed with care. "During the idea-producing phase of the process, it might be dangerous to let critical thinking play such an important role that it blocks the flow of promising ideas," wrote Leo Tornqvist. "But some control is necessary for avoiding the possibility of being caught too early by one idea when another maybe better one still awaits to be detected."

The falsification criterion in action

In the first decade of this century the British biochemist Frederick Gowland Hopkins (1861-1947) was struggling with the following problem. Carbohydrates, fats, proteins, salts and water had been identified as the main nutrients required by animals. But when researchers purified these substances, mixed them together in their natural proportions, and fed mice with this artificial diet, the animals failed to grow. Only when small quantities of milk were included in the daily diet did the mice thrive. There were five possible explanations for these facts: (a) Although the artificial diet included the right salts, it contained them in the wrong proportions. Salts in the milk compensated for this imbalance, restoring them to the correct proportions; (b) Purification of the carbohydrates, fats and proteins had introduced toxic substances into the artificial diet. These were counteracted by something in the milk; (c) The milk contained an appetite stimulant, which overcame the monotony of the artificial diet; (d) The milk contained something that promoted the digestibility of the artificial diet; (e) The milk contained "accessory food factors" (vitamins in modern terminology) which helped the body to use the other absorbed nutrients.

In 1912, Hopkins reported a series of well planned, well controlled tests, providing sufficient information to distinguish between the five options, and to enable other scientists to set out to reproduce them. He tended to favor explanation (e), but tried to falsify it if possible by seeking evidence to support the alternatives.

Hopkins eliminated possibility (a), for example, by extracting his salts from incinerated dog biscuits and the ash of burnt oats, rather than by using laboratory chemicals. This ensured that the salts were in the correct proportions, as they occur in natural foodstuffs. Any beneficial effect of milk would, therefore, not be due to its salt content. He eliminated possibility (b) by switching his animals between the diets with and without milk. Although consistent with possibility (e), these results did not support (b), according to which toxic substances would have accumulated in the animals' bodies. The newly-added milk would have had to neutralize this backlog of poisons as well as the current consumption, before any benefits became apparent. But there was no such time lag.

The most spectacular evidence for the vitamin theory came from tests in which Hopkins added much smaller quantities of milk than had been used by other investigators. He discovered that even very tiny daily amounts were sufficient to permit his rats to grow normally – suggesting that milk's beneficial quality was attributable to traces of some as-yet-unidentified substance(s) which had a catalytic or regulatory effect. It was not until 1929 that, after Hopkins' findings had finally been reproduced independently, he shared a Nobel prize for their discovery of what we now call vitamins.

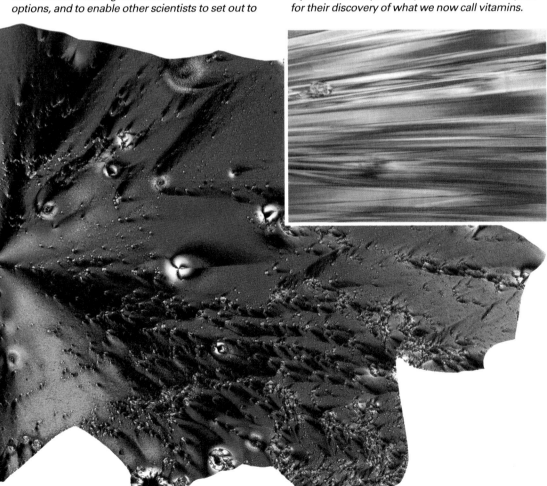

◄▲ Sir Frederick Gowland Hopkins (1861-1947) tried to distinguish between five possible explanations of the growth-promoting effect of small quantities of milk added to an artificial diet for mice. In a paper published in the "Journal of Physiology" in 1912, he even tried to falsify the explanation he most favored. Although some contemporaries were not convinced until his work had been independently confirmed, his scrupulous tests led to the isolation from milk of vitamin D3 (left – crystals of vitamin D3). It was the failure of his attempts to subject his own idea to severe examination that brought Hopkins the key advance in knowledge. Similar work led to the recognition of vitamin C and other micronutrients whose importance to health is now well known. In 1929 Hopkins shared a Nobel prize with the Dutchman Christian Eijkman (1858-1930) for their discovery of vitamins.

Modern technology provides evolutionary biologists with means to devise and test hypotheses

▲ US biologists Vincent Kerchner, Karl Niklas and Thomas O'Rourke have programmed a computer with a comparatively simple model of complex evolutionary processes in the real world. One application reflects the theory that a plant acquires competitive advantage by exposing the maximum amount of green photosynthetic surface to the Sun by branching, while retaining a structure that supports itself effectively. Simulating the earliest, leafless plants, the computer plots an "evolutionary trajectory within three-dimensional space – a universe of all possible branching structures". This it does first by determining the most primitive pattern, then selecting one with a higher ratio of light-gathering efficiency to mechanical stress. The process is repeated until the computer has identified the most efficient combination of a plant's morphological characteristics.

Testing theories of evolution

In what is perhaps an answer to Karl Popper's view that Darwinism is not a testable scientific theory, American biologists Vincent Kerchner, Karl J. Niklas and Thomas O'Rourke have developed a technique in which a computer is used to simulate the performance of primitive plants and assess their relative success rates in responding to predicted selection pressures and mutations. The game proceeds by a series of rounds in which the least successful plant species are eliminated, with the survivors at a predetermined "end" being declared winners. The simulated evolutionary trajectory does nevertheless bear a strong resemblance to the fossil record.

Science as a series of "research programs"

Hungarian philosopher Imre Lakatos has evolved a theory to meet criticism of falsification. He sees science as a series of "research programs" with a hard core of a very general theory that forms the basis from which the program is to develop in future, surrounded by a layer of subsidiary theories. The core, being the basic assumption, cannot be rejected or even modified unless a scientist decides to opt out of that particular program. But falsification is possible in the protective layer of auxiliary theories. Because these have to account for past observations and general predictions, they must be open to testing. If one of the subsidiary theories fails, however, there is no need to reject the core as well – it becomes protected as scientists formulate a new layer of auxiliary theories. The Lakatos interpretation has been influential, but one specific criticism is that it is difficult to imagine certain core theses – such as that of evolution – ever being rejected and replaced.

◄▲ *Karl Popper's interpretation of science has become increasingly controversial in recent years. Popper's philosophy categorizes Darwinism as "a metaphysical research program", because it cannot be "falsified". But some biologists have replied that it does in fact provide such opportunities to test hypotheses, since it is a continuing process – the appearance of dark forms of moth in industrial areas, for example, or of different forms of grasshopper nymph (seen here) in basalt and limestone areas of the Negev desert.*

Recent criticism of Popper

In his autobiography *Unended Quest*, Popper wrote: "I have come to the conclusion that Darwinism is not a testable scientific theory, but a metaphysical research program – a possible framework for testable scientific theories. It suggests the existence of a mechanism of adaptation and it allows us even to study in detail the mechanism at work. Its theory of adaptation was the first nontheistic one that was convincing; and theism was worse than an open admission of failure, for it created the impression that an ultimate explanation had been reached. Now to the degree to which Darwinism creates the same impression, it is not so very much better than the theistic view of adaptation; it is therefore important to show that Darwinism is not a scientific theory but metaphysical."

The fact that Popper and his philosophy categorize Darwinism as metaphysics has provoked growing hostility among many biologists. They have been especially angry because his views have been espoused by the creationists in the United States and elsewhere and distorted to discredit evolution as "not scientific". Certainly, many of the unique events of evolution – splittings of one species from another, for example – are beyond refutation because they happened at particular times in the past. They cannot be tested, or "falsified" (◀ page 64). Popper's opponents, however, argue that because evolution continues, it affords continual opportunities to test hypotheses. They also point to the powerful coherence between the evidence for evolution in many different quarters – from comparative anatomy and the fossil record, to the emergence of black moths in industrial areas, and the matching of proteins in different species of animals today. These and many other types of evidence complement each other to provide an impressive edifice of explanation. The case argued against Popper is that his philosophy must be inadequate if it relegates such a strong body of ideas to the realm of metaphysics.

Scientific Revolutions

The way in which new ideas come to be accepted in science has been described by the historian Thomas Kuhn in terms of episodes of revolutionary overhaul separated by periods of "normal" science. In "The Structure of Scientific Revolutions" (1962), Kuhn portrays a process which he believes is common to all branches of science. In the very earliest stages of human inquiry, before scientists really know anything at all about a subject, the stage is open for guesswork and even mystical speculation. Next comes the phase of discovery, precipitated by a pioneering thinker or by a practical development such as the emergence of a new experimental technique (♦ page 57). Almost by definition, the new discovery conflicts with established ideas, so the stage is set for revolution. Competing theories are formulated to explain the new findings, and the field attracts an increasing number of researchers who are drawn by the novelty and challenge of data awaiting explanation.

The key breakthrough comes when someone makes real progress in suggesting a general pattern of explanation. The ideological framework which that person puts forward – a paradigm or conceptual model of how something works – provides the basis for other scientists to make substantial advances in the same field. At this point, the new field becomes fashionable. Its practitioners may face sustained resistance from competitors who cling to outdated ideas. Eventually, disputes are resolved, and gaps in knowledge are filled. During this phase, what began by being revolutionary doctrine hardens into conventional wisdom.

Work carried out between Thomas Kuhn's "revolutions" is what he terms normal science – "research firmly based upon one or more past achievements, achievements that some particular scientific community acknowledges for a time as supplying the foundations for further practice."

▼► In the first edition of "The Structure of Scientific Revolutions", Thomas Kuhn (below) mapped out a pattern of scientific progress that could accompany chronological developments. His own analysis focused on the revolutions of Copernicus, Lavoisier and Darwin, but it is possible to see how the pattern fits with a scientific revolution of more recent times: the discovery of plate tectonics. The new paradigm put forward by the German Alfred Wegener (1880-1930) ushered in an era of controversy until the breakthroughs came in the 1960s.

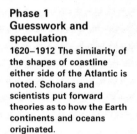

Phase 1
Guesswork and speculation
1620–1912 The similarity of the shapes of coastline either side of the Atlantic is noted. Scholars and scientists put forward theories as to how the Earth continents and oceans originated.

Pioneering discovery
1912 Alfred Wegener, German meteorologist, presents his continental drift hypothesis. He postulates the existence of a supercontinent "Pangea" which fragmented during the Mesozoic Era with the lighter rocks of continental crust floating over denser ocean rocks, powered by gravitational forces. Paleontological, geological and meteorological evidence was used to "reconstruct" Pangea.

Phase 2
Competing theories
1912–1960 Wegener's theory conflicts with the orthodox view (the lighter continental crust was in equilibrium with a denser substratum, and constrained from lateral movement). Hostility is provoked, especially in USA. Some geologists put forward alternative interpretations, while others compile evidence and formulate hypotheses in support of Wegener.

1620 Francis Bacon, English natural philosopher, draws attention to similarity in shape of Atlantic coasts of Africa and South America.

1756 Theodor Lilienthal, German theologian, noting that the coasts of Africa and South America were complementary, concludes that the Earth had been disrupted by floods.

1668 François Placet, French moralist, suggests that America might have been formed by "the conjunction of ... floating islands".

1857 Richard Owen, American scientist, proposes that, by a series of convulsive changes, the Earth expanded to the shape of a sphere, a process which involved a major displacement of continental regions.

1858 Antonio Snider, French-American scientist, hypothesizes that the continental mass was suddenly split apart by volcanic activity at the time of Noah's flood.

1801 Alexander von Humboldt, German naturalist, suggests that the Atlantic had been gouged out by an erosive current.

1885–1909 Edward Suess, Austrian geologist, concludes that several continental land masses were broken up by faulting and foundering during the Mesozoic era, forming new ocean basins.

1910 Frank B. Taylor, American geologist, publishes theory which envisages the movement of landmasses originally located over the poles towards the equator, throwing up mountain belts at their leading edges.

1879 Osmond Fisher, English physicist, proposes that Pacific Ocean Basin is a scar resulting from the tearing away of the Moon from the Earth.

1924 Foreign language editi of Wegener's book (1915), t first comprehensive accoun continental drift, are publish

1926 International sympo held in New York. Despit sympathy for the new the continental drift suffers a widespread loss of suppo

1929 Arthur Holmes, Eng geologist, proposes that continents might be displaced laterally by risi convection currents sprea out beneath the crust.

1924 Sir Harold Jeffreys, English geophysicist, oppos Wegener's theory, demonstrating that the suggested forces were inadequate.

**Phase 4
Filling the gaps**
1969– Work continues on discovering the mechanism by which plates became separated. Theories invoke convection currents, and the notion of an expanding Earth.

**Phase 3
Scientific Revolution**
1960–1968 Interpretation of ocean magnetic anomalies and evidence collected from deep-sea drilling convinces most earth scientists of the reality of spreading, though opposition persists, notably in the Soviet Union, where horizontal crustal motion is discounted in favor of vertical movements.

General acceptance
1968 Publication of papers in *Journal of Geophysical Research*, presenting a wide range of paleontological, geological and paleomagnetic evidence, marks general acceptance of continental drift theory. **1969** Data obtained from US Deep Sea Drilling Project prove conclusively that the age of oceanic crust increases away from active ridges.

General explanation
1960 H.H. Hess, American geologist, expounds hypothesis of sea-floor spreading. Drawing on results obtained from seismic refraction surveys, he concludes that continental and oceanic crust are connected and move together. New oceanic rocks are formed between separating crustal blocks at the crests of oceanic ridges, where they cool and become magnetized in the ambient direction of the geomagnetic field.

1967 W. Jason Morgan, American geologist, propounds theory of plate tectonics, in which sea-floor spreading is seen as movements between rigid plates bounded by ridge crests, transform faults and trenches.

1971 Discovery of fresh lava flows and fissures by undersea exploration of mid-Atlantic ridge during Project FAMOUS provides visual evidence of crustal formation at the ridge.

1956–60 P.M.S. Blackett, S.K. Runcorn and other geophysicists begin investigations into the magnetism of rocks, determining the relative position of the magnetic pole at the time of their formation. From a chronological series of this data, changing pole positions could be plotted, with different "paths" for different continents, indicating that they moved in different directions relative both to the pole and to one another.

1963 Fred Vine and Drummond Matthews, British geophysicists, draw on the findings of worldwide magnetic surveys, which show that periodic reversals in the Earth's polarity have taken place. They note that "stripes" of alternate magnetization, or anomalies, in the ocean floor are symmetrical by age either side of mid-oceanic ridges, and increase in age from those ridges.

1976 H.G. Owen, British geologist, constructs maps showing that the fit of continents and oceans is better when plotted on an Earth of increasing radius. He suggests that continental drift has resulted as much from expansion as from conventional sea-floor spreading.

1958 S. Warren Carey, Australian geologist, notes that continental reassembly has a more precise fit if diameter of Earth assumed to be smaller at the time of Pangea.

1965 Edward Bullard, British geologist, produces a computerized fit of continental reassembly reducing mismatch to 50 km.

1962 Vladimir Beloussov, Soviet geologist, dissents from the theory, asserting that oceanic basins are formed by a "foundering of continental crust".

Mid-1950s Mid-oceanic ridges discovered to be part of a continuous worldwide system totalling c.80,000 km in length.

1937 Alexander du Toit, South African geologist, supports Wegener's hypothesis by "reassembling" Gondwanaland using extensive geological evidence, and with the fit made at continental shelf edges.

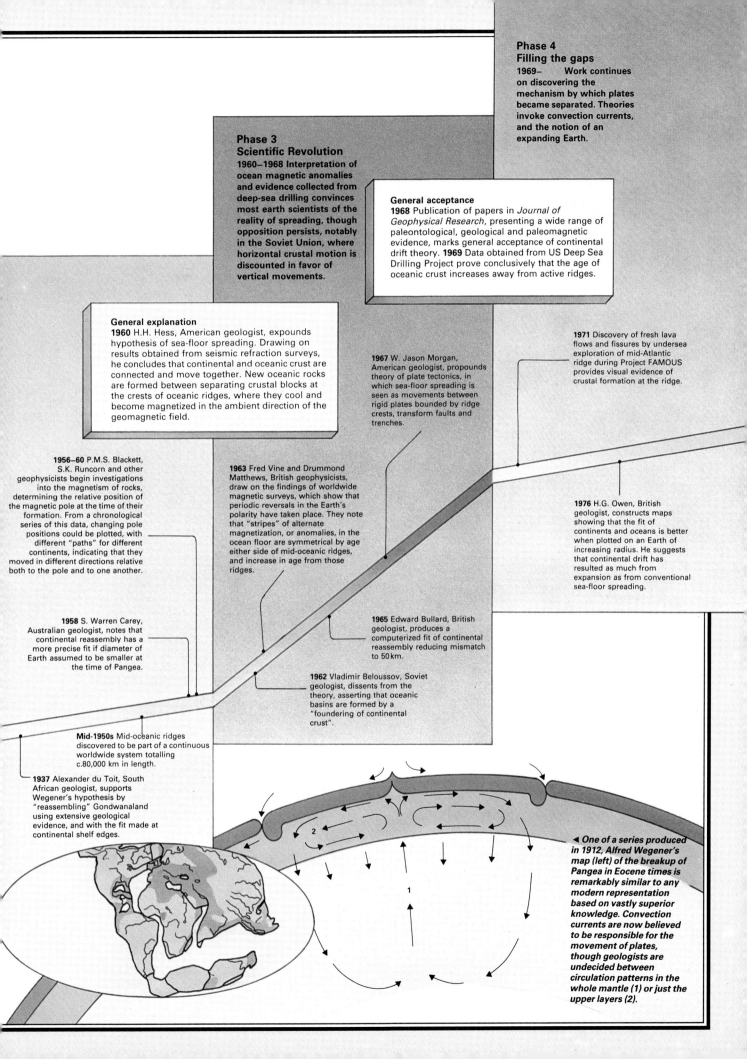

◄ One of a series produced in 1912, Alfred Wegener's map (left) of the breakup of Pangea in Eocene times is remarkably similar to any modern representation based on vastly superior knowledge. Convection currents are now believed to be responsible for the movement of plates, though geologists are undecided between circulation patterns in the whole mantle (1) or just the upper layers (2).

See also
The Central Tradition 5-24
Ideas of Science 47-56

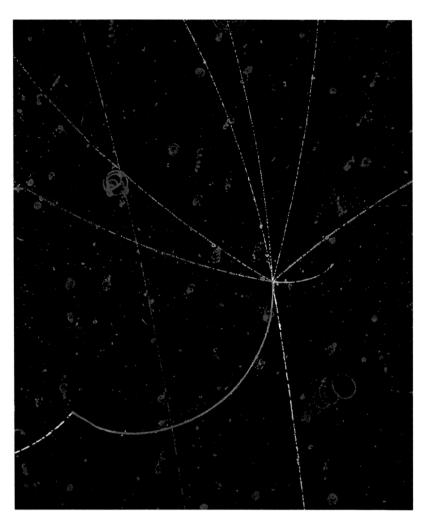

▲ Once considered
utterly implausible, the
transmutation of matter –
as in this false-color bubble
chamber photograph
showing an antiproton
(pale blue) hitting a proton
and rematerializing as four
positive pions (red) and four
negative pions (green) – is
now commonplace in
laboratories worldwide.

▶ Before the era of the
modern safety officer: the
string-and-sealing-wax
tradition of English nuclear
physics. Lord Rutherford
shows visiting physicist
John Ratcliffe (b.1902)
around the Cavendish
Laboratory, Cambridge,
during the 1930s.

Heretics in their day

Many of the central ideas of science today are so
familiar and well integrated into our understanding
of the universe that it is easy to forget that they
were highly unorthodox, even heretical, when first
enunciated, and that it was often a battle to win a
hearing. Thus we now accept without question that
certain elements can be transformed into others,
and that this process forms the basis of both
nuclear weaponry and nuclear power generation.
But in 1900, when the young chemist Frederick
Soddy (1877-1956) went from Oxford University in
England to McGill University, Montreal, to work
with New Zealander Ernest Rutherford (1871-1937),
the transmutation of the elements brought to mind
little more than ancient fancies about the upgrading
of base metals into gold. Both outside and inside
the scientific community, the whole idea seemed
highly implausible. Yet in less than three years,
working until midnight every day, the two
experimenters had demonstrated that radioactive
substances did indeed change in this way. They
tackled radium, uranium and thorium, Rutherford
doing "radioactive decay" experiments and Soddy
identifying the different substances produced. But
even when they began to achieve positive results,
doubts persisted. As one of Rutherford's
colleagues, T.E. Allibone, recalled later: "Some of
their colleagues gravely expressed the fear that
radical ideas about spontaneous transmutation of
matter might bring discredit to McGill, and
Rutherford was advised to delay publication and
proceed more cautiously. However, the senior
professor, John Cox, quietly gave support to
Rutherford and prophesied that the development of
radioactivity would bring reknown to McGill. He
went on to say that Rutherford's experimental work
would one day be rated as the greatest since that of
Faraday." Cox was right.

Equally strongly rejected by many orthodox
scientists of the day was the achievement of
American chemist James B. Sumner (1887-1955) in
being first to crystallize an enzyme and show that it
consisted of protein. That was in 1926, when, on the
authority of German chemist Richard Willstätter
(1872-1942), virtually everyone accepted that
enzymes were neither protein nor fat nor
carbohydrate. There was even a residue of
"vitalistic" thinking (♦ page 111), according to
which the molecules of life were so distinct from
inorganic chemicals that they would not be
amenable to conventional analysis. Sumner spent
nine years over his attempt to purify urease from
jack beans, but succeeded eventually through
relatively simple methods, aided by a stroke of luck
when he received a shipment of beans from Texas
that had an unusually high concentration of the
enzyme. "Soon after Sumner published his
findings, he had a lot to contend with. He was at
first ignored, especially in the European literature,
or dismissed in a footnote as having made a
preposterous claim," recorded the Czech-born
American enzymologist Carl Cori (b.1896). "He was
attacked on the basis of experiments which later
were shown to be erroneous but which made it
appear that his claim of the protein nature of
enzymes had been completely disproved."

Scientists depend on social exchange more than most...Scientists get together...Scientific publications ...Criticisms of the scientific paper...Adherence to truth ...Cheats, hoaxers and plagiarists...PERSPECTIVE...Four principles of science...Letter-writing...Citations of important papers...The importance of being first...The "Paperclip Conspiracy"...Great scientific conferences

Politicians gather for their annual party conferences. Hairdressers have hairdressing conventions, and salesmen meet to hear about their companies' latest profit performance and future plans. But none of these activities is essential. For scientists, however, social intercourse is essential. However brilliant, however disposed to the solitary life, a scientist must join in those routines – principally attending conferences, and reading and publishing papers in the journals – through which new ideas are subjected to continuous critical scrutiny. "Peer review" – the exposure of ideas, theories and speculations to the critical attention of experts in the same field – is crucially important in the advancement of science.

The ethical underpinning of this interchange was the subject of a paper published in 1938, in which the American sociologist Robert K. Merton (b.1910) wrote about "the sentiments embodied in the ethos of science – characterised by such terms as intellectual honesty, integrity, organised skepticism, disinterestedness, and impersonality". Composed at a time when the Nazis in Hitler's Germany were claiming that only Aryans could do valid science, the essay expressed the scientific community's need to clarify its own essential character. In 1942, Merton developed his theme further in a paper on "the normative stucture of science" which has become a classic for its portrayal of scientific intercourse. Defining the institutional goal of science as "the extension of certified knowledge", Merton identified "universalism", "communism", "disinterestedness", and "organized skepticism" as the imperatives or hall-marks of modern science as a social activity.

Merton's "Four Imperatives"

"Universalism" means that the acceptance or rejection of a claim made by a scientist does not depend upon that individual's nationality, race, religion, class or other personal attributes. All that matters is whether the new theory or observation accords with preestablished impersonal criteria and knowledge compiled and confirmed by other researchers in the past. An important corollary to universalism is that careers in science must be open to people of competence and talent, irrespective of their other characteristics.

"Communism", meaning the common ownership of goods, epitomizes the fact that the findings of science are the products of social collaboration between research workers and are thus assigned to that community. The scientist's claim to "his" intellectual "property" is limited to that of recognition and esteem. The antithesis of communism is secrecy. So full communication of results is de rigueur. Nonpublication can have adverse practical consequences – fruits of research may be denied to those who might benefit.

"Disinterestedness" in the sense of impartiality and honesty is central to science, but cannot be separated from the exacting scrutiny and rigorous policing to which all scientists' work is continually subjected and which is probably unparalleled in any other field of activity. Science also differs from the other professions in that its practitioners do not deal directly with a lay public. The possibility of exploiting the credulity, ignorance and dependence of laymen is correspondingly reduced.

"Organized skepticism" is crucial not only to the methods of science (◊ page 54) but also to science as a community, which should be continually open to new truths. Faced with a novel claim it is the duty of the scientific community to suspend judgement and then scrutinize that claim in terms of empirical and logical criteria. Because of this critical temper, science is always likely to find itself in conflict with institutions founded on truths drawn from other sources of authority.

◀ *The Frenchman Henri Sainte-Claire Deville (1818-1881) was renowned not only as a chemist (he was the first to prepare pure aluminum in bulk) but also as a communicator. Largely self-taught, he became a professor in the École Normale Supérieure. There and at the Sorbonne, where he also lectured, Deville was greatly loved by the students who flocked to his demonstrations. His later years were plagued by ill-health, partly caused by over-work, and he finally committed suicide.*

Communication of research findings and theories is the essence of scientific progress

Communication between scientists

Unlike other professions, the need to communicate in science is so vital that any interruption would be disastrous. Through both the spoken word (at conferences, symposia, and the telephone) and the written word (in the form of journals and books), science is in a state of continuous social intercourse. These are the channels that mediate Robert Merton's four imperatives (◀ page 71), which hold the entire enterprise together.

Cabals of scientists range from small colloquia of half a dozen people, gathered in a university department for an hour or two, to grandiose international congresses, attended by thousands of researchers and lasting a week or longer. The former will be focussed on one, highly specific topic or research report. The latter will take a synoptic view of a much wider field, such as astrophysics or biochemistry, with both introductory and final plenary sessions attended by all participants and simultaneous sessions devoted to several more specialized aspects of the subject. In each case, the objective is the same: to hear about recent research, which is then open to discussion and criticism.

Whatever the exact topic, participants' papers follow a familiar pattern and are usually illustrated with slides. The speaker begins by outlining the background to his or her problem and the methods used in performing experiments or making observations, describes the findings (often in the form of tables or graphs), and concludes by drawing conclusions. Members of the audience then discuss the presentation, with varying degrees of ferocity. They may pose questions requiring clarification, challenge the speaker's interpretation, criticize laboratory techniques, or add supportive or other information which they consider relevant.

In recent years, an alternative, arguably more efficient method of presenting research data at scientific meetings has become popular. Instead of speaking on a platform, contributors prepare "posters" which are displayed on boards alongside those of other participants. Following the same pattern of introduction, methods, discussion and conclusion, they stay in place for a day or half day. The posters can then be perused by people who wander around the room, and having located a subject of interest, they can ask the presenter questions and offer comments.

Beginning with the Solvay Conferences of the 1920s and 1930s, financed by the giant Solvay chemical company in Liège to bring together international luminaries in the physical sciences, certain gatherings have acquired an exceptional reputation for the quality of their proceedings. Unlike most conferences, which are open to the members of particular societies (or, as in the case of Royal Society meetings in London, open to anyone), most of these events are for selected invitees only. Two such series in the United States are Cold Spring Harbor Symposia and Gordon Conferences. During one of the latter, in 1973, participants sent an urgent letter to the National Academy of Sciences about possible hazards arising from the newly developed ability to join together DNA from different species of life. This historic incident triggered a wide variety of international moves to combat those supposed dangers. In Europe in particular, Dahlem Conferences in Berlin and Ciba Foundation Symposia in London are renowned for their catalytic role in bringing comparatively small numbers of scientists together for private "no holds barred" discussions.

▲ *In 1828 Alexander von Humboldt organized a meeting in Berlin of the German Association for Natural Science. It was one of a series of massive gatherings of scientists from all parts of Germany that reflected growing interest in science after the Napoleonic wars. The son of a Prussian officer, Baron von Humboldt became a major force in the emerging sciences of botany, zoology and geology through his many travels throughout the world.*

▼ *After the early, highly competitive years of the "Space Race" between the USSR and the USA, exploration of the Solar System has reflected increasing international cooperation. Here scientists from many countries meet at the Institute of Space Research at the Soviet Academy of Sciences to discuss the performance of the VEGA-1 and VEGA-2 probes which were sent by the USSR to study Halley's Comet when it became visible from Earth in 1986. The other countries that collaborated in these historic experiments were Austria, Bulgaria, Czechoslovakia, East and West Germany, France, Hungary and Poland.*

◄ ▲ *In past centuries, private letters were a favored format for scientific intercourse. Isaac Newton sent many of his musings to the Royal Society in this way, as did Dutch scientist Anton van Leeuwenhoek when describing the microbes he had seen through his remarkable microscopes. Von Humboldt (left), seen in the study from where he wrote to many great scientists of his day, was another formidable letter writer. Even in more recent times, personal correspondence has remained important – as in the letter (above) on the DNA double helix, sent in 1953 from James Watson to fellow molecular biologist Max Delbruck.*

"The truly imaginative are not being judged by their peers. They have none" – Rosalyn Yalow

Scientific publications

Most conference papers and posters describe work conducted over previous months and are known as "preliminary communications". When the author has accumulated a more substantial body of information, and after taking on board critical observations and suggestions from others, a formal paper is written for submission to a "learned journal". Originally issued by scholarly societies, but nowadays mostly in the hands of commercial publishers, journals are the lifeblood of science because they record all of the information and ideas that form the evolving corpus of scientific knowledge. The "primary journals" include the weekly *Science* and *Nature* and a few others embracing a wide range of topics, as well as the hundreds of thousands of monthlies which cover more limited territory. In contrast, even the most arcane textbooks, and journals devoted solely to articles reviewing sectors of science, are described as secondary sources because the basic information they contain comes originally from the primary journals.

Nature and *Science* are the two most widely read journals, and competition for space in them is acute. They also concentrate (though not exclusively) on fashionable frontiers such as molecular biology. A scientist will often submit a paper to one of these two journals initially and then, if rejected, turn to a more specialized title. A bacteriologist who has isolated what appears to be a new soil microbe, for example, may try the *Journal of Bacteriology* or *Journal of General Microbiology*. Individual titles have their own "instructions to authors" which dictate the format in which they will consider submitted papers. But all follow a similar sequence to that of the oral paper given at a conference – an introduction to explain the problem to be tackled and rehearse previous understanding, a description of experimental methods, a results section, and a discussion in which the author tries to interpret the findings, set them in context and perhaps raise further unknowns.

The vast majority of journals are "refereed" – they have panels of

▶ *Although the refereeing system is essential to science, this and other forms of peer review are certainly not infallible – as shown by the case of Rosalyn Yalow. Her now highly-regarded paper on radio-immunoassay was rejected by two prestigious journals. Yet it was for this work that she shared a Nobel prize in 1977 with Andrew Schally and Roger Guillemin. "The truly imaginative are not being judged by their peers," she said. "They have none."*

▶ *Just as no scientist can work effectively in isolation for more than a very short time, no country can thrive in scientific terms unless its scientists and institutes keep in permanent touch with research publications elsewhere in the world. Here scientific journals on a table in a library at the Soviet "Science City" of Akademigorodok include titles published not only in Russian but also in English, German, French and other languages. Several studies have revealed the lack of growth and vigor that occurs when, for example, French or Japanese scientists have published only in their own tongue, isolating their work from critical attention elsewhere.*

◄ The growth of scientific literature has repeatedly outstripped even the most buoyant forecasts made by publishers and science policy analysts. Dr Peter Adams, deputy editor in chief of the US "Physical Review", holds a copy of the journal as published in 1931. Beside a stack of all the issues released during that year rest the bound volumes of the journal for the year 1985. Although miniaturization techniques such as microfiche, and the storage of material electronically in databases, have had a considerable impact on the retrieval of scientific data, the human desire to browse means that the printed journal still remains very much in demand among researchers today.

advisors who act as sounding boards to help the editor assess the quality of submitted papers. A minority of journals operate without such support. A few, such as the *Proceedings of the National Academy of Sciences*, usually referee papers but exempt authors who are members of the appropriate academy or society. The prestige attached to papers that have bypassed "peer review" in these ways is correspondingly lower than for publications that have been refereed. (Papers given at meetings, orally or as posters, are sometimes published in brief by the organizing body, but they do not count as real research papers. Some editors will not even permit authors to cite such "preliminary communications" in their papers, because they have not been through the fires of critical scrutiny.)

When an editor believes a submitted paper to be appropriate for a particular journal and has space to publish it, he or she posts it off to one or more referees. They read it and send back a report of any shortcomings – ranging from dubious experimental methods or misunderstandings of earlier work, to blatant errors in statistical analysis. Having digested the referees' comments, the editor then decides whether to accept or reject it, or to return it with criticisms and a letter whose tone either encourages the author to try again or makes it plain that further efforts will be unwelcome.

Priority being so important (◆ page 79), journals keep a careful record of the date when a paper is submitted, which appears prominently at the beginning if and when it is published. Refereeing can hold up publication significantly, but most journals try to minimize the delay. There are even "rapid-publication" journals that guarantee to rush what are thought to be extremely important papers into print. Some are scarcely refereed, if at all. Electronic journals are now emerging too, with their entire contents "on line", though the difficulty of browsing with a VDU will probably ensure that their conventional paper counterparts will never disappear completely.

Referees are traditionally anonymous. With few exceptions they are not paid for their work, and it is argued that they would be less willing to criticize manuscripts properly, if at all, were their identity known. But there are complaints and suspicions that referees are sometimes needlessly obstructive. Some referees now sign their reports and insist that authors are given that information.

Making Use of Citation Data

A study of citations of scientific papers, according to authorship, discipline or other category can provide important information about a scientist, or the direction of scientific research. The individual scientist is under pressure to publish papers as an indication of his or her achievements and energy. Some years ago, what counted above all was the rate at which a scientist published papers – as immortalized in the phrase "the great paper chase". The criterion produced some unfortunate effects (◆ page 83). Today, there is much more interest in an individual's citation record – a paper that is heavily cited in the papers of other scientists is likely to have been much more useful than one that is virtually ignored (◆ page 57). Some papers are "sleepers" whose worth is not recognized (and reflected in citations) until many years after their appearance. While a citation usually indicates the confirmation or acknowledgment of a new idea or the value of a new technique, it may also mean the rejection of a statement in the cited paper.

▶ **Analysis of citations in the scientific literature in 1983 was used to reveal these successive layers of interconnections within earth sciences and biological sciences. At each level, the principle used in constructing the maps is that of co-citation strength – the degree to which research papers have been cited together by other authors, thereby confirming intellectual links between those papers. At the bottom of the page (right and left) are maps reflecting the connections between individuals papers, identified here by the names of their first authors. These clutches of papers have then been clustered together as "research fronts", on atmospheric transport of sulfur compounds (left) and plant pollination barriers (right). These and other fronts then appear in the higher level maps at the top.**

Key

☐ Subdiscipline of science

☐ Group of related research fronts

◪ Other research front

💧 Core paper (single, or first listed, author)

💧 An acid rain research front

Earth sciences

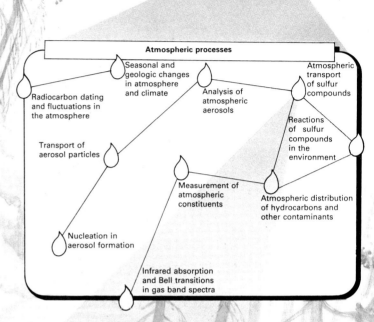

Atmospheric processes

Atmospheric processes

- Radiocarbon dating and fluctuations in the atmosphere
- Seasonal and geologic changes in atmosphere and climate
- Analysis of atmospheric aerosols
- Atmospheric transport of sulfur compounds
- Reactions of sulfur compounds in the environment
- Transport of aerosol particles
- Measurement of atmospheric constituents
- Atmospheric distribution of hydrocarbons and other contaminants
- Nucleation in aerosol formation
- Infrared absorption and Bell transitions in gas band spectra

Atmospheric transport of sulfur compounds

- Transport, deposition and atmospheric chemistry of sulfur, aerosols and other substances
- Atmospheric dispersion models for studying air-pollutant patterns
- Determination of atmospheric sulfur dioxide

- Acid rain and forest decline
- Effects of acid precipitation on aquatic environments
- Effects of acid rain components on plant growth and aquatic ecosystems

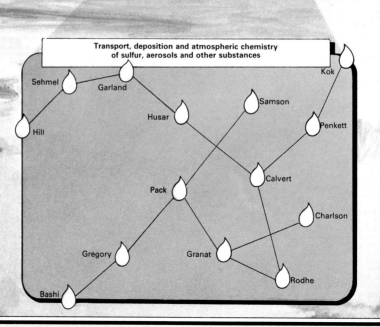

Transport, deposition and atmospheric chemistry of sulfur, aerosols and other substances

- Sehmel
- Garland
- Kok
- Husar
- Samson
- Hill
- Penkett
- Pack
- Calvert
- Charlson
- Gregory
- Granat
- Rodhe
- Bashi

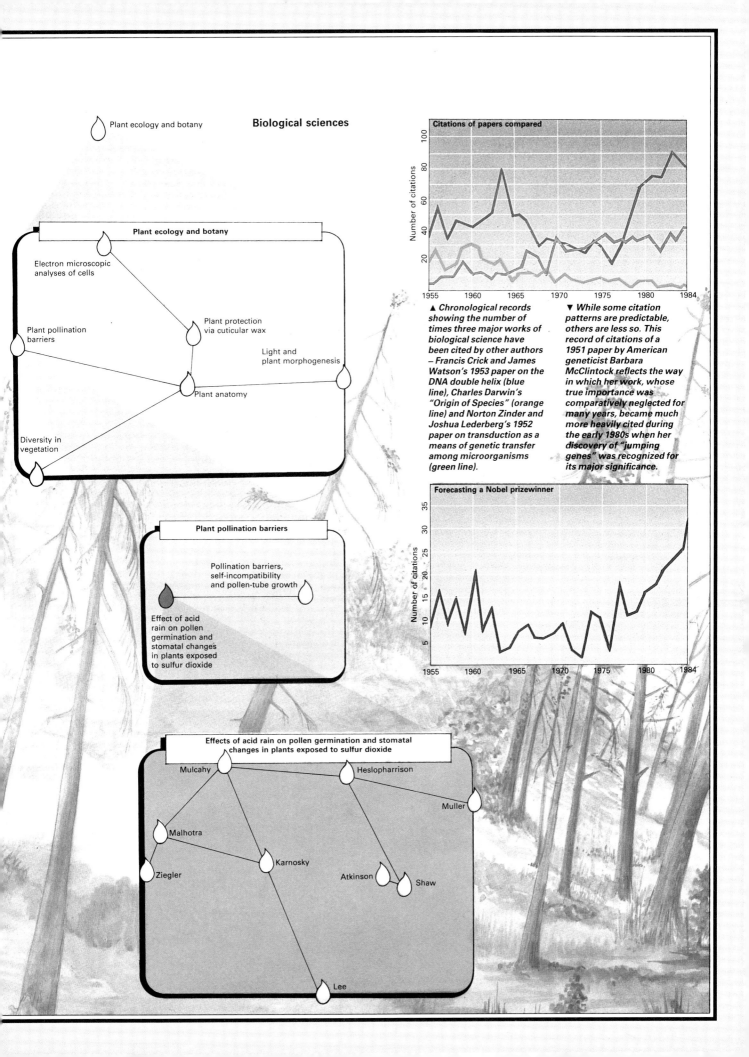

Plant ecology and botany

Biological sciences

Plant ecology and botany

Electron microscopic
analyses of cells

Plant protection
via cuticular wax

Plant pollination
barriers

Light and
plant morphogenesis

Plant anatomy

Diversity in
vegetation

Plant pollination barriers

Pollination barriers,
self-incompatibility
and pollen-tube growth

Effect of acid
rain on pollen
germination and
stomatal changes
in plants exposed
to sulfur dioxide

Effects of acid rain on pollen germination and stomatal changes in plants exposed to sulfur dioxide

Mulcahy

Heslopharrison

Muller

Malhotra

Karnosky

Ziegler

Atkinson

Shaw

Lee

Citations of papers compared

Number of citations

1955 1960 1965 1970 1975 1980 1984

▲ *Chronological records
showing the number of
times three major works of
biological science have
been cited by other authors
– Francis Crick and James
Watson's 1953 paper on the
DNA double helix (blue
line), Charles Darwin's
"Origin of Species" (orange
line) and Norton Zinder and
Joshua Lederberg's 1952
paper on transduction as a
means of genetic transfer
among microorganisms
(green line).*

▼ *While some citation
patterns are predictable,
others are less so. This
record of citations of a
1951 paper by American
geneticist Barbara
McClintock reflects the way
in which her work, whose
true importance was
comparatively neglected for
many years, became much
more heavily cited during
the early 1980s when her
discovery of "jumping
genes" was recognized for
its major significance.*

Forecasting a Nobel prizewinner

Number of citations

1955 1960 1965 1970 1975 1980 1984

Disputes about priority have reduced dramatically since Newton rowed with Leibniz over who invented the calculus

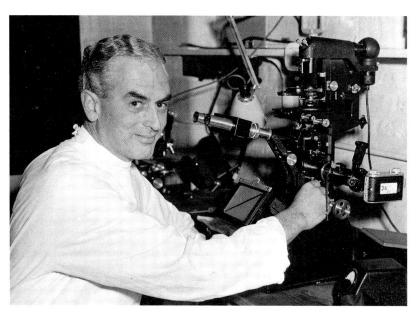

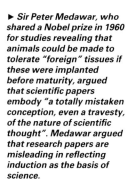

▶ *Sir Peter Medawar, who shared a Nobel prize in 1960 for studies revealing that animals could be made to tolerate "foreign" tissues if these were implanted before maturity, argued that scientific papers embody "a totally mistaken conception, even a travesty, of the nature of scientific thought". Medawar argued that research papers are misleading in reflecting induction as the basis of science.*

Critics of the scientific paper

Although the published paper is the currency of intercourse among scientists, reporting new observations and providing the information required for trying to replicate a piece of work, it has been criticized as being highly artificial. "The scientific paper in its orthodox form does embody a totally mistaken conception, even a travesty, of the nature of scientific thought," wrote the British zoologist Sir Peter Medawar (1915-1987). In setting out to write in this format, "you have to pretend that your mind is, so to speak, a virgin receptacle, an empty vessel, for information which floods into it from the external world for no reason which you yourself have revealed...and in the discussion you adopt the ludicrous pretence of asking yourself if the information you have collected actually means anything."

Medawar argued that the scientific paper is founded on the principle of induction, according to which a researcher compiles data and observations quite unthinkingly before trying to discern pattern or meaning in them. A few scientists do work in this way (◀ page 56), but most do not, and while Medawar may go too far in suggesting that scientific papers contain no hint of their authors' initial ideas, he is undoubtedly correct in spotlighting their deficiency in missing out so much that is important to the progress of science. An author writing for a learned journal must adopt a highly objective style, omitting all personal factors, mistakes and flashes of inspiration. Using the passive voice ("It has been shown that..."), he or she has to find coldly rational, logical reasons for performing a particular set of experiments and interpreting them in a particular way.

In 1963 the Cambridge physiologist Alan Hodgkin (b.1914), his collaborator Andrew Huxley (b.1917), and the Australian John Eccles (b.1903) shared a Nobel prize in recognition of their momentous discoveries about the working of nerve cells. But in 1977, looking back over his first two decades of research, Hodgkin said he now regretted that the sequence of events recorded in a published paper gave an impression of "directness and planning" which did not coincide with what had actually happened: "The stated object of a piece of research often agrees more closely with the reason for continuing or finishing the work than it does with the idea which led to the original experiments."

▲ *The German polymath Gottfried Wilhelm Leibniz (1646-1716) apparently began to develop the calculus some years after Isaac Newton – but independently of him. The question of who was the inventor created much heat, and Newton's manuscripts contain at least ten different versions of a defense of his claim to priority. He even set up a committee, packed with his own supporters, to evaluate the rival claims.*

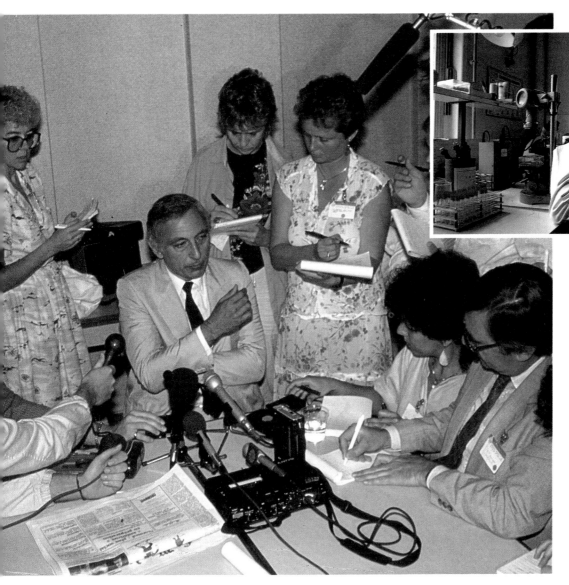

◀▲ *There was a spirited disputation between scientists during the mid-1980s, when two different groups claimed to have discovered the virus responsible for AIDS. One team was led by Dr Robert Gallo (left) at the National Institutes of Health in Bethesda, Maryland. The other was directed by Dr Luc Montagnier (above) at the Institut Pasteur in Paris. Each isolated a virus from AIDS patients, and gave them different names. The organisms were later found to be identical, and international pressure persuaded Gallo and Montagnier to accept a new name: human immuno-deficiency virus.*

The importance of priority

One consequence of the tradition that all scientific knowledge goes into a communal pool, leaving individual researchers with nothing more than recognition and esteem for their discoveries, is that they are very conscious of the need to register priority when announcing findings. Originality being central to scientific advance, it is not surprising to find throughout the history of science disputes over who was the first to make a particular discovery.

On such occasions, scientists have certainly allowed their personal feelings to propel them further in registering priority than is suggested by Robert Merton's more civilized norm of "communism" (◀ page 71). The scramble between groups on opposite sides of the Atlantic for the correct solution to the structure of DNA, described in Jim Watson's bestselling book "The Double Helix" (1968), is just one example. More recently, ferocity and pettiness characterized the rivalry between French-born Roger Guillemin (b.1924) and Polish-born Andrew Schally (b.1926) during their 21-year race toward the Nobel prize which they shared in 1977 for discovering the "releasing factors" through which the brain controls the body's hormonal system.

"It was a very bitter, unpleasant relationship. I could not stand him and he could not stand me," Schally said later about the initial five years during which he and Guillemin worked together at Houston. The partnership deteriorated much further after Schally left to run his own laboratory in New Orleans and the pair became furious competitors. Schally's inferiority complex toward his rival as a physiologist even made him recruit too many physiologists into his team, when he should have put more resources into chemistry. He also made the decision, which surprised many observers, to conduct his experiments with pigs. "Because Guillemin was working with sheep," he admitted afterwards, "I had to accept as a theoretical possibility that he would come up with a hormone first, and if I were working on sheep too my contribution would be worthless."

Despite such colorful exceptions, research carried out by Robert Merton and Elinor Barber suggests that scientists today may be less anxious about priority than they were in the past. They studied 264 multiple discoveries (in which the same finding was reported independently two or more times) and found a gradual decline in the frequency with which these led to intense arguments about personal credit. Of 36 multiples before 1700, 92 percent were contested strenuously. The figure fell to 72 percent in the first half of the 19th century, and declined to 59 percent in the second half. For multiple discoveries recorded in the first half of the present century, the percentage leading to dispute about priority was 33 percent.

Sooner or later, the degree to which scientists live by honesty, open-mindedness and cooperation directly affects whether science flourishes or stagnates

▲ "There is no sense at all in which science can be called a mere description of facts," wrote the British mathematician Jacob Bronowski in "The Common Sense of Science". "Bruno" went much further than most commentators in arguing that science not only reflects prevailing social attitudes and priorities but also (as itself a necessarily social activity) actually generates values. These include intellectual honesty and respect for rebellious individuals.

Social values inherent in science

Because science is based on objectivity, it is often portrayed – not least by its critics – as devoid of values. In particular, science and morals are said to be either opposed to each other or to have no conceivable connection. In fact, as Jacob Bronowski demonstrated in his book *The Common Sense of Science* (1951), it is not only wrong to see the pursuit of science as being amoral and ruthlessly logical. Such a view also overlooks the capacity of science itself to *generate* ethical and social values.

This follows from the nature of science as a communal activity, rather than a solitary one (◀ page 71). The intrinsic values of science include intellectual humility, an unusually acute regard for honesty, and respect for the revolutionary and the possible crank. They stress the importance of cooperation and intercourse across political and other boundaries.

Such attitudes are not optional extras for working scientists – as they are, for example, for composers, politicians and novelists. They rise inexorably out of the pursuit of research, and in the long term the degree to which scientists live by them directly affects whether science flourishes or stagnates. For example, whereas a politician can afford to denounce any opposition wholeheartedly, and make personal capital out of any situation, a scientist has to tread much more carefully.

Science is itself a revolutionary activity (◀ page 68). Many of the major branches of today's chemistry, physics and biology began with claims that were wildly out of line with contemporary opinion. Without being woolly-minded or gullible, therefore, scientists have an obligation always to take the unconventional opinions of other scientists seriously.

The overriding interest of the quest for truth

Honesty in science is at a high premium too. Without it, the entire, interlocking enterprise of science would collapse. No other profession is similarly threatened. The law, for example, is founded upon the notion of advocates pleading the best possible case for their clients. Even without indulging in blatant dishonesty, they are able to take or leave the hard facts about an alleged offence (which they term "the merits"), using them at will in setting out their arguments. Politicians, too, are able to focus only upon those facts which they find most convenient at a particular time. Some are even happy to argue that the end justifies the means. Scientists enjoy no such freedom. The facts have to be accepted and reckoned with – however awkward they may be, and however threatening to a cherished theory in which a researcher has invested years of work and from which personal prestige has flowed.

"For whatever else may be held against science, this cannot be denied, that it takes for ultimate judgment one criterion alone, that it shall be truthful," wrote Bronowski. "Whatever else they have also meant by truth, men who take pride in their conduct and its underlying values do set store by truthfulness in the literal sense. They are ashamed to lie in fact and in intention. And this transcending respect for truthfulness is shared by science. T.H. Huxley was an agnostic, Clifford was an atheist, and I know at least one great mathematician who is a scoundrel. Yet all of them rest their scientific faith on an uncompromising adherence to the truth, and the irresistible urge to discover it."

▲ An aerial photograph of the Mekong Delta shows areas (blue) affected by the spraying of Agent Orange by the US airforce during the Vietnam War. Massive quantities of defoliants were used to clear jungle, deny cover to the enemy and destroy crops. Yale University biologist Arthur Galston played a prominent role in fostering studies on the ecological effects of defoliation, leading to President Nixon's 1970 decision to phase out this technique. Galston took his stand because, 20 years earlier, he had helped to introduce similar chemicals as selective weedkillers.

▼ Arrested in May, 1945, German rocket pioneer Wernher von Braun is seen here with (on his right) Herbert Axster, whom US investigators classified under interrogation as "a notorious supporter...of the Nazi regime", and General Walter Dornberger, whom they described as "a menace to security". Despite these reports and the Nazi connections, the "paperclip conspiracy" ensured that von Braun and other valuable scientists were accepted in the USA after the war.

The Paperclip conspiracy

When Apollo 11 completed its historic voyage to the Moon in July 1969, the satisfaction was nowhere greater than among two groups of German scientists – Wernher von Braun's rocket team from Peenemünde in Germany, and a group of aviation doctors led by Dr Hubertus Strughold.

These were among some 20,000 scientists who in Hitler's Third Reich 25-40 years earlier had revolutionized the weapons of war. Their work had developed amid the violence of the Nazi regime. Indeed it had depended on it, for von Braun's V2 rockets and the tunnels in which they were tested had been built by slave labor. The experiments which led to Strughold's successful space capsule designs include fatal tests on Dachau inmates subjected to a horrible end in pressure chambers.

After Word War II considerably more resources were devoted by the victors to the hunt for German scientists than to the hunting down of war criminals. The German scientists later responsible for the United States' success in space were selected after interrogation by American officers, who identified the chosen few by attaching an ordinary paperclip to their personal file. The United States were not alone in this. In the scramble for the spoils of war, the Soviet Union, France and Britain also competed. To a greater or lesser extent each was involved in deliberately ignoring and concealing the undoubted Nazi past of many of the scientists they accepted as worthy citizens.

▲▶ "Piltdown man" was the subject of hoax, rather than of cheating for professional advancement or other reward. In 1912 solicitor Charles Dawson (right) and British Museum (Natural History) Geology Department Keeper Arthur Smith Woodward (center), here excavating on Piltdown Common in Sussex the previous year, announced that they had found some apparently fossilized remains of the cranium and jawbone of primitive man. They appeared to represent the "missing link" in human evolution. But new tests on the fragments in 1953-1954, particularly on the fluorine content, revealed that they were actually an orangutan jaw and a relatively modern human cranium, both skillfully disguised. J.S. Weiner and his colleagues announced the exposure in the "Bulletin of the British Museum (Natural History)" on November 21, 1953. Yet part of the mystery still remains. According to Dr Glyn Daniel, the editor of "Antiquity", at least ten suspects could have perpetrated the deception, including the French paleontologist and priest Pierre Teilhard de Chardin.

Cheating in science

Hoaxes apart, there had until recently been very few known cases of self-seeking fraud – open publication of claims based on fictitious or fudged experimental results. When such chicanery did come to light, exposure was usually accompanied by the diagnosis of mental illness in the researcher responsible. This was so with the French physicist René Blondlot (1849-1930), who became famous at the beginning of this century for his discovery of "N-rays".

Scientists have gradually become aware of the temptation to "massage" research data so as to enhance conclusions that are perfectly legitimate but less cast-iron than the experimenter desires. Here only a very thin – but significant – line separates the honest selection of data to support a sound line of reasoning from dishonest selection to buttress a case resting on spurious foundations. Many books about scientific method say otherwise, but any working scientist will confirm the existence of this gray area.

The response of the scientific community to the revelation of cheating during the late 1970s and early 1980s was initially hostile. Scientific journal editors too were embarrassed that the "peer review" mechanism (◀ page 74) had usually failed to bring chicanery to light. When the furore had died down, however, most people acknowledged that revelations and disclosures of dishonesty had had a purgative effect, and led to improvements in scientific intercourse.

The list of researchers suspected to have published data too good to be true includes several distinguished names. Gregor Mendel (1822-1884), the devout Moravian monk who founded the science of genetics, is one of them. As R.A. Fisher showed, some of Mendel's classic results from the crossbreeding of peas were improbably precise. The irony of this *cause célèbre* is that Gregor Mendel *was* responsible for genuine work that will stand as a major achievement for all time. His data did not need to be embellished in any way.

▲ The distinguished French physicist René Blondlot made several genuine and important discoveries, yet is best remembered for one entirely phoney piece of work. Studying X-rays a few years after they were first described by Röntgen, he claimed to have detected a new form of radiation. But Blondlot (or a faithful assistant) had invented the alleged phenomena. The truth emerged only when Robert Wood described in "Nature" how he had pocketed an essential part of the equipment during a demonstration – without affecting the results.

Recent cheating scandals: Summerlin

In April 1974, journalist Barbara Yuncker of the "New York Post" revealed that a young researcher at the Sloan Kettering Institute, New York, had confessed to fabricating some extremely dramatic research results. Over previous months, Dr William Summerlin had reported success in overcoming a phenomenon of major importance in modern surgery: rejection by the body of "foreign" tissue grafted from an unrelated donor. Summerlin claimed that merely by taking donor tissue and growing it in laboratory glassware for a short time, he was apparently able to destroy the cells' "foreignness". His most spectacular experiments involved grafting skin from black mice onto unrelated white mice without rejection.

But Summerlin's claims flew in the face not only of past evidence, but also of underlying biological principles. And other scientists tried to repeat his experiments without success. Pressure mounted on Summerlin to demonstrate the phenomenon. Then, the month before the "New York Post" revelations, he had used a black felt-tipped pen to darken some white skin grafts which he had made on white mice. He did so in the elevator on the way to see the Sloan-Kettering Institute's director, Dr Robert Good, in an effort to convince him that the aging technique was effective. A laboratory technician discovered the deception when he found that he could wipe the black skin clear with surgical spirit, and shortly afterward raised the alarm.

Human frailty apart, there seems little doubt that, at a time when cancer research was being kicked around as a political football in the United States, the incessant drive for results to secure more cash to secure more results to secure more cash was a powerful influence on scientists. At the Sloan-Kettering Institute a deficit of about $4 million for 1973 grew to $7 million by the end of 1974. It appears that just as Summerlin was guilty of deception, so the institute's director may have been negligent in not supervising such apparently revolutionary work more closely, and foolish in continuing to publicize his protégé's "discovery" when he ought to have had grounds for unease.

The high and the lowly

In 1976, it was reported that the famous English psychologist Sir Cyril Burt (1883-1971) had fabricated not only data but also the names of alleged collaborators. Burt was a powerful influence on educational policy in Britain, having demonstrated the importance of nature, as opposed to nurture, in determining a person's intelligence quotient. But diligent research by Gillie and others showed that much of Burt's data was spurious. In one "classic" paper, he had simply lifted data from studies done over 30 years previously. Two collaborators, identified as Margaret Howard and J. Conway, simply did not exist. How such deceptions went unrecognized for so long by Burt's colleagues remains a mystery.

In May 1981 a young Harvard Medical School researcher, John R. Darsee, was caught falsifying data during an experiment on some dogs in the cardiology laboratory at the Brigham and Women's Hospital, affiliated to Harvard. He was found blatantly labeling data obtained from dogs over a period of two hours to make it look as though they had been recorded over two weeks. When caught fabricating tracings, he confessed but insisted that this was a solitary, foolish act. But an inquiry into Dr Darsee's earlier work at Emory University in Atlanta concluded that Darsee had also falsified data in eight published papers and 43 abstracts, many of which were adjudged to be totally fictitious.

A super-plagiarist

Another remarkable revelation of dishonesty in science was the case of Elias A.K. Alsabti, a Jordanian doctor who went to work in the United States in 1977 and began a systematic career of lifting, verbatim, scientific papers from obscure journals, retyping them and submitting them elsewhere and thus publishing them under his own name. His tactics deceived the editors of dozens of journals all over the world. Alsabti never used the address of the institution where he was actually working, instead usually adopting the name of a fictitious laboratory. By 1979 Alsabti had apparently authored no fewer than 43 papers – and on an impressive range of different topics. Gradually, however, his deceit began to catch up with him and in 1980 William Broad exposed some of his exploits in "Science", in an article which soon led others to realize that they too had been fooled.

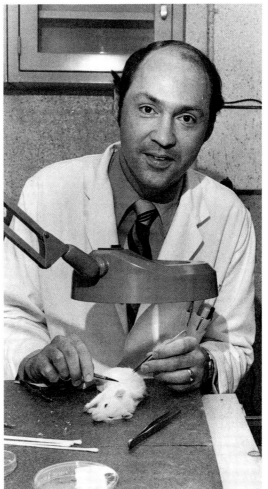

▲ In 1976, London "Sunday Times" writer Dr Oliver Gillie reported that scrutiny of work by English psychologist Sir Cyril Burt on the heritability of intelligence indicated that he had fabricated not only data but even the names of alleged collaborators. Burt's "normal distribution curve", here superimposed on genuine data (from IQ tests on US Army personnel), was so perfect that it must have been manufactured from theoretical assumptions.

◄ William Summerlin, who in March 1974 was found to have fabricated skin grafts in mice to support an apparently revolutionary method of preventing transplant rejection, may have been a victim of a drive to secure quick results in order to secure more cash for more research. The director of his institute was criticized, following Summerlin's exposure, for not supervising his work closely enough and not questioning his highly unusual results.

See also
The Philosophy of Science 63-70
Institutions of Science 85-98

▶ *Scientific exchange on a world scale is the basis of certain sciences. The International Meteorological Organization established in 1878 held its second congress in Rome in 1897 (right). Its modern counterpart is the World Meteorological Organization, an agency of the United Nations set up in 1951.*

▼ *Scientific advance has been assisted greatly since the appearance of periodicals in the 17th century. Recently, popular science magazines, specialized journals and abstracting journals have become increasingly important.*

Landmark publications

17th century Journals largely replaced letters as chief means of communication between scientists

January 1665 *Journal des sçavans*, Paris, first independent scientific (and literary) journal

1684 *Nouvelles de la républic des lettres*, Amsterdam

Breakfast-table leaflets such as *The Tatler* (1709–1712), *Spectator* (1711–1712) and *Guardian* (1713) all contained popular scientific and medical information

1679–1681 *Nouvelles découvertes* (ed. N. de Blegny), first authentic medical periodical in vernacular

1682 *Acta Eruditorum*, Leipzig

1668 *Giornale de Litterati d'Italia*, Rome

March 1665 *Philosophical Transactions* of London's Royal Society; concentrated on science from start

1670 *Miscellanea Curiosa*, first scientific journal in Germany, contained substantial medical material

1657 Accademia del Cimento; though short-lived, published results of researches in physics and natural history

1603 Academy of Lynxes, Rome; published natural history works and Galileo's *Saggiatore* (*Assayer*) on scientific method

1694 Thomas Corneille's *Dictionnaire des arts et des sciences*

1703 *Recherches de mathématiques et de physique* paid more than average attention to mathematics

1771 *Observations sur la physique*, Paris, one of the first specialized scientific journals

1771 *Encyclopedia Britannica, or, A Dictionary of Arts and Sciences*

From the 18th century ever-increasing numbers of academies and societies, national, local, general and specialized, in N Europe and N America, published their own journals

1746 foundation of *Botanical Magazine* (later *Curtis's...*), first finely illustrated such journal

1746–1761 *Monatliche herausgegebene Insekten-belustigungen*, Nürnberg, first specialized entomological periodical

1789 *Annales de chemie*, oldest chemical journal in continuous existence, ed. Lavoisier *et al.* in Paris

1751–1772 *Encyclopédie ou dictionnaire raisonné des sciences, des arts et des métiers*, eds. Voltaire and d'Alembert

1757–1758 An example of a specialized biological periodical, *Abhandlungen zur Naturgesichte der Thiere und Pflanzen*, Leipzig

1798 *Philosophical Magazine*, London, mainly physics

1782 *Almanach vétérinaire*, Paris

1780–1829 *Almanach oder Taschenbuch für Scheidkunstler, und Apotheker*, Weimar, first German pharmacological journal

1773–1780 *Journal für die Liebhaber des Steinreichs*, perhaps oldest journal in geology

1818 *American Journal of Science*

1845 *Scientific American* established

1790 *Journal der Physik*, Halle and Leipzig, first specialized physics journal

1830 *Pharmaceutisches Centralblatt* (later, *Chemisches Zentralblatt*), first abstracting journal

1778–1781 *Chemisches Journal* edited by pioneer publisher L. von Crell, Helmstedt

1781 *Annalen der Botanik*, Leipzig (later *Neue Annalen...*)

1830s Appearance of specialized journals in science and technology, coincided with industrial revolution

Annual publications of British Association for the Advancement of Science (1831) and American AAS (1848) helped popularize science

Popular science journals such as *New Scientist* (1956) and *La Recherche* (1960) also appeared in greater numbers

After World War II numbers of commercially published specialist journals increased greatly

1871–1910 Anglo-US *International Scientific Series* led the way in getting eminent scientists to popularize their own areas of science

1869 *Nature* first appeared, popular contributors included C. Darwin and T.H. Huxley

1650   1700   1750   1800   1850   1900   1950

Institutions of Science

8

*Science as a profession...Scientific training...National scientific organizations...International scientific organizations...Nobel prizes...*PERSPECTIVE*...Definition of a scientist....The supervisor-student relationship ...Laboratories and research centers...The laboratory... Bans and boycotts...Other honors to scientists...Table of Nobel laureates...Chronology*

▲ *British physicist Lord Rayleigh (1842-1919), one of the last truly amateur scientists, was a professor at Cambridge University, but worked mainly in his own laboratory. He gained a 1904 Nobel prize for studies of atmospheric density and the discovery of argon.*

In his autobiography, the distinguished British astronomer Sir Fred Hoyle (b.1915) recalls his skill in writing out multiplication tables up to 12 × 12 by the age of four, and the individualistic style of arithmetic which he had evolved long before that. Such precociousness, combined with an insatiable curiosity about the natural world, a relentless intelligence, and a marked impatience with formal education, suggest that Hoyle was destined to be a scientist – and a very good one too. Whatever the truth behind the rival psychological analyses of people's reasons for choosing science as a career (◀ page 33), it can well be argued that the very best scientists are born, not made.

Nevertheless, because science is now a profession, and because an enormous quantity of learning is required before someone can reach the frontiers of knowledge, the training of scientists today is highly organized. Centered on the first degree of bachelor of science (BSc) or similar, and the higher degree of doctor of philosophy (PhD), the present-day system originated in the 19th century. When the Cambridge classics scholar and scientist William Whewell (1794-1866) proposed the term "scientist" in 1840, science was then changing from being a pursuit for rich amateurs (Charles Darwin was one of the last) to a paid vocation – initially for academics and later also for people working in industry. Before this time, physicists, chemists and biologists were known as "natural philosophers" or "virtuosi". "Science" itself, from the Latin *scientia*, meaning, simply, knowledge, was applied to all systematic study, and embraced mathematics and theology. "Scientific", literally knowledge-making, referred to logical reasoning as used in mathematics, that is, as a synonym for "demonstrative".

Whereas formerly it had been virtually impossible to secure a formal training in science (other than by serving an uncertain and ill-organized apprenticeship as a laboratory assistant), by the end of the century the natural sciences had become formal subjects on both school and university curricula.

Germany led the way, insisting on the importance of the PhD as a measure of original scientific ability. Many new universities sprang up, competing for the cream of scholarship, within which each individual professor controlled a *seminar*. Now called a research team, this consisted of a group of assistants who were preparing dissertations on their own work in the hope of being granted a doctorate. Members of one of these teams were utterly dependent on their chief's patronage and goodwill, but the system generated high quality work and was soon to be copied – initially in the United States and later in Europe (◆ pages 86-87). That was the origin of today's graduate schools, in which students attend formal lectures and take examinations before pursuing a period of original research and preparing a PhD thesis.

What is a scientist?

The term "scientist" is of fairly recent origin, having been first coined in 1833, but not used widely until the 1930s. In the early 19th century, men of science were becoming increasingly aware of the importance of their work – and of their aspirations to be paid professionals. A contemporary account noted "the want of any name by which we can designate the students of the knowledge of the material world collectively". At a meeting of the British Association for the Advancement of Science, English classics scholar William Whewell drew the analogy with "artist" and proposed "scientist". He later wrote that "Leonardo was mentally a seeker after truth – a scientist; Coreggio was an asserter of the truth – an artist."

Paradoxically, in the years following the introduction of the word "scientist", although it was intended by Whewell to describe "a cultivator of science in general", science itself became more and more particular. As a consequence of an increase in both the amount and complexity of research, the new generation of professional scientists worked in increasingly specialist areas. Today, the enormous range of disciplines and styles of science (◆ pages 34-35) requires a common definition of "scientist" to be all-embracing: one who practices the systematic study of the nature and behavior of the universe, based on the formulation of laws to describe observed facts.

"I have finished my course work, Professor"

▲ "I have finished my
course work, Professor" – a
cartoon from "Physicists
Continue to Laugh",
published in 1968 by MIR
Publishing House, Moscow.
Although PhD training is
now usually completed
within a predictable period
of time, there have been
many occasions when the
process has been, or has
seemed to be, interminable.

▼ Jocelyn Bell was the
first to detect what we now
call pulsars. Although she
disagrees, some
commentators believe she
should have shared the
Nobel prize awarded to her
supervisor Antony Hewish.

Scientific training

Although amateurs can still make significant contributions to science
(in observational astronomy and natural history, for example), it is
now virtually impossible for someone to enter the ranks of professional science without obtaining at least a first degree (BSc), and
usually also a PhD. The former usually follows a three-year course,
leading to a degree in one of the "pure" sciences such as chemistry,
physics or botany, or an applied science such as electrical or mechanical engineering. Such courses provide a comprehensive training
within their field, though some (such as genetics, food science,
acoustics, marine biology, brewing, nuclear technology, polymer
science and nutrition) cover more tightly focused ground.

Many graduates who have taken one of the less specialized courses
go on to train as school teachers in that subject. Others choose to work
as scientists, in industry, or government institutes and elsewhere.
Their work will be closely supervised by an experienced scientist who
almost certainly possesses a PhD. A halfway house is the master's
degree (normally MSc), which is awarded for coursework and examinations more advanced than those for the BSc and/or requiring a
shorter period of original research than for a PhD. Alternatively, a
zoologist wishing to work in a specialist library, for example, might
take an MSc in information science.

Practical acquaintance with research methods is the *raison d'être* of
doctoral training. After receiving a good standard of first degree, the
postgraduate student enrols under a supervisor to tackle a defined
research project for three or four years. The supervisor, an established researcher, identifies a problem which seems likely to generate
results during that period of time. This is usually part of a wider
attack in which the supervisor directs a group of postgraduate (and
perhaps postdoctoral) students. The aim may, for example, be to
work out the food chains through which diverse living organisms in

the depths of the ocean support each other. Individual members of the group might study different members of the community, using similar experimental techniques, the supervisor being the lynchpin of the exercise in building up a coherent picture over many years of work.

Two important preliminaries tend to occupy the early months of a PhD project. First, the student has to read previous papers and books in the chosen field (which may include doing a computerized "literature search") so as to become fully informed and oriented toward existing knowledge and theories. Second, he or she requires training in methods to be used routinely once the work really starts. The student needs to become practically skilled in, for example, retrieving water samples from the ocean bottom and analyzing particular constituents back in the laboratory. Equally important is an appreciation of the strengths, limitations, and dependability of experimental equipment.

Supervisor and student then plan their campaign together, working out a program of experiments to be conducted during the allotted time. At this stage, and during regular consultations as the research proceeds, the student developes first-hand appreciation of the tactics and strategies known as scientific method (◀ page 54). It is that understanding, as much as the more obvious success of the work, which will be tested at the end when an external examiner assesses the student's thesis and asks supposedly searching questions during a viva (oral examination). Occasionally, PhD research proves to be outstandingly important – as in 1967 in Cambridge, England, when Jocelyn Bell first observed the pulsating radio signals from outer space which revealed the existence of pulsars. Her supervisor, Antony Hewish (b.1924), shared a Nobel prize in 1974 for this work. Much more often, however, doctoral studies form part of unsung "normal science" (◀ page 68).

Scientific bodies range in size from the laboratory or small trade organization to the 40,000-strong "science city" of Akademigorodok

▲ *Discoverer of potassium and sodium, Sir Humphry Davy (1778-1829) vigorously revived the flagging fortunes of London's Royal Institution at the beginning of the 19th century. In 1808, as the French and British armies were about to clash in the Peninsular War in Portugal and Spain, Davy was awarded Napoleon's 3,000-franc prize for his work on electricity. In "The Sciences were Never at War" Sir Gavin de Beer points out that during the entire intermittent conflict from the founding of the Royal Society and the French Académie des Sciences during the 1660s, to Napoleon's downfall in 1815, scientists on opposite sides of the English Channel continued to exchange information, travel to each other's countries and elect one another to membership of their learned societies.*

National scientific organizations

The principal institutions of science are the myriad national and international organizations which, through conferences, journals and other activities, facilitate scientific intercourse (♦ page 71) and provide an interface between the scientific community and other constituencies, including government. The first such national body, the Royal Society, remains the most prestigious in that election to its fellowship or (in the case of overseas researchers) foreign membership is much coveted. Election for a four-year term as president is the pinnacle of a career in British science, the post being occupied alternately by a biologist and a physical scientist. The annual quota of 40 new "FRSs", who now embrace applied as well as pure science, is based on excellence in research. The Society's activities include representing British science abroad, providing informal advice to government, awarding medals for research achievements, and holding discussions which (even today, when many conferences are commercially organized and highly priced) remain open to anyone with an interest in the subject.

The American counterpart to the Royal Society is the National Academy of Sciences. Founded in 1863 during the Civil War, it elects members in a similar way and for similar reasons. The main difference, reflecting the more adversarial nature of American society is that the Academy has lobbied more openly on behalf of science and particular science-based issues. While neither body is as radical in this respect as other, independent groups who do *not* see themselves as part of the establishment, the Washington-based National Academy of Sciences and the much newer National Academy of Engineering together sponsor the National Research Council, whose task is to conduct studies "in the public interest". In 1985, for example, the NRC surveyed the records of 46,000 veterans from atmospheric nuclear tests and revealed that, while there was no overall evidence of an increased death rate, there were significantly more cases of leukemia and prostate cancer in two subgroups.

In addition to major national and global institutions of science, the countless other bodies range from vast organizations such as the American Chemical Society, with thousands of members and an income of millions of dollars, to small groups with a fraction of the membership and resources. These are the bodies which sponsor most scientific gatherings and (increasingly in collaboration with commercial companies) publish scientific journals. Some societies interest themselves in professional issues.

Although scientists have traditionally been reluctant to join trade unions, they are more concerned nowadays to try to protect their career interests in this way. In Britain in particular, fears that central government has neglected science have driven many researchers to join unions such as the Association of Scientific, Technical and Managerial Staffs (ASTMS). Different again, and different from each other, are the American Association for the Advancement of Science (AAAS) and the British Association for the Advancement of Science (BA). Each has a considerable stake in the popularization of science, but whereas this is now the sole function of the BA (whose annual meeting *used* to provide a forum for scientists to communicate research findings to each other), the AAAS also publishes the learned journal *Science* and has a significant voice in science policy debate. The Australia and New Zealand Association for the Advancement of Science (ANZAS) is another organization with both public and political purposes.

▲ *Established by Louis XIV in Paris in 1666, the Académie des Sciences (coupled in Henri Testelin's painting with the foundation of the Paris Observatory in 1667) arose from private meetings in the Salon of Étienne Pascal (father of Blaise Pascal) some years before. Like the Royal Society and the Prussian and Russian academies, it was set up not only to foster national talent in science but also to promote national trade and manufactures. It now has a limited membership of 130, plus at most 80 foreign associates and 160 correspondents.*

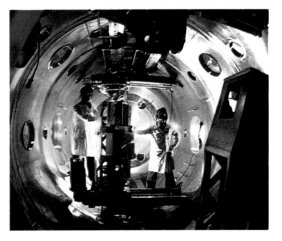

▼ Named for the French microbiologist and chemist, the Pasteur Institute in Paris has played a major part in combatting many of the world's outbreaks of infectious diseases over the past century. It has specialized in developing vaccines, such as these batches of cholera vaccine being sterilized before being flown out to fight the mysterious epidemic of cholera which occurred in Egypt in 1947.

Laboratories and research centers

Several individual laboratories and research centers are sufficiently influential and/or large to qualify as institutions of science. Some have a distinguished history and remain in the forefront of research today. They include the Cavendish Laboratory in Cambridge, England, in which Lord Rutherford and others helped to create 20th-century physics, and the Pasteur Institute in Paris, a major world center for microbiology and molecular biology. CERN in Geneva and Fermilab near Chicago are preeminent in high-energy physics – a brand of inordinately expensive "big science" in which international collaboration is increasingly essential. The Bell Telephone Laboratories of New Jersey, founded in 1925 and supported entirely out of profits from the American Telephone and Telegraph Company, are unique in providing vast resources for the quasiacademic pursuit of highly speculative ideas alongside more concertedly commercial research.

Another unique, elite center is the Tata Institute for Fundamental Research. Founded in Bombay, India, in 1945, it enjoys a mixed reputation – for the excellence of its fundamental science, and the alleged indifference of its staff to the practical challenges of the Third World. A more recent experiment was the founding in 1985 of an International Centre for Genetic Engineering and Biotechnology, with laboratories in New Delhi and Trieste, Italy. Supported by $41m from the United Nations Industrial Development Organization (UNIDO) for the first five years of development, the Centre's work will apply the latest sophisticated techniques to immediate practical problems. It will range over topics such as tropical diseases, protein engineering, and energy production from crops.

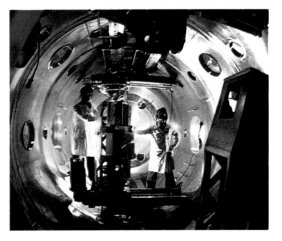

◄ In 1957, the Soviet Union resolved to turn 15km² of Siberian forest into a massive "Science City", to be devoted solely to research. Akademigorodok, near Novosibirsk, now contains some 40,000 inhabitants, and represents the deliberate creation of a scientific elite within Soviet society. The photograph shows plasma studies proceeding inside a vacuum chamber in the Thermic Physics Institute at Akademigorodok.

The Laboratory

► *The biosphere – the plant, animal and microbial life on Earth – provides one vast natural laboratory. Although individual species can be scrutinized in an artificial, enclosed laboratory, many aspects of ecology and evolution can be investigated only in the wild. Here a botanist studies Acacia in the Namib Desert of southwest Africa.*

▼ *Built in 1983, the British Antarctic Survey's Halley Station is used by visiting scientists, focusing on meteorology, atmospheric phenomena, geology and biology. The base's living modules are inside the wooden tubes, visible in the photograph, which have to be strong enough to withstand the pressure of snow that periodically buries the entire structure. The British Antarctic Survey also operates two ships and two aircraft.*

▼ *The huge Tevatron at Fermi National Accelerator Laboratory, Illinois, is 2km in diameter and contains two particle accelerators which in tandem speed protons to the high energies required for them to be used as projectiles with which to smash atoms and study the resulting products. The circular tunnel containing the Tevatron is outlined here by the lights of a car driving round a service road above the tunnel.*

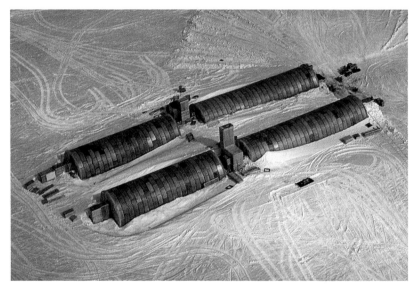

◄ Experiments – those, for example, needing more thorough mixing of chemicals than is possible under gravity – can be conducted in the weightless conditions of space. Skylab 1, here in Earth orbit during 1974, was also used for observations through its Apollo Telescope Mount, seen at the junction of four solar panels.

▼ Telescope controller John Hulse in the control room at Jodrell Bank radio observatory near Manchester, England. The instrument panel not only shows data from there but also includes data from other radio dishes at Cambridge and elsewhere in continental Europe – in effect a huge telescope 127km in diameter.

▼ Sometimes termed "the last resource", the world's oceans are a major target for scientific investigation. One of the facilities designed to study this enticing but dangerous domain is the US Navy's submersible laboratory Sealab 3, seen here attached to its surface support vessel. In 1977 another submersible, Alvin, revealed many previously unknown forms of life in warm water vents deep in the Pacific Ocean.

The International Association of Geodesy, founded in 1832, was the first global body dealing with a scientific discipline

Bans and boycotts

The tradition of openness in science continues today in the opposition of scientific institutions (though not all of them – see below) to bans and boycotts. In 1982, for example, the Australian government excluded two Soviet researchers from the International Congress of Biochemistry in Perth, in protest against Soviet military action in Afghanistan. Several senior scientists abroad, including the president of the Royal Society, Sir Andrew Huxley, protested so effectively that the rules were changed and in 1983 the International Congress of Physiological Sciences was able to proceed in Sydney without discrimination against bona fide scientists.

However, similar pleas failed two years later when the organizing committee of the Congress of the International Union of Prehistoric and Protohistoric Sciences (IUPPS), responding to local pressures in the intended venue, Southampton, England, excluded South African residents from attending the event in September 1986. After a furious row, the outcome was a shambles, the congress being transferred to Mainz, West Germany, and the British organizers going ahead with a rival meeting.

The stances of UNESCO and the ICSU

The IUPPS incident brought into focus the political stances of the two major world bodies concerned with science – the United Nations Educational, Scientific and Cultural Organization (UNESCO) and the International Council of Scientific Unions (ICSU). The IUPPS is affiliated to a UNESCO umbrella organization which advocates an academic boycott against South Africa. But its action contradicted the policy of international unions which, as members of ICSU, refuse to accept any invitation to host a congress if the country making the invitation cannot promise that scientists of all nationalities will be allowed to take part and that there will be no discrimination on political grounds.

▶ *Ethiopian farmers examine an improved variety of barley – one of the "green revolution" varieties of cereals produced by irradiation of existing types and the selection of mutants with desirable characteristics. Paradoxically, the application of this technique (and the newer methods of gene splicing) to crop improvement has increased awareness of the need to retain as wide a range as possible of naturally occurring seeds, which may be required in breeding novel varieties. In 1980, with financial and expert aid from the United Nations Food and Agriculture Organization, the Ethiopian government's Ministry of Agriculture established a gene bank to conserve such materials.*

▲ *The headquarters of the United Nations Educational, Scientific and Cultural Organization at Place de la Fontenay in Paris, France. Founded in 1945, UNESCO aims to contribute to peace and security through its three principal spheres of interest. There are 159 member states, since the withdrawal of the United States in 1985 and Britain in 1986 on grounds of alleged politicization and bureaucratic waste. From its Paris base, UNESCO fosters the development of science and technology worldwide, supports programs concerned with the human environment and global resources (preeminently "Man and the Biosphere") and fosters public understanding of science and development of science policies.*

International scientific organizations

Supporting the basic science programs on which the UN's agencies, such as the World Health Organization, thrive, the United Nations Educational, Scientific and Cultural Organization (UNESCO) is responsible for an annual expenditure of $500m on national and regional projects. Some 20,000 scientists participate in its work each year.

The International Council of Scientific Unions (ICSU) evolved in 1931 out of an International Research Council which had been formed about a decade before to provide a loose federation of international unions and links with the various national academies. Today the ICSU is the major nongovernmental organization in world science, with both scientific members (the unions) and national members (the national academies or research councils that provide most of the funds). A measure of the growth and increasing specialization of science worldwide is the diversification in just one sector, biology. In 1955 ICSU had only one biological wing, the International Union of Biological Sciences (IUBS). There are now eight more, covering microbiology (IUMS), immunology (IUIS) and other specialities. ICSU is also the major professional body through which UNESCO promotes scientific work.

Several intergovernmental organizations of the UN promote international cooperation in applied sciences. These include the World Health Organization (WHO), which was responsible for the global eradication of smallpox during the 1970s, the Food and Agriculture Organization (FAO), and the World Meteorology Organization (WMO). Separate from ICSU, several major nongovernmental organizations help to promote global action in science-related fields. The International Union for Conservation of Nature and Natural Resources (IUCN) is a typical example. The European Science Foundation, based in Strasbourg, France, is charged with assisting its members (48 academies and research councils from 18 countries) to coordinate their research programs and define priorities. As well as identifying areas in need of stimulation (particularly in interdisciplinary areas), it places considerable emphasis on the movement of researchers between different national laboratories, the joint use of expensive equipment, and the holding of specialist workshops.

▼ *While UNESCO has been under attack by many western governments for heavy expenditure in its Paris headquarters, and for policies such as a new "international information order" (which critics argue would have muzzled the media in describing developments that Third World states would prefer not to be reported), there is admiration for its field and educational efforts throughout the world. Wall charts used for an "Ecology in Action" project as part of the Man and the Biosphere program (below) illustrate this important strand of UNESCO's work.*

The inventor of dynamite founded an annual prize to go to those who "conferred the greatest benefit on mankind"

Nobel prizes

The Nobel prizes, awarded annually in physics, chemistry, physiology or medicine, literature, and peace, were founded in 1901 as decreed in the will of Alfred Nobel (1833-1896), the Swedish chemist, engineer and inventor of dynamite. The Royal Swedish Academy of Sciences awards the prizes in physics and chemistry and, since 1969, economics. The Royal Caroline Medico-Chirurgical Institute awards that in physiology or medicine. Nominations for Nobel prizes are invited from Swedish and six other universities, and from past Nobel laureates.

Although Nobel's will stated that his prizes should go to those who "during the preceding year have conferred the greatest benefit on mankind", in practice the scientific prizes have usually recognized research conducted several years previously. This has been inevitable, given the period of time that often needs to elapse before revolutionary work becomes generally accepted. But the authorities in Stockholm are frequently criticized for undue caution, sometimes allowing decades to elapse before making a decision.

Some embarrassing errors have contributed to this cautious approach. In 1926, for example, the Danish pathologist Johannes Fibiger (1867-1928) received the Physiology or Medicine Prize for discovering a parasitic worm that caused cancer – which proved to be a misapprehension. This mistake was at least partly responsible for the inordinate delay in recognizing a similar but entirely valid piece of work by the American physician Peyton Rous (1879-1970). In 1910, he found that he could transmit a malignant tumor from one chicken to another by injecting a cell-free filtrate of the cancerous tissue. His conclusion – that a virus must be responsible – has long since been confirmed, and recognized by the name Rous sarcoma virus. But the idea that microorganisms could induce cancer was alien to orthodox medicine at that time, added to which other researchers failed to replicate Rous's findings. Yet even 20 years later, when Robert Shope isolated another virus as the cause of a rabbit tumor, Rous went unrewarded. Not until 1966, at the age of 87, did he share a Nobel prize "for his discovery of tumor-inducing viruses".

▲▼ *The portrait of Alfred Nobel, by Emil Osterman, hangs in the Nobel Foundation in Stockholm. Although now rivalled by other awards of similar cash value, Nobel prizes remain by far the most prestigious for scientists. Honored in a special Swedish postage stamp (below), the first winners of Alfred Nobel's prizes, in 1901, were Wilhelm Conrad Röntgen (physics), Sully Prudhomme (literature), Emil von Behring (physiology or medicine) and Jacobus van't Hoff (chemistry).*

◄ *Owen Chamberlain, Edwin McMillan, Emilio Segrè, Melvin Calvin, Donald Glaser, Luis Alvarez and Glenn Seaborg – seven Nobel laureates from the Lawrence Berkeley Laboratory, California, pose in 1968 in front of the 940mm cyclotron magnet designed by the laboratory's founder, Nobel laureate Ernest Lawrence. In 1986 Yuan Lee became the ninth member of this major center of physics research to receive science's highest accolade.*

Nobel prizes in science 1901–1955

Chemistry	Physics	Physiology or Medicine
1901		
J. H. van't Hoff *Neth.*	W. C. Röntgen *Ger.*	E. A. von Behring *Ger.*
1902		
Emil Fischer *Ger.*	H. A. Lorentz *Neth.*	Ronald Ross *UK*
	Pieter Zeeman *Neth.*	
1903		
S. A. Arrhenius *Swe.*	A. H. Becquerel *Fra.*	N. R. Finsen *Den.*
	Pierre Curie *Fra.*	
	Marie S. Curie *Fra.*	
1904		
William Ramsay *UK*	J. W. S. Rayleigh *UK*	Ivan P. Pavlov *Russia*
1905		
Adolf von Baeyer *Ger.*	Philipp Lenard *Ger.*	Robert Koch *Ger.*
1906		
Henri Moissan *Fra.*	Joseph Thomson *UK*	Camillo Golgi *It.*
		S. Ramón y Cajal *Spain*
1907		
Eduard Buchner *Ger.*	A. A. Michelson *USA*	C. L. A. Laveran *Fra.*
1908		
Ernest Rutherford *UK*	Gabriel Lippman *Fra.*	Paul Ehrlich *Ger.*
		Élie Metchnikoff *Russia*
1909		
Wilhelm Ostwald *Ger.*	Guglielmo Marconi *It.*	Emil T. Kocher *Swi.*
	C. F. Braun *Ger.*	
1910		
Otto Wallach *Ger.*	J. D. van der Waals *Neth.*	Albrecht Kossel *Ger.*
1911		
Marie S. Curie *Fra.*	Wilhelm Wien *Ger.*	Allvar Gullstrand *Swe.*
1912		
Victor Grignard *Fra.*	N. G. Dalén *Swe.*	Alexis Carrel *Fra.*
Paul Sabatier *Fra.*		
1913		
Alfred Werner *Swi.*	Heike Kamerlingh Onnes *Neth.*	C. R. Richet *Fra.*
1914		
T. W. Richards *USA*	Max von Laue *Ger.*	Robert Barany *Austria*
1915		
Richard Willstätter *Ger.*	William H. Bragg *UK*	———
	William L. Bragg *UK*	
1916		
———	———	———
1917		
———	C. G. Barkla *UK*	———
1918		
Fritz Haber *Ger.*	Max Planck *Ger.*	
1919		
———	Johannes Stark *Ger.*	Jules Bordet *Bel.*
1920		
Walther Nernst *Ger.*	C. E. Guillaume *Swi.*	S. A. S. Krogh *Den.*
1921		
Frederick Soddy *UK*	Albert Einstein *Ger./Swi.*	———
1922		
F. W. Aston *UK*	N. H. D. Bohr *Den.*	A. V. Hill *UK*
		Otto Meyerhof *Ger.*
1923		
Fritz Pregl *Austria*	Robert A. Millikan *USA*	F. G. Banting *Can.*
		J. J. R. Macleod *Can.*
1924		
———	K. M. G. Siegbahn *Swe.*	Willem Einthoven *Neth.*
1925		
Richard Zsigmondy *Ger.*	James Franck *Ger.*	———
	Gustav Hertz *Ger.*	
1926		
T. Svedberg *Swe.*	J. B. Perrin *Fra.*	Johannes Fibiger *Den.*
1927		
Heinrich Wieland *Ger.*	A. H. Compton *USA*	Julius Wagner-Jauregg *Austria*
	C. T. R. Wilson *UK*	
1928		
Adolf Windaus *Ger.*	O. W. Richardson *UK*	C. J. H. Nicolle *Fra.*
1929		
Arthur Harden *UK*	L. V. de Broglie *Fra.*	Christian Eijkman *Neth.*
Hans von Euler-Chelpin *Swe.*		F. G. Hopkins *UK*
1930		
Hans Fischer *Ger.*	Chandrasekhara V. Raman *India*	Karl Landsteiner *Austria*

Chemistry	Physics	Physiology or Medicine
1931		
Carl Bosch *Ger.*	———	Otto H. Warburg *Ger.*
Friedrich Bergius *Ger.*		
1932		
Irving Langmuir *USA*	Werner Heisenberg *Ger.*	E. D. Adrian *UK*
		C. Sherrington *UK*
1933		
———	P. A. M. Dirac *UK*	Thomas H. Morgan *USA*
	E. Schrödinger *Austria*	
1934		
Harold C. Urey *USA*	———	G. H. Whipple *USA*
		G. R. Minot *USA*
		W. P. Murphy *USA*
1935		
Frédéric Joliot-Curie, Irène Joliot-Curie *Fra.*	James Chadwick *UK*	Hans Spemann *Ger.*
1936		
P. J. W. Debye *Neth.*	C. D. Anderson *USA*	Henry H. Dale *UK*
	V. F. Hess *Austria*	Otto Loewi *Austria*
1937		
Walter N. Haworth *UK*	C. J. Davisson *USA*	Albert von Szent-Gyorgyi *Hung.*
Paul Karrer *Swi.*	George P. Thomson *UK*	
1938		
Richard Kuhn *Ger.*	Enrico Fermi *It.*	Corneille Heymans *Bel.*
1939		
Adolf Butenandt *Ger.*	E. O. Lawrence *USA*	Gerhard Domagk *Ger.*
Leopold Ružička *Swi.*		
1940	———	———
1941	———	———
1942	———	———
1943		
Georg von Hevesy *Hung.*	Otto Stern *USA*	E. A. Doisy *Den.*
		Henrik Dam *USA*
1944		
Otto Hahn *Ger.*	I. I. Rabi *USA*	Joseph Erlanger *USA*
		H. S. Gasser *USA*
1945		
A. I. Virtanen *Fin.*	Wolfgang Pauli *Austria*	Alexander Fleming *UK*
		E. B. Chain *UK*
		Howard W. Florey *UK*
1946		
J. B. Sumner *USA*	P. W. Bridgman *USA*	H. J. Muller *USA*
J. H. Northrop *USA*		
W. M. Stanley *USA*		
1947		
Robert Robinson *UK*	Edward V. Appleton *UK*	C. F. Cori *USA*
		Gerty T. Cori *USA*
		B. A. Houssay *Arg.*
1948		
Arne Tiselius *Swe.*	P. M. S. Blackett *UK*	Paul H. Müller *Swi.*
1949		
W. F. Giauque *USA*	Hideki Yukawa *Jap.*	W. R. Hess *Swi.*
		Egas Moniz *Port.*
1950		
Otto Diels *FRG*	C. F. Powell *UK*	Philip S. Hench *USA*
Kurt Alder *FRG*		Edward C. Kendall *USA*
		Tadeus Reichstein *Swi.*
1951		
E. M. McMillan *USA*	John D. Cockcroft *UK*	Max Theiler *S. Africa*
G. T. Seaborg *USA*	Ernest T. S. Walton *Ire.*	
1952		
A. J. P. Martin *UK*	Felix Bloch *USA*	S. A. Waksman *USA*
R. L. M. Synge *UK*	E. M. Purcell *USA*	
1953		
Hermann Staudinger *Ger.*	Frits Zernike *Neth.*	F. A. Lipmann *USA*
		Hans A. Krebs *UK*
1954		
Linus C. Pauling *USA*	Max Born *UK*	J. F. Enders *USA*
	Walther Bothe *FRG*	F. C. Robbins *USA*
		T. H. Weller *USA*
1955		
Vincent du Vigneaud *USA*	Willis E. Lamb, Jr. *USA*	A. H. T. Theorell *Swe.*
	Polykarp Kusch *USA*	

Recent Nobel prize lists include more shared awards, but the emphasis is still on individuals, not teams

Nobel prizes in science 1956–1987

Chemistry	Physics	Physiology or Medicine
1956		
Cyril N. Hinshelwood *UK*	W. B. Shockley *USA*	D. W. Richards, Jr. *USA*
Nikolai N. Semenov, *USSR*	W. H. Brattain *USA*	A. F. Cournand *USA*
	John Bardeen *USA*	W. Forssmann *FRG*
1957		
Alexander R. Todd *UK*	Tsung-Dao Lee *China*	Daniel Bovet *It.*
	Chen Ning Yang *China*	
1958		
Frederick Sanger *UK*	P. A. Cherenkov *USSR*	Joshua Lederberg *USA*
	Igor Y. Tamm *USSR*	G. W. Beadle *USA*
	Ilya M. Frank *USSR*	E. L. Tatum *USA*
1959		
Jaroslav Heyrovsky *Czech.*	Emilio Segrè *USA*	Severo Ochoa *USA*
	Owen Chamberlain *USA*	Arthur Kornberg *USA*
1960		
W. F. Libby *USA*	D. A. Glaser *USA*	F. M. Burnet *Australia*
		P. B. Medawar *UK*
1961		
Melvin Calvin *USA*	Robert Hofstadter *USA*	Georg von Bekesy *USA*
	R. L. Mössbauer *FRG*	
1962		
M. F. Perutz *UK*	L. D. Landau *USSR*	J. D. Watson *USA*
J. C. Kendrew *UK*		F. H. C. Crick *UK*
		M. H. F. Wilkins *UK*
1963		
Giulio Natta *It.*	Eugene P. Wigner *USA*	John Carew Eccles *Australia*
Karl Ziegler *FRG*	Maria G. Mayer *USA*	Alan Lloyd Hodgkin *UK*
	J. Hans D. Jensen *FRG*	Andrew F. Huxley *UK*
1964		
Dorothy Crowfoot Hodgkin *UK*	Charles Hard Townes *USA*	Konrad E. Bloch *USA*
	Nikolai G. Basov *USSR*	Feodor Lynen *FRG*
	Alexander M. Prokhorov *USSR*	
1965		
Robert Burns Woodward *USA*	Richard P. Feynman *USA*	François Jacob *Fra.*
	Shinichiro Tomonaga *Jap.*	André Lwoff *Fra.*
	Julian S. Schwinger *USA*	Jacques Monod *Fra.*
1966		
Robert S. Mulliken *USA*	Alfred Kastler *Fra.*	Francis P. Rous *USA*
		Charles B. Huggins *USA*
1967		
Manfred Eigen *FRG*	Hans Albrecht Bethe *USA*	Ragnar Granit *Swe.*
Ronald G. W. Norrish *UK*		Haldan Keffer Hartline *USA*
George Porter *UK*		George Wald *USA*
1968		
Lars Onsager *USA*	Luis W. Alvarez *USA*	Robert W. Holley *USA*
		H.G. Khorana *USA*
		Marshall W. Nirenberg *USA*
1969		
Derek H. R. Barton *UK*	Murray Gell-Mann *USA*	Max Delbrück *USA*
Odd Hassel *Nor.*		Alfred D. Hershey *USA*
		Salvador E. Luria *USA*
1970		
Luis Federico Leloir *Arg.*	Louis Eugène Néel *Fra.*	Julius Axelrod *USA*
	Hans Olof Alfvén *Swe.*	Bernard Katz *USA*
		Ulf von Euler *Swe.*
1971		
Gerhard Herzberg *Can.*	Dennis Gabor *UK*	Earl W. Sutherland *USA*
1972		
Stanford Moore *USA*	John Bardeen *USA*	Gerald M. Edelman *USA*
William H. Stein *USA*	Leon N. Cooper *USA*	Rodney R. Porter *UK*
Christian B. Anfinsen *USA*	John Robert Schrieffer *USA*	
1973		
Ernst Otto Fischer *FRG*	Leo Esaki *Jap.*	Konrad Lorenz *Austria*
Geoffrey Wilkinson *UK*	Ivar Giaever *USA*	Nikolaas Tinbergen *UK*
	Brian D. Josephson *UK*	Karl von Frisch *FRG*

Chemistry	Physics	Physiology or Medicine
1974		
Paul J. Flory *USA*	Martin Ryle *UK*	Albert Claude *Bel.*
	Antony Hewish *UK*	George E. Palade *USA*
		Christian de Duve *Bel.*
1975		
John W. Cornforth *Australia/UK*	Aage Bohr *Den.*	David Baltimore *USA*
Vladimir Prelog *Swi.*	Ben Mottelson *Den.*	Renato Dulbecco *USA*
	James Rainwater *USA*	Howard M. Temin *USA*
1976		
William N. Lipscomb *USA*	Burton Richter *USA*	Baruch S. Blumberg *USA*
	Samuel C. C. Ting *USA*	D. Carleton Gajdusek *USA*
1977		
Ilya Prigogine *Bel.*	Philip W. Anderson *USA*	Roger Guillemin *USA*
	Nevill F. Mott *UK*	Andrew V. Schally *USA*
	John H. van Vleck *USA*	Rosalyn Yalow *USA*
1978		
Peter D. Mitchell *UK*	Peter L. Kapitsa *USSR*	Werner Arber *Swi.*
	Arno A. Penzias *USA*	Daniel Nathans *USA*
	Robert W. Wilson *USA*	Hamilton O. Smith *USA*
1979		
Herbert C. Brown *USA*	Sheldon L. Glashow *USA*	Allan M. Cormack *USA*
Georg Wittig *FRG*	Abdus Salam *Pak.*	Godfrey N. Hounsfield *UK*
	Steven Weinberg *USA*	
1980		
Paul Berg *USA*	James W. Cronin *USA*	Baruj Benacerraf *USA*
Walter Gilbert *USA*	Val L. Fitch *USA*	Jean Dausset *Fra.*
Frederick Sanger *UK*		George D. Snell *USA*
1981		
Kenichi Fukui *Jap.*	Nicolaas Bloembergen *USA*	Roger W. Sperry *USA*
Roald Hoffmann *USA*	Arthur L. Schawlow *USA*	David H. Hubel *USA*
	Kai M. Siegbahn *Swe.*	Torsten N. Wiesel *Swe.*
1982		
Aaron Klug *UK*	Kenneth G. Wilson *USA*	Sune K. Bergström *Swe.*
		Bengt I. Samuelsson *Swe.*
		John R. Vane *UK*
1983		
Henry Taube *USA*	S. Chandrasekhar *USA*	Barbara McClintock *USA*
	William A. Fowler *USA*	
1984		
Robert Bruce Merrifield *USA*	Carlo Rubbia *It.*	Niels K. Jerne *Den.*
	Simon van der Meer *Neth.*	Georges J. F. Köhler *FRG*
		César Milstein *UK/Arg.*
1985		
Herbert A. Hauptman *USA*	Klaus von Klitzing *FRG*	Michael S. Brown *USA*
Jerome Karle *USA*		Joseph L. Goldstein *USA*
1986		
Dudley R. Herschbach *USA*	Ernst Ruska *FRG*	Stanley Cohen *USA*
Yuan T. Lee *USA*	Gerd Binnig *FRG*	Rita Levi-Montalcini *It./USA*
John C. Polanyi *Can.*	Heinrich Rohrer *Swi.*	
1987		
Charles Pedersen *USA*	Georg Bednorz *Swi.*	Susumu Tonegawa *Jap.*
Donald Cram *USA*	Alex Müller *FRG*	
Jean-Marie Lehn *Fra.*		

Abbreviations

Arg. Argentina *Bel.* Belgium *Can.* Canada *Czech.* Czechoslovakia *Den.* Denmark *Fin.* Finland *Fra.* France *FRG* Federal Republic of Germany *Ger.* Germany *Hung.* Hungary *Ire.* Ireland *It.* Italy *Jap.* Japan *Neth.* Netherlands *Nor.* Norway *Pak.* Pakistan *Port.* Portugal *Swe.* Sweden *Swi.* Switzerland *UK* United Kingdom *USA* United States of America *USSR* Union of Soviet Socialist Republics

Nobel prize controversy

A most conspicuous omission from the list of Nobel laureates is Oswald Avery, who in 1944 proved that the substance responsible for hereditary characters is DNA. This was an essential precursor to the discovery of the DNA double helix. But while Francis Crick, James Watson and Maurice Wilkins received the Physiology or Medicine Prize for that work in 1962, Avery went unheralded.

Another celebrated mistake occurred when the authorities gave the 1923 Physiology or Medicine Prize to the Canadians Frederick Banting (1891-1941) and John Macleod (1876-1935) "for the discovery of insulin" the previous year. But Macleod had been on holiday at the crucial time. His only role had been to provide the laboratory in which Banting and the young American-Canadian Charles Best (1899-1978) carried out their historic work. Furious, Banting shared his prize with Best. In response, Macleod split his money with J.B. Collip, who had helped to purify the hormone.

Arguably the only serious criticism of Nobel and similar prizes is their emphasis on individuals rather than teams. "I was very surprised, especially so that I'm getting the prize alone," was the response of the American physicist Kenneth G. Wilson (b.1936) of Cornell University, when he learned that he was to be the 1982 Nobel laureate in physics. Wilson felt that he should share the honor with at least two other people – and took the unusual step of saying so, publicly and forcibly.

Awards to scientists

Compared with financiers, film stars, lawyers or professional tennis players, scientists are lowly paid. The sole, occasional, arguable exceptions are those specialists fortunate enough to be in demand at a time when commercial companies are burgeoning in a glamorous and potentially vastly profitable field – such as biotechnology was thought to be during the early 1980s. Career rewards for scientists have much more to do with esteem in the eyes of their peers. Although science is a cooperative, communal activity, professional esteem for a research worker is reflected in personal honors such as election to membership or fellowship of prestigious societies, the bestowing of coveted medals and honorary degrees and, at the very apex, the award of a Nobel prize. Admission to a national academy of sciences, especially at an early age, is a rare distinction.

There are countless other honors and awards, some of them with a considerable cash value. In Israel the Wolf Prizes (currently worth over $180,000 each) are given each year for work in physics, chemistry, agriculture and mathematics. Among the newest and most richly endowed are the Geneva-based Louis Jeantet Awards to support biomedical researchers in western Europe. The first awards, given in 1986, provided some $800,000 plus smaller personal prizes to scientists in Paris, Louvain and Cambridge, England.

▲ The Copley Medal, given annually by the Royal Society of London, in recognition of rare distinction in research, is particularly cherished. Accompanied by a £2,500 ($4,500) gift, the medal is awarded on the recommendation of the council of the society.

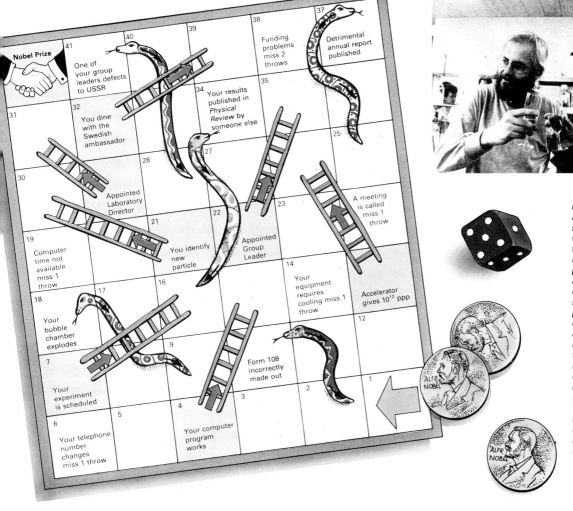

▲ ◄ Georges Köhler receives colleagues' acclaim after hearing that he has shared a 1984 Nobel prize with César Milstein for their development of hybridomas, used to produce monoclonal antibodies. Although the outcome of exacting science, these extremely pure antibodies have found diagnostic and other applications which were not the goal of the work at the time. Scientists need to have a sense of realism and even humor about the random factors involved in the path to the Nobel prize. This version of snakes and ladders (left) first appeared in the Journal of the Rutherford High Energy Laboratory, England.

See also
Scientific Intercourse 71-84

► *Fellows of the Royal Society meet in Somerset House, London, in 1840. Today the Royal Society of London remains the world's most prestigious scientific society, election to fellowship or foreign membership being a unique honor for a scientist. The Society is the principal point of contact for liaison between British science and other scientific academies throughout the world.*

▼ *The proliferation of scientific institutions bears witness to several historical changes. Firstly, the formerly amateur craft of science has become professionalized, leading to the setting up of bodies designed to represent the career interests of research workers. Secondly, the burgeoning of international collaboration is reflected in the emergence of bodies such as the World Health Organization, which have a strong scientific component in their work. Thirdly, societies devoted to "the advancement of science" have helped to encourage public interest ın science.*

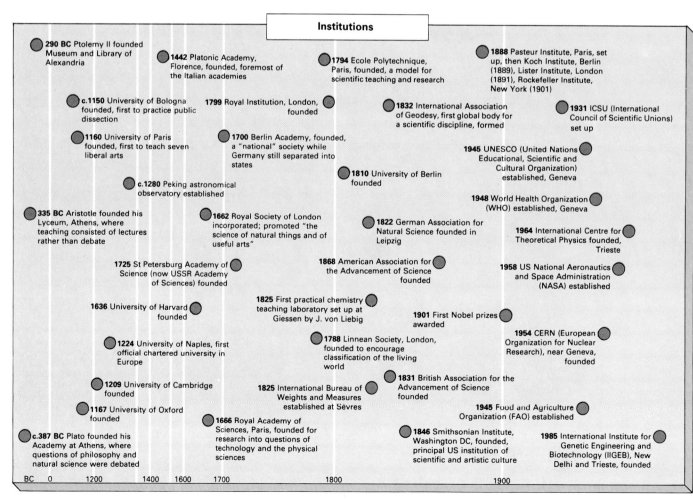

Institutions

290 BC Ptolemy II founded Museum and Library of Alexandria

1442 Platonic Academy, Florence, founded, foremost of the Italian academies

1794 Ecole Polytechnique, Paris, founded, a model for scientific teaching and research

1888 Pasteur Institute, Paris, set up, then Koch Institute, Berlin (1889), Lister Institute, London (1891), Rockefeller Institute, New York (1901)

c.1150 University of Bologna founded, first to practice public dissection

1799 Royal Institution, London, founded

1832 International Association of Geodesy, first global body for a scientific discipline, formed

1931 ICSU (International Council of Scientific Unions) set up

1160 University of Paris founded, first to teach seven liberal arts

1700 Berlin Academy, founded, a "national" society while Germany still separated into states

1945 UNESCO (United Nations Educational, Scientific and Cultural Organization) established, Geneva

c.1280 Peking astronomical observatory established

1810 University of Berlin founded

1948 World Health Organization (WHO) established, Geneva

335 BC Aristotle founded his Lyceum, Athens, where teaching consisted of lectures rather than debate

1662 Royal Society of London incorporated; promoted "the science of natural things and of useful arts"

1822 German Association for Natural Science founded in Leipzig

1964 International Centre for Theoretical Physics founded, Trieste

1725 St Petersburg Academy of Science (now USSR Academy of Sciences) founded

1868 American Association for the Advancement of Science founded

1958 US National Aeronautics and Space Administration (NASA) established

1636 University of Harvard founded

1825 First practical chemistry teaching laboratory set up at Giessen by J. von Liebig

1901 First Nobel prizes awarded

1224 University of Naples, first official chartered university in Europe

1788 Linnean Society, London, founded to encourage classification of the living world

1954 CERN (European Organization for Nuclear Research), near Geneva, founded

1209 University of Cambridge founded

1825 International Bureau of Weights and Measures established at Sèvres

1831 British Association for the Advancement of Science founded

1167 University of Oxford founded

1945 Food and Agriculture Organization (FAO) established

c.387 BC Plato founded his Academy at Athens, where questions of philosophy and natural science were debated

1666 Royal Academy of Sciences, Paris, founded for research into questions of technology and the physical sciences

1846 Smithsonian Institute, Washington DC, founded, principal US institution of scientific and artistic culture

1985 International Institute for Genetic Engineering and Biotechnology (IIGEB), New Delhi and Trieste, founded

BC   0   1200   1400   1600   1700   1800   1900

9

The "myth of objective consciousness"...Separate objective and subjective realms...The basis of "social science"...Sociology...PERSPECTIVE...Science and abstraction...A scientific look at Shakespeare...and music...The development of economics...Observation by opinion polls...Science neither "hard" nor "immature"

Scientific method is immensely powerful. It has spawned the practical and conceptual tools with which to place humans on the Moon and bring them back safely to Earth, obliterate the ancient scourge of smallpox, conquer many other appalling infections and even some forms of cancer, generate electricity through nuclear fission, and receive radio signals from space probes dispatched to Venus and beyond. In contrast to the bent spoons and card-guessing games of "parascience" (◆ page 120), these are momentous achievements. At the same time, the methodology of science has two inherent limitations. First, it rarely if ever generates findings that can be accepted as the final, comprehensive truth about a particular phenomenon or artifact. More usually, researchers express their results in cautious terms, hedging them about with caveats and qualifications.

The second limitation of science is that it is silent on such important matters as love, beauty, artistic creativity, and the intuitive understanding between one person and another. These belong to the realm of personal, subjective experience, rather than that of objective, verifiable (or falsifiable) fact. Science should not claim to adjudicate or have any currency as a guide to truth in the subjective domain – except inasmuch as subjective experience leads individuals to make apparently factual statements that have the appearance of objective claims. Thus scientific method does not permit us to rank the four symphonies of Brahms in order of artistic merit, while it does provide us with the tools with which to investigate a visionary's claim that the Moon is made of cheese.

Two approaches to mental illness
The contrast between objective and subjective knowledge is reflected in two different approaches to mental illness. A psychoanalyst seeks to understand a patient's condition by discussing, exploring and analyzing the person's deepest feelings, perhaps including their dreams and barely conscious thoughts, and often probing into experiences dating back many years previously. Whether a disciple of Sigmund Freud (1856-1939), Carl Gustav Jung (1875-1961) or Alfred Adler (1870-1937), the analyst works on the assumption that mental illness originates in the mind and may be understood and perhaps alleviated by helping the patient to comprehend what has gone wrong.

Many psychiatrists, on the other hand, focus their attention more specifically on the brain, which they believe can develop faults like any other organ in the body, producing conditions whose nature and severity reflect the location and type of malfunction. They rely largely upon physical treatments such as drugs, electroconvulsive therapy (ECT), and, until it became unfashionable, the operation known as lobotomy, in which certain nerve connections in the brain are surgically severed. Nonanalytical psychiatrists act on their own, "objective" interpretation of a patient's condition, whereas analysts are more preoccupied by the patient's own subjective thought processes.

The exponents of physical treatment can cite supportive evidence such as the capacity of long-acting tranquillizers to make life tolerable for schizophrenics. Analysts, however, claim that their opponents use treaments without understanding how they work. In one sense, the argument between the two is artificial, because brain and mind are undoubtedly intimately linked. Moreover, some eclectic psychiatrists adopt both approaches, which they believe to be complementary. Nonetheless, this is an area of clear polarization between the objective stance of science and the subjective stance of human empathy.

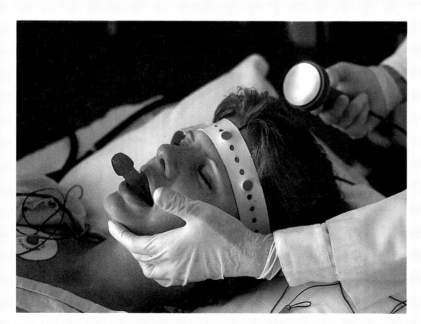

◄▲ Although some practitioners are eclectic, methods of tackling mental illness tend to polarize into subjective approaches (such as psychoanalysis) and physical treatments (such as drugs). Thus "art therapy" (above), popular in some US centers, contrasts starkly with electro-convulsive treatment (left), in which an electric current passes through the brain.

Facets of the age-old debate in western culture about science include humanism, individualism, imagination, and "quality versus quantity"

Currents counter to "objective science"

In his book *The Making of a Counter Culture* (1970), American sociologist Theodore Roszak talks of "the myth of objective consciousness". According to this myth, there is only one way of gaining access to reality – to cultivate a state of mind cleansed of all subjective distortion, all personal involvement. "What flows from this consciousness qualifies as knowledge and nothing else does," writes Roszak. "This is the bedrock on which the natural sciences have built: and under their spell all fields of knowledge strive to become scientific. The study of Man in his social, economic, psychological, historical aspects– all this, too, must become objective: rigorously, painstakingly objective." Roszak even questions the significance of reproductive physiology because "every dumb beast in the field" knows perfectly well how to reproduce.

A potent and poetic critic of the pervasive role of scientific thinking in modern society, Roszak exaggerates his case. But his analysis is significant as a modern expression of one pole of a tension that has existed for several centuries in western culture. The British historian Stephen Toulmin has identified five facets of this debate as: humanism, individualism, imagination, "quality versus quantity", and the abstract character of scientific ideas and inquiries.

▲ *French essayist Michel de Montaigne exemplified a humanism that was skeptical of objectivity and critical of the alleged indifference of scientists toward human issues.*

▼ *Nobel laureate Dennis Gabor (1900-1979) attributed his discovery of holography to an imaginative insight while watching a tennis game.*

▶▶ *Le Corbusier's proportional system called the Modulor was intended to give harmonious relationships to everything from door handles to the spaces, heights and depths in the urban environment. He hoped that industry would standardize its products according to the Modulor, which he saw as "a harmonic measure to the human scale, universally applicable to architecture and mechanics". In this way a modern architect reflects a tradition, traceable to Pythagoras and Leonardo, which attempts to reconcile science with beauty. The Heidi Weber Pavillion at Zürich (1963-1965) was one expression of the Modulor.*

Humanism

According to historian Stephen Toulmin, humanism is one of the most persistent threads in the tension in western culture between total objectivity and subjectivity. We can trace the idea of humanism back to the Greek philosopher Socrates (c.470-399 BC), who emphasized the primacy of social, ethical and humane issues, and was robustly skeptical about the possibility of achieving totally reliable, objective scientific knowledge. It was the same with the French essayist Michel de Montaigne (1533-1592) and other 16th-century humanists. While the scientific ideas evolved by the classical Greeks had survived through the Middle Ages, the humanists had to rediscover the poets, essayists and historians of antiquity. By doing so, they made a unique contribution to European sensibility. "The humanists tended – like the romantics of the early 18th century – to go on and pillory the scientists for being indifferent, and even callous, about humane issues," writes Stephen Toulmin. They did this "with the same kind of passion as any of today's antiscientists denouncing nerve-gas research or the alliance between official science and the military-industrial complex."

Individualism and imagination

The enemies of science claim that only the arts and literature provide scope for lone writers and artists to express their individual personalities. Science, by contrast, can be interpreted as a conformist occupation, research workers rigidly suppressing their personal, subjective views and feelings in favor of communally imposed orthodoxy. This is not the whole picture (♦ pages 42-3), but scientists do make a virtue of the disinterested nature of their work.

It is also argued that science is based on mechanical and stereotyped models of inquiry, which tend to starve the imagination and creativity. Again, although much normal, bread-and-butter science is pursued in this fashion (♦ page 34), inspiration comparable with that of the artist is important at many of the major turning-points of research (♦ page 33). Yet most scientists try very hard to disguise this aspect of their work when presenting and discussing new research findings.

Quality versus quantity

The fourth theme identified by Stephen Toulmin was particularly emphasized by the German romantic poet and scientist Johann von Goethe (1749-1832) and it stems from scientific method. Scientists are said to be concerned only with the common features shared by many individual objects, phenomena or living creatures – and in the last resort with statistical averages and measurable units. This leads them to neglect individual differences and to ignore qualitative variations. For the romantics, the epitome of this wrong approach was Isaac Newton's "Principia Mathematica" (1687). In this 250,000-word tome on the laws of nature, the mathematical analysis of motion, and the movement of heavenly bodies, Newton believed he had established that the universe was made by a Rational Being. Today, a particularly stark example is the sociology of mass observation, according to which we can build up an exhaustive account of society and groups within society simply by counting heads, totting up salaries, and sampling opinions through opinion polls. Many people deny the possibility that one day disciplines as sociology, economics and psychology will be on a similar footing to the "hard" or "exact" sciences, ♦ page 110).

Again, this is only part of the picture. While many scientists need to focus their minds along collective, rather than individual, lines in order to discern pattern amongst apparently confused, heterogenous evidence, others have made important discoveries by concentrating much more singlemindedly on individual specimens. The American geneticist Barbara McClintock (b.1902), who won the Nobel Prize for Physiology or Medicine in 1983 for work carried out several decades earlier, pleaded with her fellow biologists to develop "a feeling for the organism". Aided by what some critics suspected of being almost mystical contemplation of corn plants, she discovered the mobile genetic elements now known as "jumping genes". But McClintock's studies did not find favor until molecular biology had caught up and provided a theoretical framework within which her observations made sense to mainstream science.

The abstract nature of scientific investigation

This object of closely-related criticism is the characteristic which probably comes closest to indicating the psychological traits that drive young people to consider science as a vocation (♦ pages 85, 86). Many scientists tend to be ill at ease with the untidiness of politics, social intercourse and even personal relationships in the real world. They find it difficult to take the actual course of events, or a particular problem, as they find it. "They begin by imposing certain arbitrary theoretical demands and standards on the variety of nature, and they are then prepared to pay serious attention only to those aspects of nature which they choose to accept as 'significant' by those standards," argues Stephen Toulmin. "A true humanist, by contrast, will be prepared to accept each new concrete situation in all its complexity and variety, as it arises, and deal with it accordingly."

▲ ▼ Johann von Goethe (above) stressed the theme of "quality versus quantity". Scientists are generally interested in the features which things have in common – in contrast to the qualitative differences that attract artists. Yet Nobel laureate Barbara McClintock (below) made her discoveries in plant genetics by developing an almost mystical "feeling for the organism".

The area of overlap between "objective" and "subjective" spheres is neglected in many scientists' education

▲ **The leading Neo-Impressionist Georges Seurat (1859-1891) was influenced by scientific analyses of color, which led him to evolve the technique of pointillism, whereby tiny strokes of color too small to be distinguished when looking at an entire canvas, combine to create huge, shimmering images. "Quay at Port en Bassin" illustrates this attempt to develop an objective or scientific art.**

"From off a hill whose concave womb reworded
A plaintful story from a sist'ring vale,
My spirits t'attend this double voice accorded,
And down I laid to list the sad-tuned tale;
Ere long espied a fickle maid full pale,
Tearing of papers, breaking rings atwain,
Storming her world with sorrow's wind and rain."

Is it by Shakespeare?

An area where objective scientific method has been applied to the subjective domain is the statistical analysis of literature. Usage of vocabulary or the way phrases or sentences are constructed betray a style which can allow a work to be dated, and, where authorship is in question, offer clues of identity.

"The Lover's Complaint" (1609), a poem that has long been the center of such an argument, has recently been analysed in this way. Critical opinion has divided between favoring William Shakespeare (1564-1616) as author, or his close contemporary George Chapman (1559-1634). In the test, "data" in the form of frequency of usage of common words such as "and", "for", "that" and "into", are gathered for "A Lover's Complaint", together with other works known to be by the two poets –

Shakespeare's "Venus and Adonis" (1593) and "Rape of Lucrece" (1594), Chapman's "Hero and Leander" (1598) and "The Tears of Peace" – and a "control", "Hero and Leander" (1598) by Christopher Marlowe (1564-1593).

With the help of a computer, the frequency of occurrence of the common words is compared between sections of each poem, by a statistical test called the chi-squared test. A score is obtained, giving the approximate strength of comparison between the six poems (comparisons are also made between sections of the same poem) and ranked.

Although the test did not allow for the possibility of "A Lover's Complaint" being written by a poet other than Shakespeare or Chapman, the results do show that when the poem is compared with Chapman's work, strong comparison measures are obtained, similar to those from comparing sections of the poem. Comparing the poem with Shakespeare's work obtained far weaker results.

If the technique has not quite proved an objective fact, it demonstrates that scientific method, in the form of the statistical test, is capable of lending considerable weight to confirming a hypothesis in a field traditionally regarded as highly subjective.

Striking the balance

In one sense Theodore Roszak is soundly based in criticizing "the myth of objective consciousness" (◀ page 100). Scientists seldom stop to consider that *all* experience – whether of meter readings in a laboratory, of falling in love, or of a performance of Sibelius's *Finlandia* – is subjective.

"Objectivism has totally falsified our conception of truth, by exalting what we can know and prove, while covering up with ambiguous utterances all that we know and *cannot* prove, even though the latter knowledge underlies, and must ultimately set its seal to, all that we *can* prove," wrote the scientist and philosopher Michael Polanyi in his book *Personal Knowledge*. "In trying to restrict our minds to the few things that are demonstrable, and therefore explicit dubitable, it [objectivism] has overlooked the a-critical choices which determine the whole being of our minds and has rendered us incapable of acknowledging these vital choices." In addition, therefore, from the qualifications that underlie the apparently impregnable data of science, there is no justification for dismissing certain categories of experience because they are inexact or illogical.

Acknowledging the self-vindicating nature of experiences such as love and artistic inspiration brings with it the danger of suspending all critical judgment and retreating into the world of solipsism, according to which the self is the only knowable thing. Such a standpoint can indeed lead to antiintellectualism, mysticism and ultimately political fascism. In *The Social Function of Science*, the Marxist biologist J.D. Bernal (1901-1971) argued that "metaphysical scientists" and philosophers such as the Frenchman Henri Bergson (1859-1941) helped to pave the way for the fascist ideology of brute force under mystically inspired leadership. In more recent times, there have been many attacks on the very legitimacy of scientific thought – from people who believe, for example, that it is entirely a matter of personal opinion whether homeopathy works, whether influenza is causd by viruses, or whether cats and dogs dream. But here as in many other walks of life, extreme views are invariably erroneous and often dangerous. As an overall philosophy, materialistic science which tries to invalidate personal experience is just as partial and incomplete as the counterview that subjective knowledge is the measure of all things. Likewise, crude materialism is as likely to accompany and support callous indifference as is mysticism to predicate fascism.

While it is important to put reason in perspective by repudiating the application of scientific method as an arbiter in the subjective domain, therefore, it is equally important to bear in mind the fallibility of intuition and personal conviction in realms that *are* open to rational study. Unless we do so, we disparage not only the intellectual, cultural value of science but also its practical utility. This is what Theodore Roszak does in *The Making of a Counter Culture*, a book which otherwise carries an important message about the dominance and distortions of scientific thinking in modern society. "Consider the strange compulsion our biologists have to synthesize life in a test tube – and the seriousness with which the project is taken," Roszak writes. "Every dumb beast of the earth knows without thinking once about it how to create life." Thus to equate molecular biology with instinctive copulation is to diminish the intellectual triumphs of molecular biology in discerning the behavior of DNA – and simultaneously to denigrate such practical rewards as the capacity to help a woman with an hereditary disease to bear a healthy child.

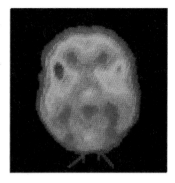
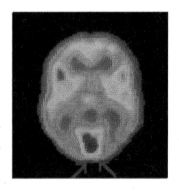
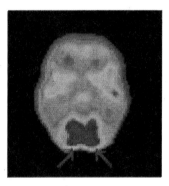

▲ *Although senses such as smells, tastes and sights are first-hand experiences, which cannot be conveyed to a second person, they can be monitored using scientific equipment. Here the technique known as positron computed tomography reveals successive increases in brain activity in an individual with eyes closed (top), with eyes open (middle) and then with eyes open and staring at a complex scene (bottom). The red color represents cellular activity where glucose is concentrated in the brain's visual cortex. The subject was injected with a radioactive "tracer" that has become bound to the sugar.*

Science and Music

Subjectivity versus objectivity

Why do we like music? The question highlights the contrast between subjective experience and objective knowledge with peculiar intensity. In recent years, many psychologists and neurologists have tried to relate the physical phenomenon of music with the effects it has on a listener. The initial steps in this analysis are straightforward. Musical sounds can be analyzed in great detail, according to rhythm and the pitch and tonal complexity of the notes. The faculty of hearing is now understood in considerable detail too. So, for example, some analysts argue that the secret of music lies in the physics of sound waves. Sequences of notes put together as scales, and chords composed of several different notes, are made up from sounds that are mathematically related to each other. Thus when we listen to a middle C, the air is vibrating at some 260 times per second. If the number of vibrations is doubled to 520 per second, we hear a note of C precisely one octave higher. If middle C is multiplied by ³⁄₂, to 390 vibrations per second, we hear the G in that octave.

We also know that musical appreciation is to some degree learned. The classical western diatonic scale, and compositions written in this format, sound "right" to most westerners' ears. But people who experience a different type of scale from an early age develop a different sense of correctness in music. There is, for example, an affinity between much traditional music in India and the folk music of the Hebrides off the west coast of Scotland, the basic scale of each differing in the same way from the diatonic scale. What we consider proper in the content of music varies widely too – from the intricately complex rhythms of subSaharan Africa to the plainsong, anthems and psalms of western church music.

Much of the writing about the physics and biology of music is based on the belief that one day it will be possible to explain musical experience on the basis of particular sounds triggering particular changes in particular nerve cells in the brain. The fallacy of this view is clear from our more detailed knowledge of vision. "Green" and "red" are the experiences that result when specific cells in the retina of the eye are stimulated by light of those colors. But the description of color vision – which is now extremely detailed – does not and cannot explain what the corresponding experience means to an individual person. We do not, and cannot, even be sure that one person's "green" is the same as another person's "green". As the theologian Ian Ramsey has pointed out, no series of "third person" accounts of a phenomenon can ever be replaced by a "first person" account.

▼ The mathematically precise relationship between sounds of differing pitches, however they are produced, have long intrigued musicians and scientists who have sought to describe music in scientific terms. The Renaissance musical theorist Franchino Gafurio is shown here (in the frontispiece to his "De harmonia musicorum instrumentorum", 1518) with three organ pipes of different lengths to illustrate the ratios of the octave, together with lines and a pair of dividers indicating that harmony is geometry translated into sound. The scroll in Gafurio's mouth ("harmony is discord concordant") propounds the old thesis that harmony results not from the consonance of two tones but from unequal consonances from dissimilar proportions.

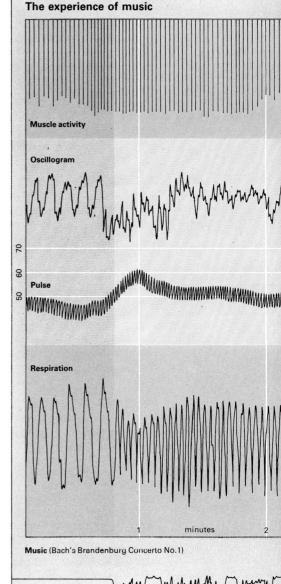

The experience of music

Muscle activity

Oscillogram

70

60

50

Pulse

Respiration

1   minutes   2

Music (Bach's Brandenburg Concerto No.1)

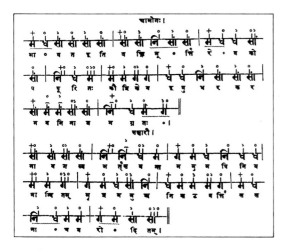

◄ ► *Two scores – a page of Indian music from "The Eight Principal Rasas of the Hindus", published in Calcutta in 1880, and an example of Italian church music dated 1532 – illustrate the wide variation that exists in musical notation and symbolism. Although written music may leave some scope to interpretation of players, the basic elements of pitch, rhythm and timing are usually represented.*

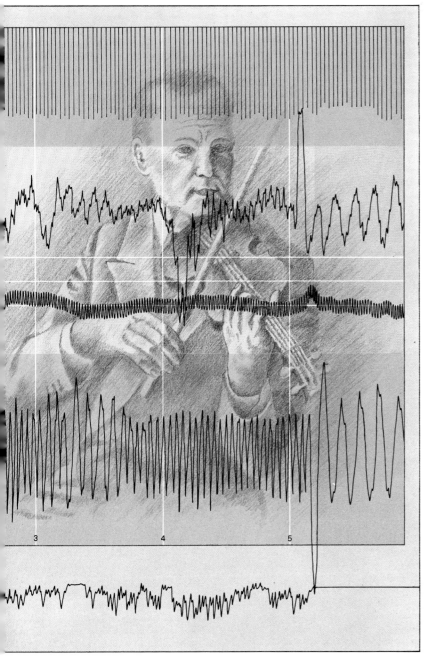

◄ *One attempt to monitor the impact of music scientifically. This is a polygraph recording showing changes in pulse rate, respiration and other physiological variables in a volunteer listening to a piece of music, in this case Bach's Brandenburg Concerto No 1. Repeated tests confirmed that the same subject responded in the same way on each occasion when listening to this work.*

▼ *Scientific and musical creativity came together in Alexander Borodin (1834-1887), perhaps best known as the Russian nationalist composer. His works include the opera "Prince Igor" as well as orchestral and chamber music. Borodin was also an outstanding chemist. Among his achievements were the discovery of aldol, and of the technique of obtaining bromine derivatives of fatty acids.*

Are social sciences scientific?

From the standpoint of the extreme skeptic in the "hard sciences", social science is almost as suspect as parascience (♦ page 120). Sometimes, the two are even coupled together as "pseudoscience". And there are many physical and biological scientists who believe that even what appear to be the the most simple issues addressed by the social sciences – the growth and migration of communities, for example, or the internal dynamics of families or business organizations – are inherently beyond true scientific investigation. Yet a considerable amount of work in disciplines such as sociology, behavioral psychology, educational psychology and even economics is based on the hope that these *are* susceptible to the same techniques of scientific investigation that are applied to chemistry, physics and biology.

Although for the most part deprived of the opportunity of mounting experiments, and with far greater difficulty in defining their material, social scientists seek pattern and significance in phenomena in the same way. Economics as a science is notable for its skill in explaining events *afterwards* rather than making accurate predictions beforehand. In this respect it resembles the "hard" science of epidemiology (the study of disease epidemics). But the economist's task is made much harder by the human elements that underly phenomena such as stockmarket price fluctuations and the flow of capital between one currency and another. Disagreement about the appropriateness of using scientific methodology to investigate individual and group behavior parallels the divide between orthodox psychiatry and psychoanalysis (♦ page 99) as to what comprises valid investigation.

Economics: a method, not a doctrine

Although the ancient Greeks used the term "economics" to describe the balancing of income and expenditure, in the 19th century it came to mean the science of wealth and exchangeable values. "Economists", beginning with the physiocracy school founded in France by François Quesnay (1694-1774), began to seek and discern laws in, for example, the movement of capital that were comparable to those enunciated by natural scientists studying the physical and biological world. Thus David Ricardo (1772-1823), following the notion of fellow-Briton Thomas Malthus (1766-1834) of population outstripping food supplies (which did not happen, thanks to advances in science and technology), wrote about the law of diminishing returns. This came into play when a burgeoning population was compelled to raise its food supplies in poorer and poorer soils, an increasing proportion of the product of people's work then going to landlords in the form of an economic rent – the difference between the productivity of the best and worst land under cultivation. This in turn led the German social philosopher Karl Marx (1818-1883) to elaborate the labor theory of value, according to which labor is the sole source of value, and capitalists appropriate part of this value in the form of profit (♦ page 5). Competition, in his view, tended to establish a uniform rate of profit throughout a particular economy, the cash prices of commodities being systematically related to their labor values.

Despite the increasingly sophisticated tools which they use (computer modeling, for example) many economists themselves now believe that economics cannot be a science. Yet there are *two* significant parallels between science and economics in (a) their incompletenesss and lack of dogmatic certainty and (b) their significance as intellectual tools to help their practitioners think.

◄ An average day on the New York Stock Exchange. Despite heavy dependence on computers for market analysis and transactions, economics remains an atypical science in being far better in interpreting events afterward than in making accurate predictions. Although the stock market collapse of October 1987 was comprehensible in retrospect, there was no way of forecasting precisely when the market would react to factors such as the burgeoning US budget deficit.

▲ "The theory of economics does not furnish a body of settled conclusions immediately applicable to policy. It is a method rather than a doctrine, an apparatus of the mind, a technique of thinking, which helps its possessor to draw conclusions" – British economist John Maynard Keynes (1883-1946).

Sociology arose as a reaction to the analyses offered by classical philosophy and folklore

Sociology

As a would-be science, sociology originated during the 18th and 19th centuries, in reaction against the analyses of social phenomena afforded by classical philosophy and folklore. One of its most conspicuous early manifestations was social Darwinism, popularized by the British philosopher Herbert Spencer (1820-1903) and others, which sought to interpret the behavior of individuals and social institutions in terms of ideas like "the survival of the fittest" which were central to Darwin's theory of evolution. But biological determinism did not find lasting favor, except among Marxists. More influential were the ideas of the Frenchman Émile Durkheim (1858-1917). He focused attention on "social facts" (such as customs and nations) that reflected group properties not found in individuals, and sought to comprehend principles underlying them (▶ page 110).

"Mass observation", pioneered in Britain during the late 1930s, was one of the earliest examples of social science attempting to mirror the exact techniques of "hard" science. Tom Harrisson and Charles Madge developed the use of questionnaires, and later interviews, in order to determine the public mind on political, social and other issues. This work has its modern counterpart in public opinion polls such as those which are employed to probe political attitudes before elections, as well as to investigate people's preferences regarding commercial products and their opinions on topical issues. Devised by American psychologist George Gallup (1901-1984) in 1935, nationwide opinion surveys began with questions such as "Are federal expenditures for relief and recovery too great, too little or about right?" On that occasion 60 percent of respondents decreed that spending was too high, and nine percent, too little. Gallup and similar polls used to gauge voting intentions have a high success rate, though occasional spectacular failures confirm the complexity and inherent unpredictability of human nature. In 1948 in the United States, for example, the Democrats won by a narrow majority when almost all of the polls had forecast a Republican victory. A more recent example is provided by the Conservative Party triumph in the British general election of 1970, after every poll except one had predicted a Labour victory.

Apart from the problem of formulating evenhanded, nonleading questions on topics other than the most elementary (i.e. political preferences), the intrinsic difficulty of gauging public opinion is illustrated by the initial task of choosing the individuals to be polled. Sophisticated techniques, such as "quota sampling", have been devised to meet this need.

Even today, however (and despite attempts by psychologists and sociologists to perform experiments by studying interactions between small groups of people), sociology has not attained the status of a mature science. It has achieved no major breakthroughs comparable to our understanding of the DNA double helix or the development of radio astronomy. Those sociologists who believe that their craft *will* become a science explain its inordinately slow progress on the grounds that sociological knowledge accumulates randomly rather than cumulatively. But others argue that, while there does exist a body of organized and testable knowledge that has accrued in sectors of sociology such as demography (the study of populations), we should never expect to understand the behavior and attitudes of human beings with the same precision that is achievable in the physical and biological sciences.

▲ *British philosopher Herbert Spencer popularized the notion of "social Darwinism", which tried to explain individuals and social institutions according to the scientific principles central to Charles Darwin's theory of evolution. Sociologists today are now mostly suspicious of simplistic analogies of this sort.*

▶ *While the opinions of a defined audience, such as a magazine's readership, can be polled easily (by quizzing, say, every tenth name on the subscription list), it is more difficult to carry out valid house-to-house surveys. Polling the residents of a large city is approached by the technique of "quota sampling", in which a statistically valid sample is sought by matching up characteristics with those of the entire "universe" that is of interest. If, for example, a recent census indicates that the city contains 52 men to every 48 women, then the sample must reflect those proportions. The exercise becomes more complex when the same principle has to be applied to age, income and every other characteristic considered relevant to the questions being asked.*

▼ ▶ *Even social scientists disagree as to whether their subject is intrinsically different from the "hard" sciences such as chemistry – because it reflects subjective, rather than objective, knowledge – or whether it is an immature discipline which will eventually attain a similar status. Émile Durkheim applied the term "anomie" to social instability related to a decline in generally accepted values and widespread feelings of alienation. But does anomie correspond with concrete qualities, such as momentum and entropy?*

Neither hard nor immature sciences

The nature of psychology and the social sciences generally in relation to the "hard sciences" such as physics and chemistry is vividly illustrated by the way in which one particular idea – anomie – has emerged since the beginning of this century. The pioneer French sociologist Émile Durkheim (1858-1917) adopted this word, derived from the Greek anomia (lawlessness), as a sociological term. He used it to describe social instability stemming from a breakdown in generally accepted values in a community, accompanied by widespread personal feelings of alienation and uncertainty. But it was Robert Merton, in his "Social Theory and Social Structure" (1968), who refined the concept and argued that anomie and some forms of deviant behavior resulted from a disjunction between "culturally prescribed aspirations" and "socially structured avenues for realizing those aspirations". If a society sets economic success as its goal, for example, and competitiveness as the method of achieving it, individuals unable to compete and win (or escape those pressures) are liable to feel both frustrated and unwanted. For them and for society as a whole, anomie is likely to be the result.

But does anomie have the analytical and descriptive power of notions such as entropy and momentum, taken from the natural sciences? It has

certainly gone through a period of refinement and increasing sophistication, as Merton and others have observed many different societies over different periods of time, hoping to match the original model of anomie increasingly closely to reality. Moreover, in order to study the phenomenon empirically, psychologists and sociologists have sought methods of measuring anomie.

During these efforts, and the accompanying debate in specialized journals and at conferences, the similarities and differences between social and natural sciences have become vividly evident. Some attempts at measuring anomie, most of which depend on use of questionnaires, have been based on clearly quantifiable figures. Thus Robert Merton believes that one variable influencing feelings of anomie is the rate at which social relationships are disrupted. Others argue that such objective figures do not indicate the true nature of anomie, which can only be felt and therefore can be described only in subjective terms. Like many other social and behavioral scientists, they are convinced that sociology and psychology are not immature sciences that will one day have the same standing as chemistry or molecular biology. They are disciplines which, resting upon subjective experiences and attitudes, will never become at one with the exact sciences.

Toward a reconciliation...Are religion and science really separated...Fate's lottery...PERSPECTIVE...Is there a "vital spark"?...An austere theology...The origin of life..."Ratomorphic" and other reductionist views... Cumulative selection

It is fashionable to write off the conflict between science and religion as outmoded. In disputations such as that between Galileo and the Roman Catholic Church, or between T.H.Huxley (1825-1895) ("Darwin's bulldog") and the Church of England hierarchy, both sides, it is argued, took up extreme, unrealistic and unwise positions. For example, some early Darwinians were overenthusiastic in claiming that their "theory" collided with and undermined biblical teaching, while antiDarwinian clerics made the contrary mistake of not recognizing the creative element in organic evolution. Today, it is said, greater understanding and tolerance allow the apparently rival claims of science and religion easily to be reconciled. Some writers even insist that there simply cannot be an inherent conflict, because the two domains are totally separate one from the other.

Countless books bear witness to this reconciliation. They adopt a variety of solutions to what their authors agree is not a problem. Some writers describe the worlds of science and religion as analogous with fact and faith – the former being exact, objective knowledge, the latter founded upon trust and intuition.

Others portray science as covering literal truth and religion poetical truth. On this basis, it is as pointless to look for evidence of divine activity in the scientific worldview as it is to expect factual certainties in holy scripture. Some draw a related distinction between fact and allegory. They see the objective literature of science as totally divorced from the morals and teaching of religion. Many fundamentalists, on the other hand, accept the verbatim accuracy of passages from the Bible, Koran or other work of revelation, and contrast this, God's totally trustworthy word, with the incomplete and insubstantial nature of scientific knowledge.

Among this diversity of standpoints, there is arguably only one area of near-consensus – the inadequacy of what the mathematician Charles Coulson called a God of the gaps. The majority of religious believers of whatever persuasion, including scientists, now agree that it is unwise to look for evidence of divine action in areas of scientific ignorance. There have been innumerable occasions when rational enquiry has rendered both superfluous and erroneous previous beliefs in a Deity tinkering with some aspect of the world. Few, therefore, now harness their religious beliefs to such shaky foundations. The most conspicuous exception to this generalization is the current interest in "creationism".

There is certainly no consensus among scientists as to the truth or otherwise of religious ideas. The scientific community includes militant atheists, cautious agnostics and devout believers. The habit, which religious apologists share with "humanist" and agnostic organizations, of citing distinguished scientists as authorities to support their philosophy, thus carries little weight.

Vitalism

In considering the proper scope of scientific enquiry, vis-à-vis religious claims and explanations, it is important to distinguish questions that are factually unanswerable from those which are simply exceedingly difficult to answer. The once popular theory of vitalism, for example, holds that living cells depend upon a mysterious, unidentified force that is peculiar to life and cannot be analyzed in terms of physics or chemistry.

Biologists believe that the DNA in the nucleus of a fertilized cell contains, in coded form, all of the information required to direct the stepwise development of a particular creature. Specific groups of genes, they suggest, are switched on and off in order to determine the differentiation of the distinct tissues and organs in the adult animal. But this far from comprehensive account of the development of even a relatively simple creature permits vitalists to claim that the key ingredient is an entelechy, or "vital spark". Orthodox science rejects any such idea, insisting that the complexity of a problem, or the lack of a comprehensive explanation of a phenomenon, does not justify invoking additional external concepts, whose explanatory power is mediocre anyway.

Distinct from exceedingly complex questions, which are unanswerable today but may be answered in the future, are others which are intrinsically unanswerable by science. For example, science is and always will be silent as to whether a house painted brown is more attractive than one painted green. In discussing topics on the boundaries of science, it is always important to consider into which of these categories fall those questions which are said to exemplify the limitations of scientific method and knowledge.

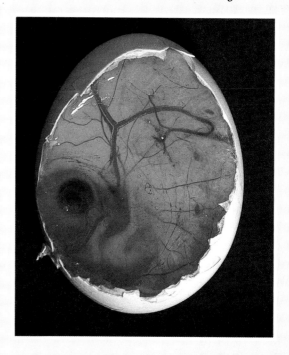

▲ How does a fertilized cell turn into a differentiated structure – like this 10-day chick embryo?

Science has little to say about the subjective aspect of religious experience but often comes into conflict with theology

The separateness of religion and science

Are efforts to separate fact from faith, or literal truth from poetic insight (◀ page 102), really convincing? Science has very little to say about the subjective aspect of, for example, religious experience. Researchers study people in trancelike and other states, in which individuals claim to have exalted visions and "oceanic feelings"; they can measure their subjects' blood pressure, brain waves and other physical parameters. They note that people of widely contrasting traditions and denominations (who may put quite different interpretations on their experiences) describe them in very similar ways. The agnostic British writer Marghanita Laski (1915-1988) drew this conclusion in her book *On Ecstasy* (1961), which covered the intense, mystical experiences of people from many different religious persuasions and of none. But no such independent, third-person observer or commentator can ever be in a position to question or discredit someone else's subjective experience.

The American psychologist and philosopher William James (1842-1910) described a man who was able to induce mystical visions by breathing laughing gas. "Whenever he was under its influence, he knew the secret of the universe, but when he came to, he had forgotten it. At last, with immense effort, he wrote down the secret before the vision had faded. When completely recovered, he rushed to see what he had written. It was: 'A smell of petroleum prevails throughout.'" This story is usually told in an attempt to undermine or ridicule the reality of religious experience. In fact, while the man's scribble scarcely tells us much about the factual content of his vision, it does not invalidate that experience.

Humans are animals who worship – people of all periods in history and geographical origins have developed systems of religious belief. For this reason, the British zoologist Sir Alister Hardy (1896-1983) argued that a "zoology of Man" which omitted religion would be incomplete. Hardy was so convinced of the importance of this dimension in human affairs and personal life that he founded a Religious Experience Research Unit at Manchester College, Oxford, to collect and collate personal affirmations about prayer, meditation and other personal experiences. Although he was criticized for attempting to extract precise, scientific data from intrinsically inexact feelings and intuitions, work of this sort has continued at Manchester College since his death.

While scientific method can never penetrate the sphere of subjective experience, it can and frequently does come into direct conflict with theology, in which religious experience or tradition is translated into specific factual propositions about the world, the universe, or personal existence. If, for example, a factual (rather than poetic or allegorical) theological proposition were to hold that girls were born with smaller adrenal glands than boys, then this would clash with the scientific evidence that the opposite is true.

Despite many efforts by theologians and others to defuse the conflict between science and religion by insisting that the two belief systems are categorically distinct, vigorous debate continues on some issues that are central to both science and religion, by far the most important of which is the existence or absence of an underlying purpose or direction in human affairs. If, for example, scientific evidence suggests that the natural order is inimical to *Homo sapiens* or life itself, then this may be seen as *prima facie* evidence against the creative or sustaining role of a benevolent deity.

▲ *Dervishes can induce a trance-like state by means of activities such as dancing and spinning at high speed, leading to exhaustion or "hystereo-epilepsy", accompanied by euphoric hallucinations. By definition, hallucinations are subjective experiences that do not correspond with the objective world as witnessed by individuals at the same place and time in whom they have not been induced.*

▶ *Theologies can be divided into those with a "transcendant" god, separate from the physical world comprehended by our senses, and those with an "immanent" god seen in nature. But agnostic biologists reject the idea that a divine designer must be responsible for ornate structures such as this rainforest passionflower.*

Immanent and transcendent gods

There is a distinction made in most theologies between an immanent and a transcendent God. Those who believe in the former version argue that divine activity may be discerned in nature and the physical world. "Natural theology" thus rests heavily upon the notion of design, according to which the exquisite structures and adaptations seen in living creatures imply the existence of a designer or creator. Such ideas are more vulnerable to attack on scientific grounds than those based on the concept of a transcendent deity, wholly "other", separate from his creation, and incapable of being experienced or understood through the natural world. Portraying God and personal immortality as mysteries approachable only through personal faith, this austere variety of theology is correspondingly less easy to criticize from the standpoint of scientific evidence.

◄ Religious ceremonies such as this spring Hindu festival sometimes entail activities that would normally be extremely painful but which are rendered tolerable as a result of hysteria, ecstasy or trance-like conditions induced by prayer. As observed on the battlefield, individuals can be rendered insensitive to very serious injuries – until the cessation of the conditions that have produced the analgesia. According to the gate theory of pain, this occurs because part of the brain blocks off impulses that would otherwise cause a sensation of pain. Opiate-like endorphins in the brain may be involved in this effect.

Creation

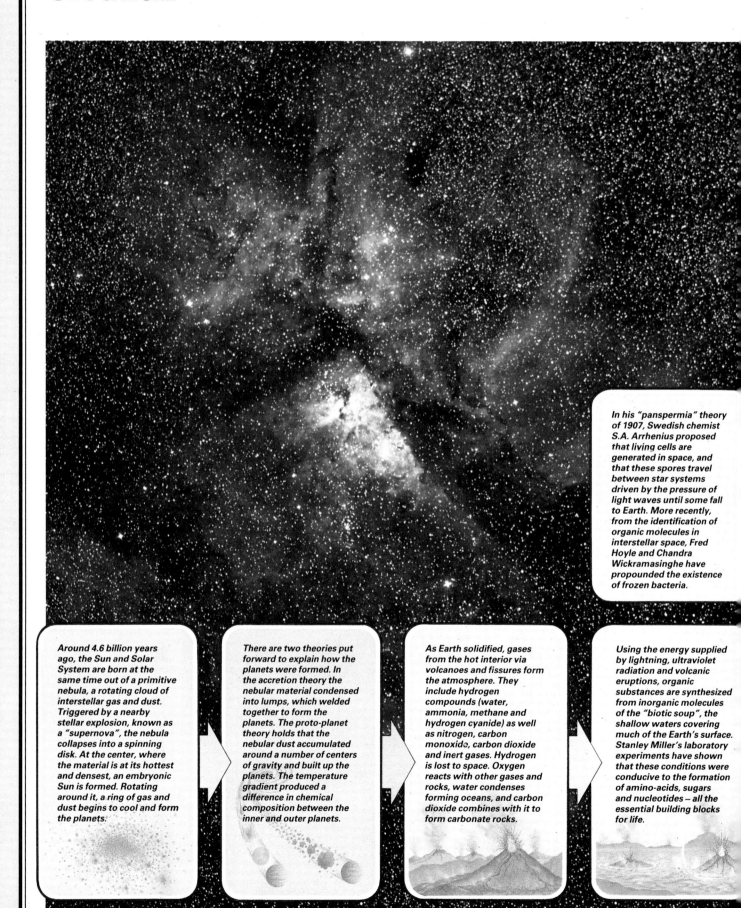

In his "panspermia" theory of 1907, Swedish chemist S.A. Arrhenius proposed that living cells are generated in space, and that these spores travel between star systems driven by the pressure of light waves until some fall to Earth. More recently, from the identification of organic molecules in interstellar space, Fred Hoyle and Chandra Wickramasinghe have propounded the existence of frozen bacteria.

Around 4.6 billion years ago, the Sun and Solar System are born at the same time out of a primitive nebula, a rotating cloud of interstellar gas and dust. Triggered by a nearby stellar explosion, known as a "supernova", the nebula collapses into a spinning disk. At the center, where the material is at its hottest and densest, an embryonic Sun is formed. Rotating around it, a ring of gas and dust begins to cool and form the planets.

There are two theories put forward to explain how the planets were formed. In the accretion theory the nebular material condensed into lumps, which welded together to form the planets. The proto-planet theory holds that the nebular dust accumulated around a number of centers of gravity and built up the planets. The temperature gradient produced a difference in chemical composition between the inner and outer planets.

As Earth solidified, gases from the hot interior via volcanoes and fissures form the atmosphere. They include hydrogen compounds (water, ammonia, methane and hydrogen cyanide) as well as nitrogen, carbon monoxide, carbon dioxide and inert gases. Hydrogen is lost to space. Oxygen reacts with other gases and rocks, water condenses forming oceans, and carbon dioxide combines with it to form carbonate rocks.

Using the energy supplied by lightning, ultraviolet radiation and volcanic eruptions, organic substances are synthesized from inorganic molecules of the "biotic soup", the shallow waters covering much of the Earth's surface. Stanley Miller's laboratory experiments have shown that these conditions were conducive to the formation of amino-acids, sugars and nucleotides – all the essential building blocks for life.

The origin and development of life

The principal area in which science and theology continue to wage war, despite attempts at demarcation between them, is the origin and development of life on Earth.

In one sense, the actual emergence of the first self-reproducing cells is a barren area for debate because the issue can never be resolved conclusively. The conventional view, accepted by many biologists, is that conditions on Earth were at one time such that the appearance of life in a lifeless world was inevitable. The planet is said to have been enveloped in a vast primeval soup, containing a rich and varied mixture of simple chemicals. Catalyzed by lightning, radiation or other physical phenomena, these gave rise to more complex molecules of the sort we now describe as "organic" because they are associated with metabolic processes and living cells. In the course of time – and an important plank of the argument is that eons of time were available for rare, unlikely events to occur – mixtures of these substances came together in such a way as to generate units with the capacity of replication.

There is some evidence to support these speculations. Laboratory experiments with simulated primeval soup have proved that the crucial building blocks of protein and nucleic acid (key macromolecules upon which life depends) can be synthesized under the supposed conditions of the early Earth. Other scientists have demonstrated artificial microspheres which grow to a particular size and then divide – possibly precursors of the first cells. And geological studies suggest that the planet was in a highly favorable state for the emergence of life – not least because it lacked both the oxygen that would otherwise have oxidized newly synthesized substances and living creatures which would have gobbled up the earliest cells.

But such evidence is far from conclusive. Indeed, controversy about the origin of life has broken out anew among biologists themselves in recent years. After several decades during which the primeval soup hypothesis was accepted without question, alternative explanations have been put forward. Also being taken seriously again is the venerable theory of "panspermia", according to which the Earth was initially seeded with living organisms from space. This approach does not, of course, answer the question of the actual mechanism of the origin of life, but merely moves the event to another location at another time.

Given such uncertainty, it is open to religious believers to hold that terrestrial life began as a particular act of special divine creation. Many biologists feel that there is no need to invoke this explanation. They are content with the mixture of speculation and factual evidence which supports the theory that living, organic matter arose from dead, inorganic matter, without supernatural intervention or paranormal influence. But believers could continue to believe in special creation even if human experimenters created real, vital, self-reproducing cells in the test tube. They could argue that scientists had simply learned how to copy God's handiwork. That being so, the issue seems destined to remain beyond resolution.

▲ All societies have speculated over our origins – as in this Aztec painting. It shows Texcatlipoca, from whose body the Earth was supposedly created, tempting the Earth Monster to the surface of the great waters.

◄ The Eta Carinae nebula. Cosmologists Sir Fred Hoyle and Chandra Wickramasinghe have energetically publicized the view, first suggested by Svante Arrhenius, that Earth's living organisms arrived from outer space. The far more widely accepted theory, strongly supported by evidence that "organic" chemicals can originate from nonliving precursors, is that life emerged spontaneously.

Organic molecules are stored away inside comets, which shed this material when closest to the Sun (in the region of the Earth). Frozen material thaws at the comet's surface, gas and particles producing the coma and tail. Cells which fall to Earth make "soft" landings cushioned by the atmosphere and "take root" in hospitable surroundings.

Organic molecules evolve into more complex chemical systems, growing at the expense of their surroundings. By a number of processes, high levels of concentration are achieved. These may have included evaporation or freezing; the enclosure of molecules in colloidal droplets, which coalesce in water under the right conditions; adsorption on solid particles; the organization of amino-acid chains into membrane-coated "microspheres".

Organic chemical systems are organized into cells that can replicate and so pass on genetic information. How this started is unknown. Cells make DNA or RNA with the help of enzymes and a nucleic acid template, both of which are made with DNA. Possibly there was chance interaction of amino-acid chains and polynucleotides (structural unit of DNA or RNA), or of primitive enzymes which enhanced the replication of polynucleotides.

The role of chance

Many scientists who are nonbelievers affirm the random nature of the processes upon which all life depends. This viewpoint is set out in *Chance and Necessity* by French biologist Jacques Monod (1910-1976), who shared a Nobel prize in 1965 for charting the intricate, elegant and sensitive mechanisms by which living cells regulate their own metabolism. Monod's case hinges upon such "telenomic" mechanisms – those in which apparently goal-directed behavior suggests design and purpose but which can be adequately accounted for in terms of physics and chemistry. Despite persuasive evidence to the contrary, Monod argued, the entire phenomenon of life on Earth, from its beginning to the appearance of Man, is based on fortuitous happenings among chemical molecules. Beginning in the primeval soup, chance has also dominated evolution through the blind forces of Darwinian natural selection, acting on mutations thrown up by equally blind, random forces.

The randomness upon which Monod builds this philosophy is illustrated by the way in which parental genes are mixed and allocated to offspring when germ cells unite in reproduction. Termed "fate's lottery" by American biologist Garret Hardin (b.1915), this is a process in which pure chance determines whether a particular selection of genes will come together or not. Given that some such combinations of genes can doom a child to disease, wretchedness or early death, it is not easy to see divine benevolence or purpose here. Likewise the mutations which lead not only to new and improved structures and behaviors, but also to disabling and lethal malfunctions, are also entirely random. Jacques Monod insisted that chance is embedded so deeply in living processes, whether those of microorganisms or humans, that it renders meaningless even our social institutions and concepts such as education and justice. Only by endorsing "the essential message of science" – the intrinsic purposelessness of life – can Man break free from self-deception. "He wakes at last to the realization that, like a gypsy, he lives on the margin of an alien world. A world that is deaf to his music, just as indifferent to his hopes as it is to his suffering or his crimes."

The reactions of American sociologist Theodore Roszak (page 100) to this diagnosis is: "How sad to be Jacques Monod: to stare so expertly at miracles and meanings, and never see them." Monod's bleak diagnosis is equally unpalatable and incredible for many religious believers. They answer him in a variety of ways. Some Christian theologians argue that a creation which enshrines both freedom and creativity *and* pain and suffering is precisely what the Christian gospel leads one to expect. Some concede the entire, materialistic picture as an honest expression of biological science, but insist that such a description of the living world is not equivalent to an explanation. They argue that, whatever the mechanisms, it is still miraculous for a dead, lifeless world without feeling or self-awareness to have given rise to consciousness, morality, and artistic and intellectual creativity. This leads them to embrace the scientific and religious viewpoints as complementary. Such eclecticism is made more palatable and enticing by the recognition that even the scientific worldview includes paradoxes to baffle common sense. Modern physics, for example, teaches that electrons behave as both particles and waves. Relativity provides several equally bizarre ideas. Why then, religious believers may ask, should not the conflict between modern biology and religious significance be accepted as a paradoxical necessity?

▲ *According to Frenchman Jacques Monod, there is "pure chance, absolutely free but blind, at the very root of the stupendous edifice of evolution". As a result of the past century of research, "Man knows at last that he is alone in the universe's unfeeling immensity, out of which he emerged only by chance." Not all biologists would agree with this analysis.*

▲ *The complexity and beauty of so many natural structures – such as this fossilized nautilus shell from the lower Jurassic period – is at first sight seriously at odds with the idea that randomness is at the heart of evolution. But as demonstrated by English zoologist Richard Dawkins (b.1941) in "The Blind Watchmaker", complex and ornate forms can arise on the basis of underlying disorder.*

Reductionism under attack

Within science itself too, there have been several recent attacks on reductionism (◀ pages 99-101), mostly though not entirely coming from scientists who are religious believers. The analysis of Jacques Monod is one expression of reductionist thinking. Another is the behaviorist view that mental evolution is the result of nothing but "random tries" preserved by "reinforcements" (as when a rat is rewarded with food after pressing a particular bar in a cage and is punished by an electrical shock when it presses the wrong lever). Critics do not question that reductionism is valid as a technique of investigation; problems often need to be reduced to their simplest essentials in order to further scientific understanding. The error is in treating an explanation afforded by such atomistic dissection as an exhaustive account of a particular phenomenon or type of behavior.

One example comes from psychologists who see nothing in human conduct that is not explicable on the basis of studies with rats in mazes, and thus construct what the Hungarian-born British writer Arthur Koestler (1905-1983) termed a "ratomorphic" view of Man. This is clearly anathema to religious believers. As the British animal ethologist W.H. Thorpe (1902-1986) commented: "If reductionism were right in the sense that the mental, spiritual and ethical values which we experience really are in the electrons and other primary components of which the world is made, then all one can say is that they don't appear to be there. It follows that a great and unjustified leap of faith is required, a leap without any scientific evidence, to believe it".

▼ The use of rats as "models" for laboratory studies, has encouraged biologists to draw analogies with the mental skills and phenomena found in humans. The writer Arthur Koestler argued that this tendency had gone much too far, substituting an anthropomorphic view of animals for a simplistic and misleading "ratomorphic" interpretation of Homo sapiens as a species.

▲ *In "The Selfish Gene" and "The Blind Watchmaker", Oxford University zoologist Richard Dawkins has achieved the difficult feat of discussing complex ideas in a manner that appeals to experts and nonexperts alike. Born in 1941, Dawkins is a Fellow of New College, Oxford.*

▶ *It is not easy to believe that the exquisite sensitivity of the eye of a bird of prey, such as this prairie falcon (Falco mexicanus), emerged on the basis of capricious, random, purposeless mutations. The odds against such an organ arising in a single step are many billions of times greater than the number of atoms in the universe. But evolutionary biologists do not argue that this happened. The evidence indicates rather that successive mutations over eons of time, and their preservation through natural selection, caused gradual, stepwise improvements in performance.*

How random events can be creative

There is a formidable amount, and variety, of evidence to support the idea that life evolved by means of natural selection. Yet many people, contemplating the beauty of a peacock's tail, the sensitivity of the eye of a bird of prey, the uncanny precision of bird migration, or the mystery of human consciousness, still find it hard to believe that these things evolved "by accident".

Religious apologists from the time of the English theologian William Paley (1743-1805) onward have used the inherent unlikelihood of randomness spawning complexity to argue that life must have been created. If you found a watch, Paley reasoned, the intricacy of its cogs and springs would show that it must have been designed. The same thing applied to the plants and animals on planet Earth.

In his book "The Blind Watchmaker", the British zoologist Richard Dawkins explained the fallacy behind the argument that random events ("mutations" in biological terms) can never be creative. Consider the familiar notion of whether a monkey, bashing away aimlessly at a typewriter keyboard, would ever produce the works of Shakespeare.

Take only one line, "Methinks it is like a weasel", and consider just the first letter. There is a one in 27 chance (a space counts as a letter) that the monkey will get this right the first time. But the chances of the first two letters being correct is one in 27

multiplied by one in 27 – which is one in 729. Following this through, the chance of the monkey coming up with the entire sentence – still an astronomically tiny part of the Bard's output – is the astronomically large figure of one in 10,000 million million million million million million million (10^{39}).

But no one has ever seriously suggested that a peacock's tail or an eagle's eye was ever produced as a result of a constellation of simultaneous capricious events of this sort. What actually seems to happen during evolution is "cumulative selection". Random changes – mutations – are selected over many generations, some of the altered organisms being preserved for subsequent stepwise modification. Dawkins has devised a computer program to illustrate this process. In one experiment based on that same line of Shakespeare, the computer chose a totally random sequence of letters. But it then "bred" from this repeatedly, with occasional mistakes (equivalent to mutations) in the copying. At each stage the computer examined the nonsense phrases and selected the one that was closest to the target sentence. After ten generations it had produced MDLDMNLS ITJISWHRZREZ MECS P. A further ten generations later, this had become MELDINLS IT ISWPRKE Z WECSEL, and after another ten generations the line was METHINGS IT ISWLIKE B WECSEL. By generation 40 it was just one letter short of the target line, which was reached in generation 43.

On the Margins of Science

Scientists' attitudes to the paranormal...When the paranormal disappeared...ESP and the quest for a repeatable experiment...PERSPECTIVE...Scientists who believed...Do plants have feelings?...Telepathy... Parapsychology...The Soal controversy

"Parascience has so far failed to produce a single repeatable finding and, until it does, will continue to be viewed as an incoherent collection of belief systems steeped in fantasy, illusion and error."

These words formed the introduction to a review of "parascience" by the New Zealand psychologist David Marks, published in *Nature* magazine in 1986. They reflect the predominant attitude of orthodox scientists toward a wide range of phenomena – from extrasensory perception to paranormal metal bending – which would, if authenticated, call for a radical reappraisal of the scientific view of reality. Those who believe in claims of this sort find the scientific community's generally dismissive attitude both puzzling and reprehensible. Given that the principles upon which science is founded include intellectual tolerance and respect for revolutionary ideas (◀ page 70), the unwillingness of many scientists even to examine paranormal claims is indeed difficult to justify.

At the same time, their attitude stems from other important principles, of rigorous investigation and progress through reproducibility (◀ page 52), which they believe have not been satisfied by the exponents of parascience. The wisest research workers will always concede that the most bizarre phenomenon or idea *could* be assimilated into mainstream science. But they tend to be biased against this possibility by the long history of parascience, during which the same, inconclusive claims have been made over and over again without reaching the requisite degree of proof, while mainstream science has provided ever more sophisticated and dependable analyses.

Gullible scientists

Some scientists have proved remarkably gullible toward the paranormal. In France during the early years of this century, the intellectual climate was open and revolutionary, anything seemed possible, and there was considerable interest in so-called psychical research.

Among researchers who investigated "métapsychique" and attended seances were Marie (1867-1934) and Pierre (1859-1906) Curie, discoverers of radioactivity. Also keenly interested was the physiologist and 1913 Nobel laureate Charles Richet (1850-1935).

In 1905 Richet discovered a medium called Marthe Beraud, the prospective daughter-in-law of Madame Noel, wife of the colonel in charge of the garrison at Algiers. Richet took part in several of Marthe Beraud's seances at the Noel home, during which a ghost called Bien Boa manifested itself, apparently dressed in a sheet, false beard and coal scuttle. The distinguished scientist even tested the ghost's physiological behavior, proving that it exhaled carbon dioxide just like a human being. Richet was quick to report the results of his researches in the journal "Annales de Science Psychique".

But the appearance of Richet's paper was the very moment when the principal characters in what had been an elaborate joke decided to admit their deception. Marthe Beraud and the other hoaxers, who had simply set out to fool the credulous Mme Noel, were concerned that the story had received such weighty scientific approval. So they made a full confession during a public lecture in Algiers. This was generally accepted – except by Richet, whose belief in Bien Boa if anything seemed to deepen:

"In treating seriously these phenomena, their strangeness had, in spite of all proofs, occasioned some doubts in my mind," he wrote. "But now, in view of the poverty of the objections which could be brought against them, many of those doubts have disappeared."

▶ Definitely beyond the pail – Bien Boa dressed in sheet and coal scuttle. Although attested by distinguished physiologist Charles Richet, the "ghost" turned out to be an elaborate hoax.

◀ The vast majority of scientists continue to be deeply skeptical toward "unidentified flying objects" like these, photographed in 1952 in Massachusetts. So many alleged sightings have had unremarkable causes – from clouds to balloons – that there is great reluctance to accept the possibility of "real" UFOs.

Merely thinking about burning a leaf evoked the plant's emotional response, claimed Cleve Backster

Parascience and scientific inquiry

Clearly, some scientists who *are* believers in the paranormal have an attachment to belief which is as impervious to rationality as is the belief of nonscientists. There have been many other occasions when they have persisted with their faith even after the perpetrators have been shown to be charlatans or merely extremely talented magicians. Occasionally, however, they are able to put on a brave face and admit their mistake. When the Israeli entertainer Uri Geller appeared for the first time on British television screens in November 1973, the expert panel included the mathematician and relativity expert John Taylor. "Not only did he cause a fork to break after a minute's gentle stroking, but he was able, without touching it, to cause the bending of another one lying nearby on the table," Professor Taylor, of King's College, London, wrote later in his bestselling *Superminds*. But Geller's performance was not conducted under laboratory conditions, and Taylor had not reacted to it in the way he would have responded to the same feats accomplished by a conjurer. Taylor resisted the implications that demonstrations of Geller's apparently paranormal achievements could indeed be duplicated by entirely normal means, and set out to study "the Geller effect" in the laboratory.

Gradually, however, Professor Taylor began to revise his opinions. In 1980, five years after *Superminds*, his *Science and the Supernatural* appeared. "Our investigations are finally over. We have searched for the supernatural and not found it. In the main only poor experimentation, shoddy theory and human gullibility have been encountered," were the opening words of his final chapter. "Everything that I investigated turned out either to have a scientific explanation, or did not occur at all under careful test conditions. The earlier results of others in these latter cases were found to be explicable under the headings of mischief, fraud, credulity, fantasy, memory, cues and fear of death."

▼ *Hamish Miller allegedly dowsing the Merry Maidens stone circle, Land's End, Cornwall. Although a few scientists have suggested that the ancient practice of dowsing for water may be explainable by practitioners responding to variations in magnetic field strength, the majority view remains highly skeptical. Such disbelief is supported by the American magician James Randi's demonstrations that dowsers sometimes make claims which they cannot substantiate – though as always in science it is possible that proof of the reality of dowsing will emerge in future.*

◄ The 1973 television demonstration by Israeli Uri Geller, here holding a bent key, convinced scientist John Taylor that paranormal metal-bending was involved. "Geller's demonstration of his amazing powers produced other effects which were even more incredible than those he achieved himself," he wrote in "Superminds". "In hundreds of homes throughout Great Britain cutlery has been bent and timepieces restarted."

▼ Professor Taylor, seen below with a selection of bent cutlery, was criticized for abandoning stringent standards of inquiry when he accepted Uri Geller's claims of paranormal powers. Taylor later studied children apparently capable of such feats, but concluded that "everything that I investigated turned out to have either a scientific explanation...or did not occur under careful test conditions."

The "feelings" of plants

The alleged "feelings" of plants, publicized in Peter Tomkins and Christopher Bird's "The Secret Life of Plants" (1973), illustrate particularly clearly the contrast between scientific and parascientific approaches. During the late 1960s Cleve Backster, an American exponent of lie detection using the polygraph, decided to see whether he could measure the electrical resistance of plant leaves using the same instrument. Placing the two electrodes on opposite surfaces of leaves of a common potted houseplant, Dracena, he found that the basic reading was drifting upward, with variations superimposed on top of an erratic signal.

Backster decided at once that his plant must have been experiencing something like human emotion, and went on to investigate its response to stress. He exposed Philodendron cordatum – a plant with broad, stiff leaves – to an emotional shock by scalding brine shrimps to death nearby. These maneuvers led Backster to conclude that plant cells "have a primary sensory system." His data have, however, been widely criticized on grounds such as statistical significance (◀ page 50) and an absence of adequate controls (◀ page 52). For example, he began with only 21 recordings, discarded eight of them for one reason or another, and was left with allegedly positive results, the significance of which is highly dubious.

The response to Backster's findings

Orthodox botanists were totally skeptical about Backster's findings and felt it would be a waste of valuable time to try to test such absurd ideas. But improbability is not an adequate reason for rejecting a claim. To withdraw from debate is disloyal to the spirit of science and leaves the field open for exploitation. It also inevitably polarizes believers and disbelievers, with convictions based on ignorance rather than real evidence.

For such reasons, Dr E.L. Gasteiger and colleagues at Cornell University decided to repeat the brine shrimp tests, with Backster's advice but under more carefully controlled conditions. Statistical analysis of their results demonstrated that there was no association whatever between the polygraph readings and the shrimp killings.

Another independent researcher, Dr J.M. Kmetz of the Science Unlimited Research Foundation in San Antonio, Texas, found – after 168 trials on 42 plants, and with 84 shrimp killings and an equal number of control tests – no meaningful correlation between signal variations and the shrimp killings. Using a control circuit which included two electrodes like those Backster had attached to his leaves, Kmetz also discovered that the records were every bit as "active" as when a leaf was included. He then found that water evaporating from the electrodes produced deflections on the polygraph.

Is ESP possible?

Is it possible for one person to communicate with another without using the recognized senses? Can certain people know what is happening at a distance or predict the future apparently without any information to go on? All these possibilities (telepathy, clairvoyance and precognition) are aspects of extrasensory perception (ESP). In the late 19th century there were "mediums" in every western country who claimed to be able to make tables move and levitate, voices speak from the "other side" and even create "ectoplasm" in the shapes of the dead. Today controversy over such phenomena continues. Studies of spontaneous cases and naturally-occurring "psychic experiences" are dogged by the problems of the vagaries of human memory, the lack of reliable corroboration of accounts and the difficulty of studying events after they have happened. Experimental studies continue in many countries but with mixed results. Card-guessing experiments were rarely successful; possibly because they are so boring for the subjects. In the 1960s American psychologist Stanley Krippner and others pioneered dream-telepathy experiments. Sleepers were woken after a period of dreaming (detected by electroencephalogram) and asked to report their dreams. The dreams were then compared with a series of pictures, only one of which had been looked at by someone in another room. At first this method seemed highly successful but later proved impossible to reproduce.

The search for a repeatable experiment

One of the severest problems of parapsychology is the difficulty of replicating the most successful experiments. Remote viewing was an initially-successful technique used by psychologist Charles Tart and physicists Russell Targ and Harald Puthoff, in California. An experimenter traveled to a previously determined location while the subject stayed in the laboratory reporting on what he could "see" or imagine. Afterward judges used transcripts of the imagery to try to select, from a group of possible places, where the experimenter had been. The successful results were published in the journal *Nature*. However, the Australian psychologists David Marks and Richard Kammann pointed out that the transcripts contained vital cues to the target order which the judges might have used. Tart reanalyzed the results to claim that the cues could not have been effective. Nevertheless the matter is not closed.

The most recent candidate for a repeatable experiment is the Ganzfeld, the idea of which is to mask out all normal patterned stimulation so as to allow the ESP input to get through. After half an hour or so, the subject is given four or more pictures and asked to decide which one most closely matches his experiences.

American parapsychologist Charles Honorton and British psychologist Carl Sargent independently reported outstanding results with this technique. Others tried it with lesser or greater success. In 1985 the American sociologist Ray Hyman analyzed every published psi-ganzfeld experiment and listed all the methodological flaws. He argued firstly that no study was free of flaws and secondly that the number and type of flaws correlated with the outcome; the more flaws in an experiment, the more "successful" it was likely to be. Honorton countered this with his own analysis, arguing that there was no correlation and some of the flaws were trivial. More errors were subsequently found in Sargent's methods; tending to confirm Hyman's analysis.

▼ *Investigations of spirit phenomena by the great scientist Sir William Crookes, who testified to the genuineness of several mediums (and claimed to have walked arm-in-arm with one apparition), caused a sensation in Victorian England. They were welcome to believers but an embarrassment to more skeptical scientists.*

▲ *Persuaded of the existence of fairies by this and other photographs provided by two young girls, author Sir Arthur Conan Doyle convinced many others through his book "The Coming of the Fairies". Sixty-five years later, in 1983, the two cousins, Mrs Elsie Hill and Mrs Frances Griffiths, admitted publicly that they had faked the images. The "Cottingley fairies", which deeply influenced a whole generation of spiritualists, were drawn and colored in watercolor by Mrs Hill.*

Early psychical researchers
The highly respected British physicist Michael Faraday (1791-1867) devised experiments which showed that "tapping tables" were pushed by the hands of the sitters rather than pulled by some unseen force. He concluded that the effects were due to "unconscious muscular action".

On the other hand the British chemist, Sir William Crookes (1832-1919) was convinced by the claims of Florence Cook and D.D. Home that they could materialize spirit forms or levitate heavy objects. He even measured the forces exerted and took photographs of the events (although these look less than convincing to the modern eye).

In 1882 the Society for Psychical Research was formed. Under the presidency of the British philosopher Henry Sidgwick (1838-1900), the founders set up research committees, including one on "thought transference" (or telepathy). Some experiments were initially successful but became less so as the controls were improved. One series was only exposed when one of the "psychics" admitted using a code.

Parapsychology
The problems of experimental design and fraud continued but gradually the methods were improved. In the 1930s American biologists J.B. Rhine (1895-1980) and Louisa Rhine (1891-1983) set up a laboratory for parapsychology at Duke University in North Carolina. They coined the term ESP and devised new methods for testing it. They developed ESP cards which consisted of five designs – square, circle, wavy lines, cross and star – with five of each in a pack of twenty-five. In telepathy experiments an "agent" looked at a random series of such cards while a "percipient" tried to guess the order. In clairvoyance experiments there was no agent, just a pack of shuffled cards. After nearly 100,000 trials Rhine was able to show, with simple statistical techniques, that the subjects were getting more guesses right than would be expected by chance.

The critics instantly objected to their methods and statistics. In response the Rhines showed that their statistical techniques were essentially correct. However, there remained problems with the quality of the cards (some of which could be read from the back), the shuffling, and the effective separation of agent and percipient.

The Soal controversy
Meanwhile others around the world tried to replicate the findings. One was Samuel Soal (1889-1975), a mathematician at Queen Mary College, London. From 1934 for five years he carried out similar experiments, accumulating even more data than the Rhines but with far tighter controls. The results were compatible with chance, and showed no signs of any ESP. Perhaps Soal would have given up, but a colleague suggested that the subjects might have been guessing "one ahead" in the lists of target cards. Soal reanalyzed his thousands of guesses and confirmed this. So he repeated the tests with his best subject, Basil Shackleton. Respected observers constantly watched both agent and percipient and there were elaborate controls over the cards and their randomization. He found the same effect. Shackleton was guessing one card ahead so effectively that the odds against the results being due to chance were calculated at 10^{35} to 1. Obviously something other than chance was going on. But what?

Critics immediately accused Soal of fraud despite the exemplary controls. Others argued that at last the ESP controversy was over and that no reasonable person could any longer doubt the existence of ESP.

It took nearly 30 years to resolve this particular controversy. Only then did a laborious search through all of Soal's data, by a British computer analyst, Betty Markwick, reveal that Soal had indeed fraudulently manipulated the target lists. The outstanding results, which had convinced so many people for so long, had been faked.

▲ In an experiment conducted under Ganzfeld conditions, the subject tries to receive "psi" information while under partial sensory deprivation, with uniform soothing sounds played through headphones and only a dim red haze visible through split ping-pong balls. A distant "sender" concentrates on, for example, one of four different images, the subject (here Heidi Bartlett) trying to discern which one. Working at Cambridge University, England, Carl Sargent has claimed results from such experiments that were much more significant than would be expected from random guesses. But other experimenters have failed to achieve similar results.

124

See also
Scientific Intercourse 71-84
Objective and Subjective Science 99-110
Science and Religion 111-18

▲ **Nativities or birth charts of Louis XVI and Marie Antionette of France,** published in 1795 but based on fanciful ideas still used by astrologers today. If care is taken to avoid self-fulfilling prophecies (as when individuals, asked questions about their personalities, give answers already affected by their knowledge of their "star signs"), no significance can be discerned in personal horoscopes.

▶ **The planet Saturn, we are assured in one popular work in astrology, is** associated with skin, teeth, bones, gall bladder, spleen, vagus nerve, crystallization and acid formation in joints, old age, perseverance, tenacity, cold, slow change, inhibition, restriction and intolerance. Enough said.

Testing astrology

Astrology is another variety of parascience which the majority of scientists (especially astronomers) are prone to reject on a priori grounds. It is very difficult indeed to see how a horoscope, showing the positions of the "planets" (the actual planets, the Sun, Moon and other heavenly objects defined by astrologers), could afford information about personality or predictions about events surrounding a person's life.

There have been many attempts to establish the validity of astrology which have been deeply flawed. For example, many experimenters have overlooked the fact that the answers of people given personality questionnaires are likely to be influenced by their own awareness of what, on astrological grounds, their character and attitudes are supposed to be. Pragmatically, however, it can also be argued that a body of ideas with no inherent validity would scarcely have survived so long, being taken seriously by millions of people each day and making large amounts of money for astrologers.

A refutation of astrology

In an attempt to resolve the question unambiguously, Professor Shawn Carlson of the University of California set up a massive and meticulously-planned "double-blind" investigation. His aim was to determine whether natal charts (the name given to horoscopes based on the place and time of an individual's birth) could indicate personality traits accurately. To avoid the criticisms leveled against numerous previous studies by either believers or skeptics, he engaged the assistance of astrologers, scientists and statisticians in planning experiments which met the tight specifications of each group. Carlson took care to ensure that no hidden clues were available which astrologers or their subjects could use to choose correct answers not based solely on astrological information. He even eliminated all biases which could tend to arrange the results in a way that simulated chance distribution and thus favored scientific skepticism over the astrological interpretation.

There were two sets of experiments. Volunteers tried to select their own natal charts and associated interpretations from three – one prepared by astrologers from information provided by the subject, the other two picked at random from the whole group. Second, the astrologers were invited to decide which of three "personality inventory" results most closely matched a randomly selected individual whose natal chart they were also given. The results, reported in the premier international scientific journal "Nature" in 1985, showed that none of the astrologers performed at a level higher than that expected on the basis of pure chance and guesswork. "Tested using double-blind methods, the astrologers' predictions proved to be wrong," Professor Carlson concluded. "Their predicted connection between the positions of the planets and other astrological objects at the time of birth and the personalities of the test subjects did not exist. The experiment clearly refutes the astrological hypothesis."

Glossary

Absolute zero
The temperature at which all substances have zero thermal energy.

Academy
Plato's Academy was named for the garden where he taught; medieval academies were schools; new academies of the 15th to 18th centuries were associations promoting science, literature and technology.

Accelerator
In particle physics, a research tool used to accelerate subatomic particles to high velocities.

Acid rain
Precipitation, in rain and mists, that bears sulfuric and nitric acids formed in the atmosphere from sulfur dioxide emitted by burning coal, oil and gasoline; it can severely damage plant (forests) and animal (fish in lakes) life.

Acquired characteristics
It was the view of Jean Lamarck (1744-1829) that changes which took place in a plant or an animal in its lifetime could be passed on to later generations.

AIDS
Acquired immune deficiency syndrome, an epidemic disease whose virus wrecks the immune system, rendering the body vulnerable to potentially fatal infections.

Amino acid
A basic chemical unit, from which proteins are synthesized by the body.

Anomie
Term applied by Émile Durkheim to social instability stemming from a breakdown of generally accepted values accompanied by widespread personal feelings of alienation and uncertainty.

Antibiotic
A chemical produced by a microorganism and used as a drug to kill or inhibit the growth of other microorganisms.

Antibody
A defensive substance produced by the immune system to neutralize or help destroy a specific foreign substance or ANTIGEN.

Antigen
A foreign substance that provokes the body to produce ANTIBODIES.

Applied science
Science intended to produce clearly identified returns, as opposed to PURE SCIENCE.

Astrology
The science-art of divining the future from study of the heavens.

Atomic clock
A device using the constant frequencies of electron spin reversals of the cesium atom to define an accurate and reproducible time scale.

Bacteria (singular bacterium)
A large and varied group of MICROORGANISMS, unicellular and 0.3μm-2μm in diameter, classified by their shape and staining ability. They live in many environments; only a few are PATHOGENS.

Bacteriophage
See PHAGE.

Binomial system
The system of NOMENCLATURE introduced by Carolus Linnaeus (1707-1778) comprising two Latin names, generic and specific, for each plant (or animal), e.g. *Homo sapiens*.

Biometry
The statistical analysis of biological observations and phenomena.

Bubble chamber
A device used to observe the paths of subatomic particles, by reducing pressure as the particles pass through so that bubbles form along the paths.

Calculus
Mathematics dealing with continually changing quantities.

CAT
Computed axial tomography; a diagnostic use of X-rays, which scan the body, the data being computer-stored to build up the image of a "slice" which is color-coded to show up slight differences between different parts of the body.

Cell fusion
A technique of fusing different types of cells together in order to combine their genetic material; it has led to the creation of HYBRIDOMAS.

Chlorofluorocarbons
Gases used to propel aerosol sprays; they are accumulating in the atmosphere, where they appear to be destroying the protective layer of ozone.

Chromosome
A thread of genetic material contained in the cell nucleus and duplicated when the cell divides.

Citation
The reference in one scientific paper to another; co-citation is the citation together of papers in a third paper.

Classical science
Generally taken to be that period in western science between the publication of Isaac Newton's *Principia Mathematica* in 1687 and the discovery of radioactivity and the overthrow of Newton's ideas on time and space, by Albert Einstein and others, in the years around 1900.

Classical world
The Mediterranean civilization centered first on Greece then later on Rome between about the 8th century BC and 4th century AD.

Control
In scientific experiments, a group or individual (animal, plant or inanimate) that affords a standard of comparison with a similar item subject to a variablle to which the control is not.

Creationism (creation science)
A form of FUNDAMENTALISM, emerging in the USA in recent years and claiming equal time with evolutionary biology in school curricula.

Deduction (deductive method)
A form of logic in which particular conclusions are reached by reasoning from certain general principles assumed to be true. An alternative process is INDUCTION.

DNA
Deoxyribonucleic acid; its structure contains the blueprint that contains genetic information.

Electromagnetic radiation
RADIATION consisting of an electric and magnetic disturbance which travels in a vacuum at a constant speed known as the speed of light (about 300,000 km/s). Visible light and radio waves are examples.

Electron micrograph
A highly magnified image obtained by using a beam of electrons rather than light.

Element
Defined in 1787 by A. Lavoisier as a substance that was chemically "simple", i.e. could not be decomposed; 2,000 years earlier, Empedocles defined four elements: earth, fire, air, water.

Empiricism
In philosophy, the view that knowledge can be derived from sense experience. Empirical: relying on experience, observation and experiment.

Enzyme
An organic catalyst, composed of a protein.

ESP (extrasensory perception)
Perception using senses other than those generally recognized.

False-color photography
The processing of special photographic or other emulsions to display information, using added or "unnatural" color.

Falsification principle
As suggested by Karl Popper: a single unambiguous piece of evidence against a general statement is enough to destroy its credibility; scientific laws cannot be proved, only tested; much of science is devoted to systematic attempts to refute or falsify laws and hypotheses.

Fission
In nuclear physics, the changing of an element into two or more elements of lower atomic weight, with the release of energy.

Fundamentalism
A religious movement developed in the USA after World War I; fundamentalists insist on the absolute truth of the Bible, including the Creation story.

Fundamental science
Pure science.

Fusion
In nuclear physics, the merging of two nuclei to form a new element of higher atomic weight, usually resulting in the release of energy.

Futurology
The study of what developments, particularly on a global scale, are possible or likely in the future.

Gene
The unit of heredity, made up of DNA and located on a CHROMOSOME in a cell nucleus.

Gene-splicing
A method of taking a piece of DNA-carrying hereditary GENES from one living organism and inserting it into another organism.

Germ theory
The theory pioneered by L. Pasteur (1822-1895) and Robert Koch (1843-1910) that diseases are spread by living germs (microbes).

Gravitation
The force of attraction existing between all matter.

Green Revolution
The use in the 1960s and 1970s of high-yielding varieties of grain (notably wheat and rice) developed by scientists, and the ensuing changes in agriculture, society and food output.

GUT (grand unified theory)
An attempt to explain theoretically the forces of nature in terms of one underlying force.

HeLa cells
Cells which originated with tissue taken from a US victim of cervical cancer in 1951 (HeLa being the first two letters of her first and family names). Potentially immortal, the cells are widely used for cultivating viruses.

HIV
Human immunodeficiency virus, infection with which may result in AIDS.

Homeopathy
The treatment of medical symptoms by giving minute amounts of a drug which produces similar symptoms.

Humanism
The individualistic and critical spirit, and emphasis on secular concerns, that was a characteristic of, for example, the RENAISSANCE.

Hybridoma
A fusion of malignant and ANTIBODY-generating cells, with wide pharmaceutical, medical and research uses; can produce MONOCLONAL ANTIBODIES.

Ice-minus
A strain of the BACTERIUM *Pseudomonas syringae* bred to remove the GENE responsible for producing a substance that triggers ice nucleation when the bacterium is present on the leaves of crop or other plants.

Induction
a) The process of reasoning from particular instances to make general propositions; as a scientific method, it requires accumulation of quantities of information in the hope or expectation that conclusions will emerge.
b) The phenomenon in which an electric current is generated when a conductor passes through an electric field.

Industrial Revolution
The major change in national economies which began with the introduction of power-driven machinery in the late 18th century in England, and continued through the 19th century.

Integrated circuit
A structure on which a large number of electronic components are assembled on one SEMICONDUCTOR wafer; has largely replaced the TRANSISTOR.

Intercropping
A "low-tech" farming practice whereby two (or more) crops are grown together; it can increase yields, and limit pest damage.

Irradiation of foods
The exposure of foodstuffs to ionizing RADIATION to preserve the food and/or destroy microbes responsible for causing food poisoning.

Isotopes
Atoms of an element with the same number of protons in the nucleus but a different number of neutrons.

Laser
Light Amplification by Stimulated Emission of Radiation; a device producing a very intense beam of parallel light with a precisely defined wavelength.

Macrophage
A white blood cell specialized to circulate through body tissues and consume foreign bodies and cell debris.

Magnetohydrodynamic generation (MHD)
A procedure in which electric current is created by passing high-temperature ionized gases through a magnetic field.

Mechanics
The study of the action of forces on bodies.

Meltdown
An accident in a nuclear plant in which (as at Three Mile Island), following failure of cooling systems, core fuel rods and grid spacing melt down.

Metaphysics
The study of or speculation on the fundamentals of existence or reality.

Meteorology
The study of the atmosphere, weather and climate.

Microbe
MICROORGANISM.

Microorganism
A living organism too small to be seen without a microscope.

Monoclonal antibodies
Extremely pure versions of ANTIBODIES assembled by the body in response to infection; produced by HYBRIDOMAS.

Mutation
A change in genetic material (GENE or set of CHROMOSOMES).

NASA
National Aeronautics and Space Administration, the US government agency responsible for space exploration, artificial satellites and rockets.

Natural philosophy
Until the 19th century "natural philosophy" meant something similar to our word physics.

Natural selection
The mechanism of evolution discovered by Charles Darwin (1809-1882).

NMR
Nuclear magnetic resonance; technique of imaging the interior of the body using the magnetic resonance of the atoms comprising the elements of the tissues.

Nomenclature
In biology, an internationl system of Latin names used for plants and animals. See BINOMIAL SYSTEM.

Nuclear winter
The lower temperatures, and their consequences, forecast as following on a nuclear war and the consequent absorption of solar RADIATION by smoke from fires.

ORT
Oral rehydration therapy; administration of a mixture of water, sugar and salt to children suffering from diarrhea.

Paleomagnetism
The study of past changes in Earth's magnetic field by examining the magnetic properties of old rocks.

Panspermia theory
An explanation of the origin of life according to which the Earth was initially seeded with living organisms from space.

Paranormal
Describes a phenomenon that is not explicable in terms of acceptable science.

Parascience
A loose term covering the study of PARANORMAL phenomena.

Pasteurization
A technique of heating milk, beer, wine etc. to destroy bacteria it may contain; named after L. Pasteur (1822-1895).

Pathogen
An organism that produces disease.

Peer review
The process by which scientific papers are assessed by REFEREES or members of advisory panels of periodicals, also, the assessment of grant applications by fellow experts.

Periodic table
A table of elements arranged by atomic number (the number of protons in the nucleus) to show similarities and trends in physical and chemical properties.

Phlogiston
One of three varieties of "earth"; a combustible material lost by the substance that burns (18th century).

pH
A measure of the acidity of an aqueous solution.

Phage
A VIRUS that attacks BACTERIA; also known as a BACTERIOPHAGE.

Pneumatic chemists
Chemists of the 18th century who studied airs released from solids and fluids, including J. Black, J. Priestley, H. Cavendish, C. Scheele.

Priority
The condition of publishing or announcing a scientific discovery before anyone else.

Protozoa
The single-celled animals.

Pure science
Also known as basic or fundamental science; the disinterested quest for information to compile and the process of compiling, accurate pictures of the physical and biological world (also called "curiosity-oriented").

Quantum theory
A theory developed at the beginning of the 20th century to account for certain phenomena that could not be explained by CLASSICAL physics.

Radiation
The emission and propagation through space of ELECTROMAGNETIC RADIATION or subatomic particles.

Radioactivity
The spontaneous disintegration of unstable nuclei, accompanied by the emission of RADIATION of alpha particles, beta particles or gamma rays.

Rationalism
A theory that reason alone, unaided by experience, can arrive at basic truth; in the 17th century the rationalism of R. Descartes, G. von Leibniz and B. Spinoza stood in opposition to the EMPIRICISM of J. Locke.

Reductionism
A viewpoint expressed by, for example, J. Monod (1910-1976), that life's mechanisms, including apparently goal-directed behavior, can be explained in terms of physics and chemistry.

Referee
One of a panel of advisors who help a periodical editor to assess the quality of submitted papers, a process known as PEER REVIEW.

Relativity
The theory of space, time and matter, enunciated by A. Einstein (1879-1955).

Renaissance
The transition between medieval and modern times in Europe, beginning in Italy in the 14th century and continuing to the 17th century, marked by a HUMANISTIC revival of CLASSICAL learning, and the beginnings of modern science.

Research front
A cluster of co-cited papers. See CITATION.

RNA
Ribonucleic acid; a single-stranded nucleic acid that cooperates with DNA for protein synthesis.

Scanning electron microscope
An electron microscope in which the electron beam scans the specimen's surface; this emits secondary electrons that are focused as a three-dimensional image, a scanning electron micrograph or SEM. See TRANSMISSION ELECTRON MICROGRAPH.

Scholastics
In western Christendon in the 9th-17th centuries, a movement combining religious dogma first with the mystical and intuitional tradition of philosophers such as St Augustine (354-430) and, from the 13th century, with the ideas of Aristotle, mainly translated into Latin.

Semiconductor
A material whose electrical conductivity is intermediate between that of an insulator and a conductor at room temperature and increases with rising temperature and impurity concentration. See TRANSISTOR.

Spectroscopy
The production, measurement and analysis of SPECTRA, much used by astronomers, chemists and physicists.

Spectrum
The distribution of the intensity of ELECTROMAGNETIC RADIATION with wavelength. The visible spectrum encompasses those wavelengths to which the human eye responds, the different wavelengths corresponding to the different colors.

Staphylococcus
A BACTERIUM responsible for many skin, soft tissue and bone infections.

Strategic science
Basic science carried out because its results may help solve foreseeable practical problems in the future.

Strata
The various layers in which sedimentary rock is formed. The singular "stratum" is rarely used.

Stratigraphy
The study of the chronological sequence and the correlation of rock STRATA in different districts.

Superconductor
Material which, when cooled to low temperatures, conducts electricity with little or no resistance.

Teleology
The use of predetermined purpose to explain the Universe.

Thermodynamics
The science of the interconversion of heat, work and other forms of energy.

Transistor
An electronic device made of SEMICONDUCTOR materials used in a circuit as an amplifier, rectifier, detector or switch. See INTEGRATED CIRCUIT.

Transmission electron micrograph
Or TEM; an image from an electron microscope based on the notion of replacing light with electrons, focused by magnetic fields rather than through glass lenses.

Transmutation
Alchemists believed that one substance could be transmuted into another – hence their efforts to transmute into gold. The same term was used by Darwin to label the process of one species giving rise to another.

Trigonometry
The study of the ratios of the sides of right-angled triangles.

Uncertainty principle
A principle of subatomic physics, enunciated by W. Heisenberg (1901-1976), that it is impossible to determine simultaneously the position and the momentum of a particle.

User pays
A system whereby the cost of research and development is borne by their beneficiaries rather than by government or another public funding agency.

Vaccination, vaccine
Originally, the introduction of matter from cowpox pustules to lessen the danger of catching smallpox; by extension, vaccines. Vaccines contain attenuated (weakened) or killed microbes or their fragments, which are used to confer immunity but do not cause disease.

Virus
A submicroscopic parasitic MICROORGANISM comprising a protein or protein/lipid sheath enclosing nucleic acid (DNA or RNA); those that attack BACTERIA are BACTERIOPHAGES.

Vitalism
A once-popular theory that cells depend for life on a mysterious force that cannot be analyzed in terms of physics and chemistry.

Vitamin
An essential nutrient found in low concentration in food. Vitamins are organic substances which perform vital functions in the body.

X-ray diffraction
The process by which the X-ray diffraction patterns of crystals are translated into pictures showing the relative positions of the atoms in a crystal, as in a photomicrograph of very high magnification.

Index

Credits

Key to abbreviations: AP Associated Press;
ARPL Ann Ronan Picture Library; BCL Bruce
Coleman Ltd; BHPL BBC Hulton Picture Library;
FSP Frank Spooner Pictures; MEPL Mary Evans
Picture Library; OCD Oxford Chemical Designs Ltd;
RFL Rex Features Ltd; SPL Science Photo Library;
TCL Telegraph Colour Library; TPL Topham Picture
Library; b bottom; bl bottom left; br bottom right;
c center; cl center left; cr center right; t top; tl top left;
tr top right; l left; r right.

5t SPL 5b J-L Charmet 6l, 6r, 7t M. Holford 6-7b
J-L. Charmet 8l Phaidon Archive 8r BPCC/Aldus
Archive/British Museum 9 Scala/Museo Nazionale,
Naples 10tl, 10tr ARPL 10bl J-L. Charmet 10-11b
Mansell Collection 11r J-L. Charmet 12l Scala 12tr
J-L. Charmet 12br Thomas Photos, Oxford 13t
Mansell Collection 13b, 14bl ARPL 14-15b J-L.
Charmet 15 Scala 16t Royal College of Physicians 16b
British Museum (Natural History) 17l J-L. Charmet
17r Giraudon 18tl, 18tr Tom Tracy 18bl M. Holford
19l British Library 19r East Asian History of Science
Trust 20b Popperfoto 20t ARPL 20-1t Illustrated
London News 21t MEPL 22l Popperfoto 22r Bettman
Archive/BHPL 23l MEPL 23r ARPL 25l J-L.
Charmet 25r ARPL 26b Sir Alexander Gibb and
Partners, Reading 26t BHPL 27 ARPL 28t J-L.
Charmet 28b Royal Albert Memorial Museum, Exeter
28-9t ARPL 29b Keystone Collection 30b M. Holford
30-1t, 31b ARPL 31tr MEPL 32b U.S. Department of
Energy/SPL 32 inset Imperial War Museum 33
Hammer/Kobal Collection 36l St. Mary's Hospital,
London, Medical School/SPL 36r Heather Davies/SPL

37t Smith, Kline and French 36-7b OCD 38 CERN/
SPL 39 CERN 40l British Antarctic Survey/ Vallance
40-1 British Antarctic Survey/A. Moyes 41t British
Antarctic Survey/L.D.B. Hernod 41b British
Antarctic Survey/R.A. Price 42 L'Express-Lautier 43
BCL 46l Photosource 46r Solo Syndication and
Literary Agency Ltd 47 Royal Astronomical Society
48t J-L. Charmet 48-9b Dr. Tony Brain/SPL 49r
CNRI/SPL 50l Jerome Yeats/SPL 50-1 FSP 51b U.S.
Office of Earthquakes 52l, 52r Professor C.O. Alley 53
James Kilkelly/DOT 55 OCD 56l National Portrait
Gallery 56r Photosource 57 CNRI/SPL 58b D.
McMullan/SPL 58t Ernst Ruska 58-9 Siemens
Museum, Munich 59 Synaptek/SPL 60tl Professor
Henry Harris 60br J. Burgess/SPL 60-1t Rob
Stepney/SPL 60-1b CNRI/SPL 62l Darwin Dale/SPL
62r National Archive for the History of Computing,
Manchester University 64l A.R. Mew 64-5 BCL/A.
Pasieka 65c D. Parker/SPL 65r World Health
Organisation 66tl, 66tr, 67tl, 67tr Professor Karl
Niklas, Cornell University 66-7, 66b Premaphotos/
K.G. Preston-Mafham 68 J. Kuhn 70t Lawrence
Berkeley Lab/SPL 70b Cavendish Laboratory 71
Giraudon 72 Equinox Archive 73tl Royal Geographical
Society 73tr Weidenfeld and Nicolson 72-3b FSP 74
RFL 75t John Schulz for PAR/NYC 75b Popperfoto
78l Photosource 78br BHPL 78-9 FSP 79tr RFL 80
Popperfoto 80-1 Pixfeatures 80 inset Professor A.
Galston 81b National Archives, Washington 82tl
Popperfoto 82tr British Museum (Natural History)
82br J-L. Charmet 83t Keystone Press 83b Sygma/
J.P. Lattor 84 World Meteorological Organisation 85
MEPL 86t MIR Publishing House, Moscow 86b

Jocelyn Bell Burnett 86-7 Fermilab/SPL 87r Guy
Gillette/SPL 88, 88-9t Bridgeman Art Library 89cr
TPL 89br RFL 90t Ardea 90c Dong Allan/SPL 90b
D. Parker/SPL 91tl NASA/SPL 91tr D. Parker/SPL
90-1b Rondi/Tani/SPL 92b FAO Photo Library/
F. Botta 92-3 TPL 93b UNESCO 94t Nobel
Foundation 94b Lawrence Berkeley Laboratory 97bl
P. Duke 97tr Royal Society 97br Popperfoto 98 Royal
College of Physicians 99l W. McIntyre/SPL 99r L.
Mulvehill/ SPL 100l Fondation Le Corbusier 100tr
BHPL 100cr Photosource 100-1b Privat Museum,
Heidi Weber Haus 101t Giraudon 101b Popperfoto
102l, 102-3 Bridgeman Art Library 103 Dr. M. Phelps
and Dr. J. Mazzaiotta/SPL 104 Bodleian Library,
Oxford 105tl, 105tr Royal College of Music, London
105br Novosti 106 Photosource 107 National Portrait
Gallery, London 108 BHPL 109 TCL 110l J-L.
Charmet 110r FSP 111 BCL 112, 113t, 112-13
Hutchison Library 114-15 Kitt Peak National
Observatory 115t Werner Forman 116 AP 116-17t
S. Stammers/SPL 117b BHPL 118t R. Dawkins 118b
Zefa 119l Popperfoto 119r R. Brandon 120 Fortean
Picture Library 121l BHPL 121r MEPL 122 BHPL
122-3t R. Brandon 123tr MEPL 124t ARPL 124b
NASA

Artists Alan Hollingbery; Kevin Maddison; Colin
Salmon; Mick Saunders; David Smith; Del Tolton
Production Joanna Turner, Clive Sparling
Index Barbara James and John Baines
Media conversion and typesetting Peter MacDonald,
Ron Barrow